OCCUPIED CITY

GERALD M. CAPERS

OCCUPIED CITY

NEW ORLEANS
UNDER THE
FEDERALS
1862-1865

UNIVERSITY OF KENTUCKY PRESS

COPYRIGHT © 1965 BY THE UNIVERSITY OF KENTUCKY PRESS
COMPOSED AND PRINTED AT THE UNIVERSITY OF KENTUCKY
LIBRARY OF CONGRESS CATALOG CARD NUMBER: 65-27007

To the memory of my grandmother

RACHEL HUTCHINSON DEANE
1841–1936

Louisiana matriarch, native and long-time resident of St. Helena Parish

PREFACE

LIKE MANY of my generation of southerners, I learned about the Civil War from my grandmothers, who were eyewitnesses to the ordeal. Anna Misroon (Capers) as a sixteen-year-old girl witnessed the firing on Sumter from her house on the Battery, and her silver was later confiscated by Sherman's soldiers. Rachel Hutchinson (Deane), being some years older, suffered more acutely. Her husband Albert was one of the Louisianians wounded at Shiloh, and many years later he died from an infection caused by the bullet he carried in his leg. After the battle of Baton Rouge in August, 1862, she rode down a Yankee sentry in order to comfort her mortally wounded brother, Samuel. Despite my best efforts I was never able to convince either of them that Lincoln was a great man.

I have always regarded military history, whatever its appeal to the layman, as intellectually sterile. For a century southerners have made a fetish of the Civil War, using it to fulfill their penchant for self-pity and to justify their racial caste system. Brave men have often died for causes in which they believed; they should properly be commemorated for their courage. But this does not belie the basic fact that all wars, civil and national, are inhuman, barbaric, and stupid; or that the people of both South and North must share equally the responsibility for the tragedy of 1861. Unlike some of their descendants, many Confederate soldiers freely admitted that they were rebels; most of those who survived accepted the hard gage of battle and took up life where they had left it.

Surely a century of commemoration of their valiant deeds is sufficient. Let us hope that with the orgy of the centennial the dead will at long last be laid quietly to rest.

In retrospect, life in New Orleans during the Civil War does not seem to the present generation—despite the rule of Beast Butler—as dramatic as that in Washington and Richmond, which Margaret Leech and Alfred H. Bill have described so vividly. This impression is due to a basic contrast in the history of these three cities during the hostilities. Washington, though threatened, was never captured, and beleaguered Richmond did not fall until the end of the war. New Orleans, on the contrary, was taken at the start of the second year of the struggle, and it was never recaptured. From the viewpoint of those living in the 1860s, however, the New Orleans story was quite dramatic. Suspense there was just as great, for a good chance of its recapture existed even as late as 1864 when Banks led his unsuccessful campaign up the Red River.

I do not intend this as a book about the Civil War in the traditional sense, though it is so in point of time. What I have tried to do is to examine, in a specific instance, the problems of the conqueror and the response of an urban population to military occupation.

Professor Ralph Gabriel of Yale, on the faculty of the School of Military Government during World War II, summarized our national experience in military occupation in an incisive article in the *American Historical Review,* July, 1944. In 1860 we as a nation had carried out but one brief occupation of foreign territory—that of General Winfield Scott in Vera Cruz, Mexico in 1846. Scott's brilliantly successful performance was largely the result of his General Orders No. 20, laying down the rules for American martial law which won him the support of the Mexican people against Santa Anna. This order was largely the basis in our next conflict for the even more famous General Orders No.

100, published April 24, 1863, written by Francis Lieber and a board of officers.

But any historical study of our national experience with military occupation must concern itself equally with the other side of the story: instances in which Americans themselves fell under the rule of a conquering enemy. The British occupied several American cities during the Revolution, notably New York; yet by the 1860s the memory of that ordeal was dim, if not forgotten. New Orleans is the largest American city ever occupied by enemy forces for a considerable period.

For many periods in the history of individual American cities the sources are scanty, but for New Orleans in the 1860s they are plethoric and frequently redundant. In the location of these sources, and for certain conclusions about the occupation, I wish to express my indebtedness to two works in particular: Fred Harrington's biography of General Banks, and Elizabeth Doyle's unpublished doctoral dissertation on civilian life in occupied New Orleans. I am under obligation, as well, to several of my Tulane colleagues for their critical reading of the manuscript: my wife Roberta, Albert Cowdrey, and Marguerite Bougere.

I am also indebted to the staffs of the following libraries for their assistance: the Howard Tilton Memorial Library at Tulane and the New Orleans Public Library; the Louisiana State University Library at Baton Rouge; the Sterling Library at Yale, the Houghton at Harvard, and the Essex Institute at Salem, Mass.; and to Dr. Philip M. Hamer of the National Archives. My research was facilitated by grants from the Research Council of Tulane University and the John Simon Guggenheim Foundation.

CONTENTS

Preface	*page* vii
Maps	xiii
One: The Crescent City on the Eve of the Civil War	1
Two: The Capture	25
Three: Enter General Butler	54
Four: The Rule of the Beast, May to December, 1962	77
Five: Changes in Command, 1862-1865	98
Six: Unionist Politics and Reconstruction Government	120
Seven: The Economy of a Conquered Metropolis	145
Eight: Press, Church, and School	172
Nine: Civilians and Soldiers	191
Ten: The Negro during the Occupation	214
Epilogue	232
Bibliography	239
Index	245

MAPS

New Orleans in 1860   *pages* 16 *and* 17

Geography of the Capture of New Orleans   32 *and* 33

ONE THE CRESCENT CITY ON THE EVE OF THE CIVIL WAR

WHEN THE PELICAN FLAG of the Independent State of Louisiana was raised in New Orleans on January 27, 1861, it was the fourth flag to fly over the city. The Stars and Bars of the Confederate banner at the end of March was the fifth. From the founding of the city in 1718 until near the end of the Seven Years War, the Island of Orleans had belonged to France, and from 1762 to 1800, to Spain. Then Spain secretly returned it to Napoleon, who in turn sold it to the United States in 1803. Changes in national allegiance were an old story to Louisiana Creoles.

In the middle of the nineteenth century, residents of the Crescent City had reason to expect it to become the largest city in an America which was rapidly moving west. From less than 10,000 in 1803 when Jefferson bought it from France, the population of New Orleans had soared by 1840 to 102,000, making it third in rank in the entire nation. In that year it led the nation in value of exports, ahead even of New York; and it handled twice as much of the western produce exported as all other ports together. The tonnage at its wharves was more than double that of its rival on the Hudson. In the year of Lincoln's election 3,500 steamboats docked at its wharves, an average of ten a day; its total trade, exports and imports, amounted to a stupendous $324,000,000.

Louisiana banks ranked first in capital stock, deposits, and specie among the fifteen slaveholding states.[1]

This growth and wealth resulted from the richness of the great interior valley of the United States and from the Mississippi River which flows down its center. Located 120 miles from the mouth, between a crescent bend in the river and Lake Pontchartrain a few miles to the north, New Orleans became a transhipment point for all exports coming downstream. The mountain barrier of the Appalachians long gave New Orleans a monopoly of the commerce of the interior valley. The invention of the steamboat early in the century, by making it possible to ship goods up the river in quantity, cinched this monopoly, which lasted until the completion of the Erie Canal in 1825 and of the canals between the Ohio and the Great Lakes two decades later.

In the larger sweep of civilization, towns have a natural history of their own in which less dramatic factors like geography and climate are more significant than diplomatic incidents. These factors are basic to the culture of cities and go far in determining their social and political characteristics. Economically New Orleans was more a western than a southern town—though it slowly became less so. Before 1850 its chief source of business was the vast variety of goods brought downriver for export or for distribution to its southwestern hinterland. Fur led the exports in value in the eighteenth century. All along, but in lesser volume, New Orleans received by sea imports which it sold upriver or in the immediate area. By 1860, however, it concentrated more on marketing cotton and sugar from the lower valley and on

---

[1] Harold Sinclair, *The Port of New Orleans* (New York, 1942), is a good general description of the economy of ante bellum New Orleans. The following articles give more detail: R. D. Way, "Commerce of the Lower Mississippi Valley in the Period, 1830-1860," Mississippi Valley Historical Association *Proceedings*, X (1919-20), 57-69; E. P. Puckett, "The Attempt of New Orleans to Meet the Crisis in Southern Trade with the West," *ibid.*, 491-98; J. E. Winston, "Notes on the Economic History of New Orleans," *Mississippi Valley Historical Review*, XI (1924-25), 200-27. The same sources are the basis for subsequent paragraphs on the economy.

trade with Texas. In that year it handled two million bales, the largest cotton market in the world.

"A contest has been going on between the North and the South," said *De Bow's Review* in 1847, "not limited to slavery or no slavery—to abolition or no abolition, nor to the politics of either whigs or democrats as such, but a contest for the wealth and commerce of the great valley of the Mississippi— a contest tendered by our northern brethren, whether the growing commerce of the great West shall be thrown upon New Orleans or given to the Atlantic cities."[2] Even before Abraham Lincoln was elected, eastern cities led by New York had won this contest. Their southern rival was already foreordained—as Harold Sinclair says in his *Port of New Orleans*—to become "a midget with a prodigious personality rather than one of the world's great cities."[3] Between 1854 and 1858 western products, which in previous years had averaged 61 percent of total receipts, declined to a mere 18 percent.

If this outcome was largely the result of changes in technology, it was also a consequence of apathy on the part of New Orleans businessmen. Every port on the Atlantic and the Gulf of Mexico, from Boston to nearby Mobile, resorted to railroads in an effort to offset the natural advantage of the Louisiana metropolis. Thanks to the railroads, by 1850 Charleston and Savannah together handled almost as much of the southern cotton crop as New Orleans. During the next decade New York, Philadelphia, and Baltimore completed railroad connections with the upper valley, as did Charleston with the lower. In 1859 the Mobile and Ohio reached its destination at Cairo. About the same time New Orleans, upon completion of its own road to Canton, Mississippi, also attained rail access to the middle valley, but it

[2] *De Bow's Review*, III (1847), 98. This leading business journal of the Old South was published in New Orleans.
[3] Sinclair, *New Orleans*, 203. Robert G. Albion, *The Rise of New York Port* (New York, 1939), gives the New York side of the story.

had built only eighty miles on its western route to Texas when the war began.

Snags and low water in the river frequently interfered with shipping, impediments which the railroads could avoid. More serious were conditions on the 120 miles of river between the port and the gulf. Though year by year the bar at the mouth grew shallower, local businessmen did little but petition the national government for aid. (The final solution came with the construction of the Eads jetties in the 1880s.) In addition, the service of the bar pilots was unsatisfactory, and rates for towing sailing vessels upstream were almost prohibitive.

Most of all, no direct shipping lines from New Orleans to Europe were established (New York had begun her famous Black Ball packet line in 1816), and little of the ocean shipping using the port was locally owned. Rates to Europe from New Orleans were higher than from the Atlantic ports. To make matters worse, storage facilities and docks were inadequate; for more than twenty years cotton and tobacco were simply unloaded on the levee without protection from the weather, causing an annual loss on tobacco alone of $100,000. Overconfident, New Orleans therefore never developed its import potential, nor for all De Bow's urging did it develop any appreciable industry. As long as the annual volume of trade continued to increase, local merchants—unaware of or indifferent to the rapidly changing world—assumed that the future would take care of itself.

THE MOST ACCURATE of the many contemporary comments on ante bellum New Orleans appeared in the *Illustrated London News* during the yellow fever epidemic of 1853. The city had been built, said the *News,* "upon a site that only the madness of commercial lust could ever have tempted men to occupy."[4] Habitation was confined to the higher ground along the crescent of the river formed through the centuries by alluvial deposits. North of this milewide strip stretched a great dismal swamp to the shores of Lake Pontchartrain, into which drainage from the settled area, such as it was, had to flow. The heat and humidity of the subtropical climate, coupled with inadequate drainage, made it the most unhealthy city in the United States, with a soaring disease rate and frequent epidemics of yellow fever and cholera.

Then too, existence was ever threatened by other physical calamities. Hurricanes and floods were not uncommon, and for months in 1849, for example, a crevasse in the levee inundated most of the town to a height of several feet. Thus the social ills common to any growing metropolis were immensely aggravated in New Orleans by numerous adverse physical conditions. The danger and discomfort in such a location, particularly before the advent of modern medicine and modern engineering, can hardly be exaggerated.

That it was sixth in size among the urban centers of the nation in 1860 (although only seventeenth in industrial output) indicated its many economic advantages. Only New York, Philadelphia, Brooklyn, Baltimore, and Boston were larger, the last two not greatly so. With its 168,000 residents the Louisiana river town dwarfed its southern rivals like Charleston (40,000) and younger Memphis up the river (22,000). In it resided three out of every seven white persons in Louisiana, though New Orleans accounted for only a quarter of the state's total population due to the much heavier concentration of Negro slaves in plantation areas. Included among its populace were more than 13,000 Negro slaves and almost 11,000 free persons of color. Thirty-eight percent of its citizens were foreign-born, the largest groups being Irish (24,398), German (19,572), and French (10,564).

[4] *London Illustrated News*, XXIII (Sept. 10, 1852), 203.

It should be noted that the percentage of foreign-born was much lower than in St. Louis (60), Chicago (50), or New York (47). Most of its white residents were born in Louisiana, but striking evidence of its commercial promise was the fact that New Yorkers and Pennsylvanians were more numerous than natives of any other southern state.[5]

These statistics reveal the fallacy in the popular conception that New Orleans was more "foreign" than the average American city in the nineteenth century. It was less so than many, particularly those in the upper Mississippi Valley. The misconception that it was mainly a "French" city is refuted by the fact that the Anglo-Americans very early came to match in numbers the few thousand inhabitants of French or Spanish birth, the *ancien population* and their descendants; by 1860, immigrants from other nations in Europe were far more numerous than those from France. The extent to which it was a "Creole" city depends entirely upon the definition of the word "Creole," a semantic problem of considerable complexity. All old towns have a local mythology of their own, but it is doubtful if any American city has been so erroneously romanticized by its own natives as New Orleans. Not until a generation after the Civil War was the fiction concocted that its early social history involved a conflict between "cultured" Creoles (descendants of French and Spanish settlers) and "crude Americans." If anything, the reverse tended to be truer as a generalization. In ante bellum days "Creole" simply meant native: "all who are born here . . . without reference to the birthplace of their parents," stated a local directory of 1873, *Jewell's Crescent City Illustrated*.[6] Thus in 1860 there were Creole French, Creole Anglo-Americans, Creole Negroes, and even Creole

---

[5] These statistics are from *Eighth Census of the United States* (1860). In addition to the data on New Orleans in the section on Louisiana, this census includes a more detailed breakdown on the twelve largest cities in the nation.

[6] Edwin L. Jewell, ed., *Jewell's Crescent City Illustrated* (New Orleans, 1873), 15.

Germans and Irish. For the sake of accuracy some other terminology must be used.

The question can be approached more simply from the point of view of old families and newer ones, a phenomenon common in most nineteenth-century American cities because of their rapid growth. Urban aristocracies which had arisen by midcentury were based both upon birth and property. Older families had many advantages over later arrivals for the accumulation of wealth—the tremendous increase in the value of real estate, for instance. Often resentment arose between the two groups, but usually there was considerable intermarriage and the end product was an amalgamation. To some extent this happened in New Orleans, but the process was complicated by a distinct division of the older families on the basis of national origins.

The white residents of 1803, French and Spanish, might be called Latin Creoles. Since the population tripled in the first fifteen years of American occupation, however, there were many old Anglo-American families also, though only their children were Creoles. Meanwhile, French migration from the continent and the West Indies continued, and these "foreign French" formed a third "old" group. By the 1850s, intermarriage and business partnerships among the three were not uncommon at the upper levels. The foreigners who arrived after 1840, most of them German and Irish, had not had on the eve of the Civil War sufficient time to gain entrance into the aristocracy. To distinguish them from the other main groups they might simply be called immigrants.

Much of the confusion results from the assumption that the city acquired by the United States in 1803 was a mature city. Actually it was a rough frontier town out in the wilderness, by no means on a par in the cultural essentials with Boston, Philadelphia, or Charleston. Highly provincial, many of its inhabitants were unlettered (more than half of the 8,000 were Negroes); its tastes and manners did not compare with those of Paris, though some circles tried to copy continental courtliness. Both Anglo-Americans and foreign French who arrived subsequently had broader cultural backgrounds and more education than the Latin Creoles.[7]

To cite a few examples, one of the richest and most philanthropic merchants, John McDonogh, came to the city from Baltimore in 1801.[8] Acquiring various properties which made him in time a millionaire, he eventually moved across the river to his plantation. The famous jurist Edward Livingston, heavily burdened by debt, arrived from New York in 1804 and shortly married the widow of a French officer from Santo Domingo. Another migrant from New York City was John Slidell, lawyer and politician, who married a Latin Creole, Mathilde Deslonde. Finally elected to the United States Senate in 1853, he fought Pierre Soulé in the fifties for the leadership of the state's Democratic party. James Robb, later a rich banker, railroad promoter, and art collector, arrived from Pennsylvania in 1837 with a few hundred dollars in his pocket. Christian Roselius came from Germany in 1823 under indenture to pay for his passage. First an apprentice printer, he soon turned to law and attained prominence on the legal faculty of the University of Louisiana (later Tulane University). Though he was accepted into the society of wealthy Latin Creoles, Roselius did not marry one of them but, instead, the American directress of a girls' school.

Judah P. Benjamin, born into a West Indian Jewish family and reared in Charleston, arrived fresh out of Yale in 1828 to take a job as a clerk in a mercantile house. In time Benjamin became probably the ablest of local lawyers; he was

---

[7] Joseph G. Tregle, "Early New Orleans Society: A Reappraisal," *Journal of Southern History*—hereafter cited as *J.S.H.*, XVIII (1952), 20-36. This incisive article by a careful scholar explodes the whole Creole myth, and in preceding paragraphs I have been following his conclusions.

[8] *Dictionary of American Biography*, Allen Johnson and others, eds. (New York, 1928-1958)—hereafter cited as *D.A.B.*, has been used for statements in these brief sketches.

elected to the United States Senate in 1852 and during the war held three different posts in the Confederate cabinet. The brilliant attorney and orator Etienne Mazureau, exiled from France because of opposition to Napoleon, reached the city by way of New Jersey in 1804. Prosecuting a sensational case as attorney general of the state, he dared attack the practice of dueling. Most prominent of the foreign French was Pierre Soulé, Democratic senator and party leader of the 1850s. Imprisoned in France for republican activities under Charles X, he escaped to America in 1825 and came south after a brief stay in Baltimore. Marrying into a Latin Creole family, he became prominent because of his oratorical powers and his skill in politics. Charles E. A. Gayarré of French and Spanish descent, noted for his four-volume history of Louisiana, was one of the few gifted Latin Creoles. But when he remarried later in life, Gayarré picked as his wife an Anglo-American woman from Jackson, Mississippi.

So much for the aristocracy. In any large commercial city —particularly one which increased twentyfold in population in half a century—the middle class was bound to be much more numerous. In New Orleans it consisted of the vast majority of Latin Creoles and Anglo-Americans who were not as able or as lucky as their aristocratic fellows, and an increasing number of immigrants who worked their way upward in the 1850s. Within its ranks were professional men, managers of business enterprises, skilled workers, clerks, grocers, and similar groups. By no means as homogeneous as the upper class, it never exerted the influence that it did in most American cities because of the highly transient nature of local society. By 1860 the proletariat—the largest group among the populace—consisted mainly of the immigrant Irish, who replaced Negro slaves as the hewers of wood and carriers of water. Their abject poverty, their rowdiness, and their clannishness caused them to be hated and feared by the classes above them; but their labor was needed, and it was used because it was cheap and available. The masses and the middle class usually followed their gentleman leaders. In wartime both groups would assume more importance because of sheer numbers.

Negroes, slave and free, constituted a fourth main social class in the metropolis, though they declined in numbers—both absolutely and relatively—in the two decades before the war because of the increasing rigidity of the caste system and cheaper immigrant labor for rough work. Earlier they had enjoyed considerable freedom despite the letter of the law. Many of them were house servants, but a large number were skilled workers, hired out by their masters if they were slaves or easily attaining employment if they were free. By no means were they the proletariat in 1860.

The local community of free Negroes, 80 percent of whom were mulattoes, included numerous small businessmen and skilled artisans, many of whom were educated and well-to-do. Quadroon women, taken as mistresses by aristocrats, were set up in small white houses on Rampart Street; but the practice was by no means as extensive as has been claimed, and the romanticized "Quadroon Balls" were more often interracial orgies. As the slavery dispute heightened, the state legislature put more and more legal restrictions on free persons of color and finally in 1857 forbade manumission, causing some of the more sensitive and ambitious to migrate to Haiti or to France. All Negroes, bond and free, had good reason to welcome the "bluecoats" upon the Federal capture of the city.

"Let no one judge of America from New Orleans," wrote the much-traveled Captain James E. Alexander in his *Transatlantic Sketches,* "for it is altogether *sui generis.*"[9] All travel accounts agree that it was the *most different* American city. These differences were both in kind and in degree, the consequence of many diverse factors which cannot be meas-

[9] James E. Alexander, *Transatlantic Sketches* (London, 1833), II, 31.

ured with any accuracy. Basic, however, was the fact of disease, chiefly yellow fever, which appeared almost every year and frequently became epidemic, taking a tremendous toll of lives (estimated at more than 6,000 in 1832 and at 9,000 in 1853). As a result New Orleans had the most transient population of any metropolis, far more so than the average port or river town.

In fact, it was a six-months-a-year town. Natives either had contracted the disease and died or, surviving, had acquired a degree of immunity. Few outsiders dared enter the city between May and October (normally slow months for an economy based on cotton and sugar). Residents who could afford to do so left during these hot months; the aristocracy went to Europe and the East, the middle classes to closer sites like Covington across the lake or to the Mississippi gulf coast.

In the busy season a large percentage of the male population were bachelors or men who had left their wives up north. Living in boarding houses or hotels, they departed as soon as they had transacted their business; eager for pleasure, they lacked any concern for the welfare of the community. "It is a striking peculiarity of New Orleans," wrote the editor of *Harper's* in 1853, "above even all other American cities, that it has worn no air of home; its citizens have worn the bustle and nervous activity of men who were only *staying* a little longer."[10]

By a process of natural selection the extreme danger of residence in New Orleans tended definitely to determine the quality of the Americans who came there to live and of the immigrants who stayed upon their arrival from Europe. By and large the Americans were men, however able and ambitious, willing to gamble for high stakes at the risk of high losses. Because cotton ships returning empty from Europe offered cheap transportation to New Orleans, many immi-

[10] *Harper's New Monthly Magazine*, VII (1853), 846.

grants arrived only to go straight on up the river, while others stayed simply for lack of funds to move on. Perhaps this is why the local German émigrés never produced a leader of the caliber of Carl Schurz of Missouri, though Christian Roselius might be considered such. After the epidemic of 1853, Irish immigration almost ceased for a decade. In any event, many men of intelligence and sober judgment looking for a home for their families were disinclined to select the Crescent City over healthier and in many ways superior places in the Mississippi Valley. Certainly, such adverse conditions for half a century affected the character of the local populace.

Generalizations about cities are always subject to some exceptions and they must be comparative, but the scores of travel accounts by observers, both American and European, who also visited New York, Memphis, Cincinnati, Philadelphia, and St. Louis, must be granted a high degree of objectivity because of their general agreement about New Orleans. They pronounced it the dirtiest city in the country. Dead animals, garbage of all kinds, and even "night soil" were dumped on its mostly unpaved streets, which intermittent subtropical rains turned into quagmires and even lakes. They pronounced it equally the most lawless—half of the inmates of the state penitentiary had been arrested in the city.[11] Nowhere was the consumption of alcoholic liquor heavier or more widespread, prostitution more accessible and open, or gambling of all kinds at all social levels more common—from the more fashionable houses to the dives on Gallatin Street in the Vieux Carré which the police dared not invade.

Political corruption and illegal voting were customary. The historian Gayarré left the Democratic party because it condoned such practices (chiefly the voting of unnaturalized

---

[11] Robert C. Reinders, *End of an Era* (New Orleans, 1964), is an excellent social history of the city in the 1850s, and I have relied upon it heavily.

immigrants), and formally charged that his defeat as an independent candidate for Congress in 1853 resulted from the several thousand fraudulent votes cast in the election. Senator Slidell never lived down the notorious "Plaquemine Frauds" which he initiated. Thus many observers found fun-loving New Orleans excessively vicious and violent, a community where laws were violated with impunity.

Yet it was a town of great contrasts, and the very heterogeneity which ever worked for social disintegration produced an unusual tolerance and gave it much color and charm. In the better areas its varied architecture was both pleasing to the eye and functional; exquisitely furnished homes were set against a background of live oaks and bright foliage of semitropical flora. Visitors and residents who had the means could easily find opportunities during the winter season for the gratification of their aesthetic tastes and of less refined pleasures of the flesh. The public and private cuisine was excellent. Social activities reached their height during Mardi Gras and other holidays. One could attend the theater —either the older Théâtre Orléans, where the plays were in French, or several larger American playhouses like the St. Charles, where actors and offerings were easily on a par with those of eastern cities. New Orleans led the nation in the opera, sung by some of the best talent in Europe; in fact, it was the first American city to have a regular opera season. The first opera house was built in 1813 by the gambler John Davis. Concerts were frequent in the fifties, by singers like Jenny Lind or pianists like Louis Moreau Gottschalk, a native who left for Europe at an early age. One could attend balls at the sumptuous St. Charles or the St. Louis hotels, bet on the horses at the Metairie Track, and hunt, fish, or sail within a short distance of the settled area.

Pleasure was by no means a monopoly of the rich, for the masses found equivalent means of enjoyment. Since entertainment was a big local business, it had to appeal to popular tastes and pocketbooks. Upper class habits were often copied by the masses, and good taste tended to seep down through the strata of society. Even the Negroes could enjoy various amusements and cavort at their "Congo" Square. In this quest for pleasure, however, was a large element of conspicuous waste on the part of the well-to-do and of a desperate effort by the less fortunate to forget the grim realities of a highly uncertain and uncomfortable existence.

More than half the church members in New Orleans were Roman Catholics, and the largest of the Protestant denominations was the Episcopalian, followed closely by the Methodist. Since French Catholics were liberal and even inclined towards deism (they joined Masonic lodges and the Know-Nothing party), conflict arose between them and the militant, devout Irish immigrants. Organized religious bodies made the customary efforts to mitigate social ills, but in general they displayed less zeal for reform than their brethren elsewhere in the United States. Numerous fraternal organizations, like the Masons and the Odd Fellows, made some effort to cope with problems arising from poverty. Outstanding in the fight against disease were the services of the Catholic sisters who operated Charity Hospital and of the nondenominational Howard Association which fearlessly tended the stricken during fever epidemics. Volunteer fire and militia companies supplemented the small, underpaid police force in the preservation of order when the community was threatened by natural or social catastrophe.

Some conflict was bound to arise between groups of different national origins, and such strife was frequently exploited by politicians. A concerted civic effort to solve basic problems was long delayed by a physical as well as a municipal segregation. Latin Creoles settled in the First Municipality (Latin Quarter) below Canal Street, Anglo-Americans in the Second Municipality above Canal, and immigrants in the poorer area downriver from the Creoles in the Third Municipality (Faubourg Marigny). An act of the state legislature in 1836 divided the city into three municipalities under one mayor and a general council with severely limited powers. Not until 1852 were they consolidated with the addition of a fourth district, Lafayette (see map).

By 1860 segregation had diminished a bit, for Americans had moved into the old quarter and immigrants into all districts. English had probably become the dominant language, although French was still used in the schools below Canal; none of the newspapers were printed exclusively in French, but three had both English and French editions—the *Bee-Abeille* for instance. Led by the banker James Robb, consolidation had been accomplished by more progressive businessmen (mostly Whigs). It was primarily to prevent municipal bankruptcy, but under this leadership other civic improvements dictated by enlightened self-interest were launched. Most important of these was the progress in the public school system, which was soon superior to the older private and parochial educational institutions already in existence. Efforts were also made to improve the drainage system and the wharves.

It is not true, therefore, that the city made no attempt at civic betterment, nor is it fair to judge it by the paucity of accomplishment—even in comparison with the generally poor record of American cities as a whole. None faced the numerous and in some cases insurmountable obstacles that the Louisiana metropolis did. But the effort was definitely retarded by the complacency of its aristocracy, who escaped six months a year and had the means to afford cesspools and cisterns while the rest of the populace drank river water. The expense of civic progress was far greater than property holders were willing to pay. The local middle class, often the backbone of a community, was too weak and divided to

NEW ORLEANS IN 1860

MUNICIPAL DISTRICTS

In 1836 the city was divided into three separate municipalities, each with their own mayor. The old city (Vieux Carré) between Canal and Esplanade streets was named the First Municipality. The area settled mainly by Anglo-Americans above Canal—between Canal and Felicity streets—was named the Second Municipality. The area below Esplanade—the old Faubourg Marigny—was named the Third Municipality.

But when the municipalities were united in 1852, the Second Municipality was designated the *First* District, and the First Municipality became the *Second* District. The Third Municipality became the Third District. The separate town of Lafayette was added as the Fourth District. Thus the third and fourth districts were at the opposite edges of the city. In present-day New Orleans, *uptown* means *above* Canal Street (generally west) and *downtown* means below Canal (generally east).

TRANSPORTATION ROUTES

(1) The Carrollton Railroad followed the crescent of the river up to the town of Carrollton. There it joined—
(2) The Jefferson and Lake Ponchartrain Railroad, which ran out to the lake.
(3) The New Orleans, Jackson, and Great Northern Railroad later Illinois Central.
(4) The New Basin Canal, on the western edge of the city, ran north to the lake.
(5) The Carondelet Canal and Bayou St. John (a natural bayou) also ran out to the lake, but on the eastern edge of the city.
(6) The Ponchartrain Railroad, east of and parallel to the bayou, ran north to the lake along Elysian Fields Avenue.
(7) The Mexican Gulf Railroad ran out Good Children Avenue to Proctorville, on the south shore of Lake Borgne.
(8) The Opelousas and Great Western Railroad, across the river in Algiers, ran westward eighty miles to Berwick Bay.

THE ACCOMPANYING MAP was drawn from several contemporary maps, one of the best of which is that of Gardners' in 1861.

For perspective, see also the larger map of southern Louisiana in Chapter Two.

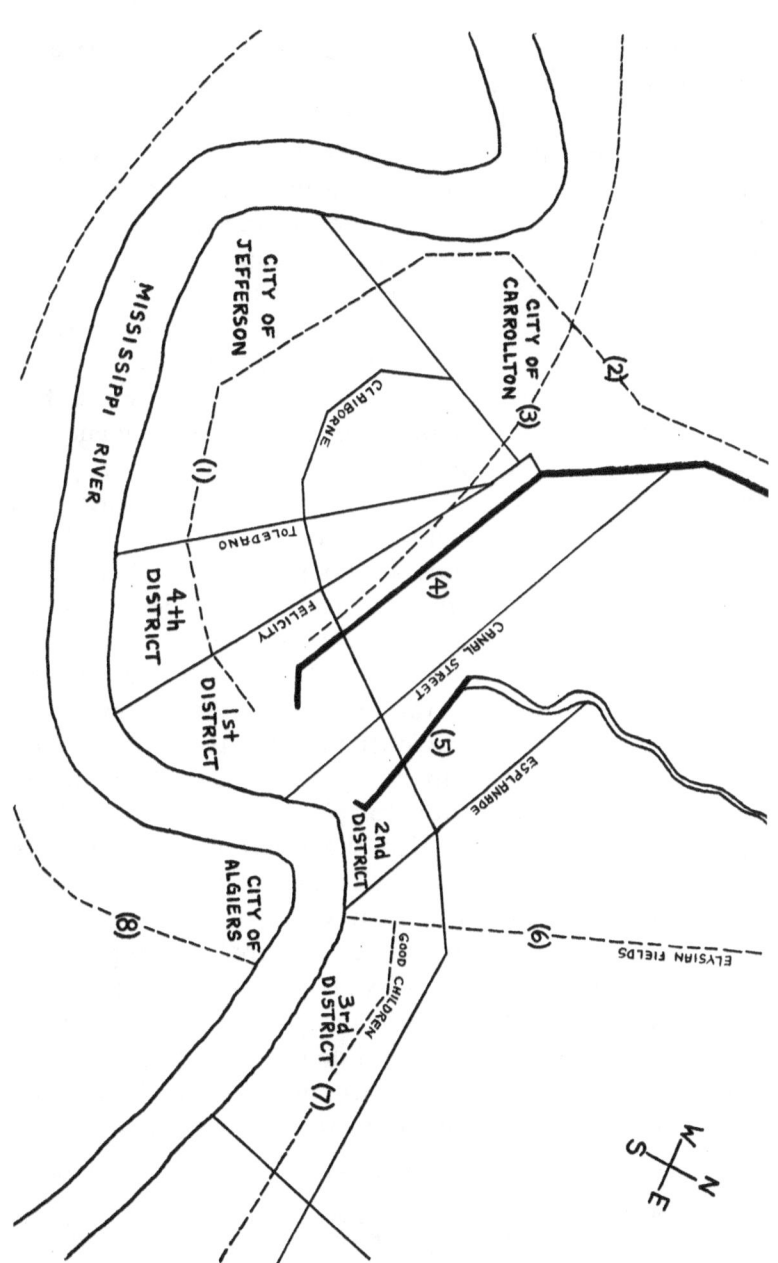

carry the costly burden alone. Resignation and complacency was contagious, and even enterprising Yankees in time surrendered to the debilitating climate.

Certainly one might have expected from New Orleans, if anywhere in America, some significant contributions to the arts. The closest it came were the histories of Gayarré and its architecture, more a folk creation than anything else. In the 1850s its artists were mediocre portrait painters and its musical composers were writers of popular songs. Local geniuses who later attained fame moved to the continent early in life. Creative work, as one critic states, "was stifled in the vigorous business-like atmosphere."[12] Evidence of intellectuality was equally lacking; no museum or citywide library existed, and William T. Sherman, president of a Louisiana college, complained that he could not find the books he needed in New Orleans bookstores. The University of Louisiana, founded in 1845, had an excellent medical faculty and a good law school, but it attracted only a handful of students to its undergraduate college. On the eve of the Civil War the earlier observation of Prince Achille Murat in his *America and the Americans* was still true: intellectual conversation was met with rarely in the city, "but ample means are afforded for eating, playing, dancing, and making love." A harsher critic called the community a "halfway house between California and civilization."[13]

As much like Caribbean as it was like other American and southern towns, despite its cosmopolitan appearance New Orleans had a provinciality all its own. The comments of its newspapers left no doubt that it felt an intense local pride, resented any criticism, and denied all charges that life there was in any way more hazardous than elsewhere. The dollar and pleasure were its gods. It liked itself pretty much

---

[12] Harriet Cale, "Cultural Life in New Orleans in the 1850's" (M.A. thesis, Louisiana State University, 1945), 127.
[13] Achille Murat, *America and the Americans* (New York, 1849), 247; Robert G. Barnwell, *The New-Orleans Book* (New Orleans, 1851), preface, i.

as it was, and it intended to stay that way as long as possible. Through the years it had indeed exhibited an amazing vitality in resisting vicissitudes. Had the United States possessed a choice in the matter, it could not have chosen a more difficult city for an experiment in military occupation.

POLITICS in the United States operates at three different levels: local, state, and national. Even when the same party label is used, issues and individual affiliation often differ at these levels; such was the case in New Orleans. During the decades before the Civil War the Whigs nationally favored a policy which benefited business interests and stood stanchly for the Union. The Democrats, who also supported the Union but opposed their rival's economic policy, usually received most of the votes of small farmers, laborers, and immigrants. It is not surprising, therefore, that in every presidential contest from 1836 to 1860 save one, the commercial metropolis of Louisiana gave its vote to the Whig candidate, even though the state went Democratic several times. However confused the national party situation after the Whigs broke up early in the 1850s, the same local conservative groups who voted for Zachary Taylor in 1848 won the election of 1856 for the Know-Nothing candidate Millard Fillmore and that of 1860 for the Constitutional Union nominee John Bell, both of whom were former Whigs. Some Democrats, of course, were conservative, and several former Whigs like Benjamin joined their ranks. Three senators from Louisiana in the 1850s, Soulé, Slidell, and Benjamin, were New Orleans residents.

In state politics New Orleans merchants might squabble with planters over the method of representation in the legislature, but they united with them in the protection of property interests against the smaller farmers and workers, as in the adoption of the conservative constitution of 1852. In

1856, at the municipal level, progressive merchants used the Know-Nothing party and intimidation to break up a Democratic coalition of Latin Creoles and immigrants which had held control, though individual personalities and ambitions were also involved. But labor soon became the dominant local political force and took over the Know-Nothing organization; the last two prewar mayors were skilled laborers, Gerard Stith a printer (1858) and John Monroe a stevedore (1860).[14]

The city's opposition to secession manifested itself clearly in every presidential election after the issue arose in the crisis of 1850. It gave overwhelming support to the compromise of that year and condemned the Nashville Convention. In 1852 a Whig candidate met defeat locally for the first time by a narrow margin because the party platform and possibly its candidate were lukewarm in support of the compromise. In 1860, when secession was the main question, New Orleans voted three-to-one against the Southern Democratic candidate: John Bell 4,978, Stephen A. Douglas 2,967, John C. Breckinridge 2,533.[15] The same pattern was repeated in Memphis up the river for the same reason; both cities regarded their trade with the upper Mississippi Valley as essential to their prosperity, which secession might destroy. Yet this opposition did not indicate the slightest doubt about the virtue of slavery—nowhere in the South was it defended more vigorously than in the Crescent City—or southern rights; local opinion simply did not regard secession necessary for the protection of either. As a matter of fact the South as a whole agreed. The Unionist candidates Bell and Douglas together received more popular votes in the region than Breckinridge, and only a minority of slave states—seven out of fifteen—seceded before the firing on Sumter. Since Lou-

[14] Leon C. Soule, *The Know Nothing Party in New Orleans* (Baton Rouge, 1961), is a detailed study.
[15] Merle E. Owen, "Presidential Elections in New Orleans, 1852-1860" (M.A. thesis, Tulane University, 1956), is a careful analysis.

isiana was one of these seven, Lincoln's election obviously caused immediate change in attitudes.

In times of crisis, public opinion changes rapidly as the impact of events stirs emotions to a frenzy. Though in November New Orleans voted overwhelmingly for compromise, the following January it gave secessionist candidates to a state convention the small minority of 380 votes out of a total of 8,336 over the "cooperationists," who opposed immediate secession by the state. Before the election the *Picayune* (which followed more than it led public sentiment) had warned against the delusion that secession could be peaceful. "Oh for an hour of Henry Clay!" cried the editor of the Whig *Bulletin*. "I have been asked, when I would consent to a dissolution of the Union. I answer never, never, NEVER, NEVER!"[16] But *De Bow's Review* openly advised the South to get out of the Union as quickly as possible unless the North agreed to protection of her rights, and Democratic leader Slidell admitted that he might favor secession in the event of Lincoln's election. Secession sentiment mounted daily after the election, reaching a climax in the stirring sermon of the prominent Presbyterian minister Benjamin Palmer in December. After delegates were elected to the convention on January 7, which three weeks later adopted the ordinance of secession, only the *True Delta* among major local newspapers continued to oppose such action.[17]

The explanation of New Orleans' amazing shift in attitude lies in the real meaning of the votes cast in the presidential election. In supporting Bell and Douglas, Orleanians expressed their desire for and their belief in the possibility of compromise. The editor of the *Bulletin* to the contrary, they did not vote for the Union at all cost nor did they reject secession as a subsequent resort. Their preference for compromise at the moment did not indicate what would be their

[16] *Commercial Bulletin*, Nov. 6, 1860.
[17] Dwight L. Dumond, ed., *Southern Editorials on Secession* (New York, 1931), xx.

position in the event of a Republican victory. President-elect Lincoln had stated positively in his speeches that he favored nonextension of slavery partly as an initial step to its ultimate extinction where it did exist. At his direction Republican members of the Senate Committee on Compromise, appointed on the day that South Carolina seceded, rejected the moderate Crittenden proposal which had the best chance of adoption. Infuriated by Republican intransigence, many New Orleans citizens by January had simply lost all hope of the acceptance of their minimum demands. They then had to face the question of whether their state should follow those of the Lower South in an immediate departure from the Union or whether they should proceed by a convention of all the southern states which would make a final effort at compromise before withdrawal of the entire region.

The close vote in the January election suggests that on this issue planters outside the city may have forced the adoption of the first alternative over the reluctance of urban commercial interests and that some Unionist sentiment existed locally, much of it suppressed by various methods. The state as a whole gave secessionist candidates 20,488 votes to 17,296 for the cooperationists, but twice as many of the former were elected. Since the convention, meeting in Baton Rouge, refused to publish the official returns for more than two months—despite the constant demands of the *Picayune*—the possibility of some juggling cannot be ruled out entirely.

Cooperationists were not Unionists *per se,* but they definitely wanted to delay action until a southern convention was called. After being defeated on several motions within the first three days, however, they surrendered, and most of them voted for the ordinance on January 26. Two motions were introduced by delegates from New Orleans. One, by John A. Rozier, called for a regional convention at Nashville to propose amendments to the Federal Constitution; and a second, by Charles Bienvenu, who represented part of the city along with neighboring parishes, would have required submission of the action of the convention to ratification by the electorate. Seven of the more than one hundred delegates refused to sign the ordinance, three of the nonsigners being from the city. On January 29 the convention moved to New Orleans, where it continued its deliberations for two months.[18]

Unquestionably there were irregularities in the procedure. None of the three crucial decisions were submitted to the voters of the state for approval, though the *Picayune* continually demanded submission: not that of the special session of the legislature in December to hold a convention, nor the act of secession in January, nor the formal entrance of the state into the Confederacy in March. This was not necessarily proof of a conspiracy of the planter oligarchy of Louisiana. Only a small percentage of the state's white freemen had voted in the past, and the oligarchy was once again acting in the manner to which it was accustomed. Some perspective may be gained by a comparison of Louisiana with Tennessee, where Memphis had partly undergone the same shift of opinion as New Orleans and had voted affirmatively in a plebescite on the calling of a convention.[19] But Whigs in the central and eastern parts of that state had defeated the call, probably because they owned far fewer slaves than their fellow planters in Louisiana. The refusal of Louisiana to secede in January would hardly have changed the course of events, since it would certainly have withdrawn with the states of the Upper South when Lincoln called for troops after Sumter.

More significant is the fact that one-fourth of the Louisianans who voted in the presidential election in November did not cast votes in January on the more important question

[18] The secession movement and the convention in Louisiana are discussed in Willie M. Caskey, *Secession and Restoration of Louisiana* (Baton Rouge, 1938), 1-43; Jefferson D. Bragg, *Louisiana in the Confederacy* (Baton Rouge, 1941), 1-32; Roger D. Shugg, *Origins of the Class Struggle in Louisiana* (Baton Rouge, 1939), 157-70.

[19] Gerald M. Capers, *Biography of a Rivertown* (Chapel Hill, 1939), 136-41.

of the convention. Either they had not made up their minds or they were Unionists; in either case most of them would have opposed immediate action. Many of them may have refrained from voting for fear of retaliation. A New Orleans printer, DeWitt Roberts, and other Unionists were banished from the city,[20] though German-born Christian Roselius on the law faculty of the University of Louisiana openly challenged the constitutionality of secession at the convention and afterward with impunity. Irish and German immigrants elsewhere in the nation were lukewarm if not hostile to the institution of slavery, but on the other hand they had no liking for the Negro. If they had voted in New Orleans as they did in Memphis, where the *Appeal* blamed the victory of Unionist delegates upon the almost solid support of immigrants, local newspapers would surely have called attention to that fact. The term "Unionist," it should be remembered, was highly relative; many who opposed secession in November no longer did so in January, and some who in that month still sought to prevent separation ceased to do so after Sumter. Even the approximate number of residents who remained Unionist cannot be determined.

In any event New Orleans was bound to go along with the decision of the state. However much it valued its trade with the upper valley, its main economic ties were with the cotton and sugar planters of Louisiana. In view of the actual situation and the prospects in January, 1861, commercial interests could easily rationalize the action on grounds of self-interest. At that time war was by no means certain, and a majority believed that it would be short in duration if it came and that it would end in a victory for the South. As the largest city of an independent confederacy with closer ties to England, its economic position might well be improved rather than hindered.

[20] DeWitt Roberts, *Southern Sketches* (Jacksonville, Ill., 1865), 27-28, 35-38.

TWO   THE CAPTURE

THE STORY of the Civil War has been told and retold many times. A major episode in that story was the battle at the forts near the mouth of the Mississippi and the consequent fall of the city of New Orleans in April, 1862. Just as local history has little significance unless it is woven into the larger national epic, so any single battle attains meaning only against the major events of the entire war. The fighting near the mouth of the river, like the bloody battle of Shiloh which preceded it by two weeks and the naval capture of Memphis which followed it within five, was part of the successful Federal campaign to seize the control of the river and cut off the western portion of the Confederacy.

This attack, down the valley from Cairo and up from the Gulf of Mexico, produced the only major victory for the United States during the first two years of hostilities. It contrasted with the Union rout at Bull Run in the summer of 1861 and George B. McClellan's failure to take Richmond by his Peninsular campaign in the spring of 1862. Whatever the strategic value of the conquest of the Mississippi (not complete until Vicksburg fell in July, 1863), there can be little doubt of its effect upon American morale. Without this victory the North might well have abandoned the effort at coercion; even if it had not, Europe would probably have recognized the independence of the Confederacy.

One of the many similarities between the Confederacy and the American colonies in the rebellion of the 1770s was the lack of a fully organized national government at the outbreak of hostilities. In both instances the existing local and state governments necessarily had already initiated military preparations and planning. Considerable time was required before the Confederate cabinet could establish the agencies essential for coordination of the martial effort and for the crucial decision on overall strategy. Inevitably conflicts in authority arose, some of which were never resolved. This was a main reason for the decision of the Davis government to fight a defensive war, but what alternative was possible in view of the disparity of population between the belligerents and the general southern insufficiency in war material, ships, or factories to produce them? As in 1776, the broad plan was to repel invasion wherever it was attempted until entrance of other nations into the war against the enemy or foreign aid was forthcoming.

The colonies succeeded in their strategy with the victory at Saratoga and the French alliance, but the South failed in the defeats at Shiloh and New Orleans. On the basis of hindsight, military historians, like Monday morning quarterbacks, have advanced various criticisms of both southern strategy and tactics on the unprovable assumption that a different course of action would have reversed the outcome.[1] In any war of long duration where the odds were obviously so even as in this one, the variable factors are too numerous to single out any one as being conclusive. Nor can the element of mere chance be ignored, or the numerous instances in the history of warfare when the most intelligent

---

[1] Typical of these is British General J. F. C. Fuller, who argues in his *Grant and Lee* (Bloomington, Ind., 1957) that the Confederates should have retreated to North Carolina in 1861, which could have been held by a smaller force than Virginia, and massed their strength in Tennessee.

judgments have turned out contrary to expectations. The authorities in Richmond, as well as in Tennessee and Louisiana, were aware from the outset that an attack in the West would come in time, and they jointly took steps to repel it. The wisdom of their actions should be judged, if it is to be judged at all, on the basis of the situation as they saw it in 1861. The ultimate responsibility for the disposition of forces, of course, lay with the Confederate government, which had to resist demands from the states that the highest priority be given to local defense.

Faced with an uncertain future, human beings are always inclined to wishful thinking, but too much emphasis cannot be placed upon the many events of the first year of the conflict which increased southern confidence in an early victory. The northern panic which followed the wild retreat at the first battle of Manassas, and the imminence of war between the United States and England when Confederate commissioners were taken off the *Trent,* buttressed the conviction that the Yankees could not fight and that Europe would intervene shortly. The expectation of southern success was even stronger in London and Paris, where government circles and public opinion generally favored the Confederacy.

Should sentiment alone not induce foreign aid and loans, the South believed that economic pressure would do so when the embargo on cotton produced a shortage of that commodity in England. Enough ships ran the blockade of the Atlantic and Gulf coasts in 1861 to make it as yet only a slight inconvenience, and even that would be ended by foreign intervention. Such was the atmosphere in which the plans were made and executed which would determine the course of the second year of the conflict.

President Jefferson Davis, a West Pointer who had fought in the Mexican War and had served as secretary of war under Franklin Pierce, possessed unquestioned military competence and experience. Knowing firsthand the military power and potentiality of the United States better than any official in the Union, unlike his fellow southerners he did not expect an easy or quick triumph. Because of insufficient arms for the available volunteers, he had to disperse his smaller forces where the enemy concentrated theirs for attack, and at other points where—on the basis of intelligence reports and his own considerable knowledge of war and of the terrain—subsequent attacks were indicated. Such a dispersal involved a large element of calculated risk.

Most of all, the geography of the southern region was basic to its defense. Since the Federals early revealed that their main drive would be directed against Richmond, Davis and his cabinet in the first months moved troops from all over the South to Virginia, leaving smaller forces in the ports along the coasts to protect them from invasion by sea. In no area was the Confederacy so exposed to attack as in the middle Mississippi Valley, where there were no mountains and where railroads and three rivers (the Mississippi, Tennessee, and Cumberland) extended deep into the interior. By contrast, none was more protected than the mouth of the Mississippi, where extensive fortifications had long existed and where the shallow bays and swamplands would require a difficult amphibious operation.

MOST MILITARY DEFEATS set off a controversy about responsibility which, from the very nature of war, cannot be settled. Major General Mansfield Lovell, in command of local military defenses after October, 1861, was made the immediate scapegoat for the fall of New Orleans, and soon President Davis and his secretary of the navy justly received much of the blame. More details than usual are available in this instance because at Lovell's insistence in 1863 a special court of inquiry was held which exonerated the general with some slight criticism. All of its testimony, as well as the correspondence between the Confederate War Department, Lovell, and the governor of Louisiana, was published at the time by the Confederate Congress, which also conducted a full investigation into the local activities of the Navy Department. Even this was *ex post facto*. Davis apparently directed unfair censure at Lovell to protect his cabinet officer and himself.[2]

As a matter of fact, throughout the first year of hostilities the vast majority of local residents were confident that no attack would be attempted and, even if one were, that the defenses were impregnable. When word came in April, 1862, that the Federal fleet had crossed the bar at the mouth of the river, the *Picayune* assured its readers that "Forts Jackson and St. Philip are armed with one hundred and seventy guns. . . . The navigation of the river is stopped by a dam about a quarter of a mile from the above forts. No flotilla on earth could force that dam in less than two hours, during which it would be within short and cross range of one hundred and seventy guns of the heaviest calibre."[3] It went on to list other redoubts along the river manned by troops "in discipline and

[2] *Proceedings of the Inquiry Relating to the Fall of New Orleans* (Richmond, 1864)—hereafter cited as *Court of Inquiry; Correspondence between the War Department and General Lovell Relating to the Defenses of New Orleans* (Richmond, 1863)—hereafter cited as *Lovell Correspondence*. These are also in *Official Records of the Union and Confederate Navies in the War of the Rebellion* (Washington, 1894-1922), Ser. 2, I, 639-716—hereafter cited as *O.R.N.;* the omitted letter of Jan. 3, 1862, is in *War of the Rebellion. A Compilation of the Official Records of the Union and Confederate Armies* (Washington, 1880-1901), Ser. 1, LIII, 765—hereafter cited as *O.R.* (Ser. 1 unless otherwise indicated). They are supplemented by a congressional investigation of the Navy Department in New Orleans, *O.R.N.*, Ser. 2, I, 433-809. A conclusive defense of Lovell on the basis of these records is Gustavus V. Smith, *Confederate War Papers* (New York, 1884), 59-144. President Davis' congressional enemies joined the bitter delegates from Louisiana in forcing these investigations and publications upon him. Davis removed Lovell from command in December, 1862, delayed his request for a court of inquiry—as well as publication of the court's findings—and falsely charged that Lovell had not warned him in advance about the weakness of local defenses. The fullest account of Confederate New Orleans is Charles L. Dufour, *The Night the War Was Lost* (New York, 1961), and the most recent general study is John D. Winters, *The Civil War in Louisiana* (Baton Rouge, 1963).

[3] *Picayune*, April 5, 1862 (the daily edition is cited, unless otherwise specified).

drill far superior to the Yankees." Three months before, after Federal forces had landed on Ship Island over in Mississippi Sound, the *Crescent* had asked, "Why do they not come along? . . . Chalmette's glories will be repeated, with the difference only between defeating a brave and manly foe, and such a race of sneaking imbeciles as the Bull Runners of the North."[4]

Such remarks can be discounted as the boasting of the press. But the more dispassionate Davis knew the situation firsthand; he and his closest adviser in the cabinet, Judah P. Benjamin, whose plantation was just across the river from New Orleans and who would soon become secretary of war, were also confident. No army could march against the city overland but must be carried within striking distance by transports, as the British had done in 1815. General Edward Pakenham had chosen the route through Mississippi Sound, marching across the narrow swampland between Lake Borgne and the river, and had suffered a devastating defeat when he attacked Andrew Jackson's entrenchments below the city. Should the Federals try the same route, Fort Bienvenu would stop them; Fort Pike on the Rigolets and Fort Macombe on Chef Menteur would check their advance if they chose to move through the passes into Lake Pontchartrain for an attack from the north. Both lakes were too shallow for the entrance of large vessels. If, for that reason, the enemy came up the river, their deep-draft warships must pass the shallow bar at the mouth and the two forts twenty-five miles upstream. As the President told panicky and petulant Governor Thomas O. Moore, much had been done since 1815 to improve all these defenses.[5]

When the war began, southern Louisiana was already one of the fortified points on the American coastline. Since the state had seized these fortifications before secession was completed, for six months after Sumter little was done because it

[4] *Crescent*, Jan. 10, 1862.
[5] *O.R.N.*, Ser. 2, I, 705.

was believed that nothing really needed doing. Geography and forts protected the city in all directions. Had not the British been routed in 1815, and did not Bull Run prove that the Yankees could not fight? Surely the war would be over before preparations for an attack upon New Orleans could be completed; in any event England would not permit the fall of so important a cotton port. As a gesture to local pride the War Department placed in command seventy-one-year-old General David Twigg, a semi-invalid. With public approval Louisiana troops were sent to Virginia or to other points on the gulf coast like Pensacola, for it appeared that only an attack on the city by river from the north had any chance of success. Until the spring of 1862 both General Lovell, Twigg's successor, and Governor Moore regarded an attack from that direction as more likely. Even there, Memphis and Vicksburg must fall before any local danger would exist.

The arrival of the first blockading ships at the mouth of the river in May and the seizure of Ship Island by the Federals in the autumn disturbed the more timid, particularly the governor, leading to Lovell's appointment and the strengthening of defenses. The initial ocupation of the island, however, was designed merely to implement the blockade. Not until November was the top secret decision made in Washington for an attack up the river from the passes, and not until the following February did Captain David G. Farragut and General Benjamin F. Butler arrive at Ship Island.

At the end of 1861 Lovell informed Richmond that in his opinion any invasion from the gulf would be directed against Mobile and that despite his difficulties, chiefly the slow progress of the navy on its part of the defense program, he remained confident of repelling any land attack on New Orleans. "We do not apprehend much danger of an attack from the sea," observed the *Crescent* upon learning early in February of Ulysses S. Grant's capture of Fort Henry in Tennessee. "We think we can beat off the enemy if he

GEOGRAPHY OF THE CAPTURE OF NEW ORLEANS

(1) *Ship Island,* where the Federals massed their forces for the attack. It is fifty miles from Lake Pontchartrain and eighty miles from the mouth of the river.
(2) *Southwest Pass,* used by Farragut's warships because it was the deepest of the passes, though obstructed by a shallow bar off its mouth.
(3) *Fort Livingston,* guarding an alternate water approach through Barataria Bay and bayous to the vicinity of the city.
(4) *Fort Jackson,* and
(5) *Fort St. Philip,* where the battle actually occurred.
(6) *Chalmette Battery,* on the site of the battle of 1815.
(7) *Fort Bienvenu,* on Lake Borgne along the route taken by the British in 1815.
(8) *Fort Macombe,* on Chef Menteur, a deep pass between Lakes Borgne and Pontchartrain.
(9) *Fort Pike,* on the Rigolets, another deep pass between those lakes.

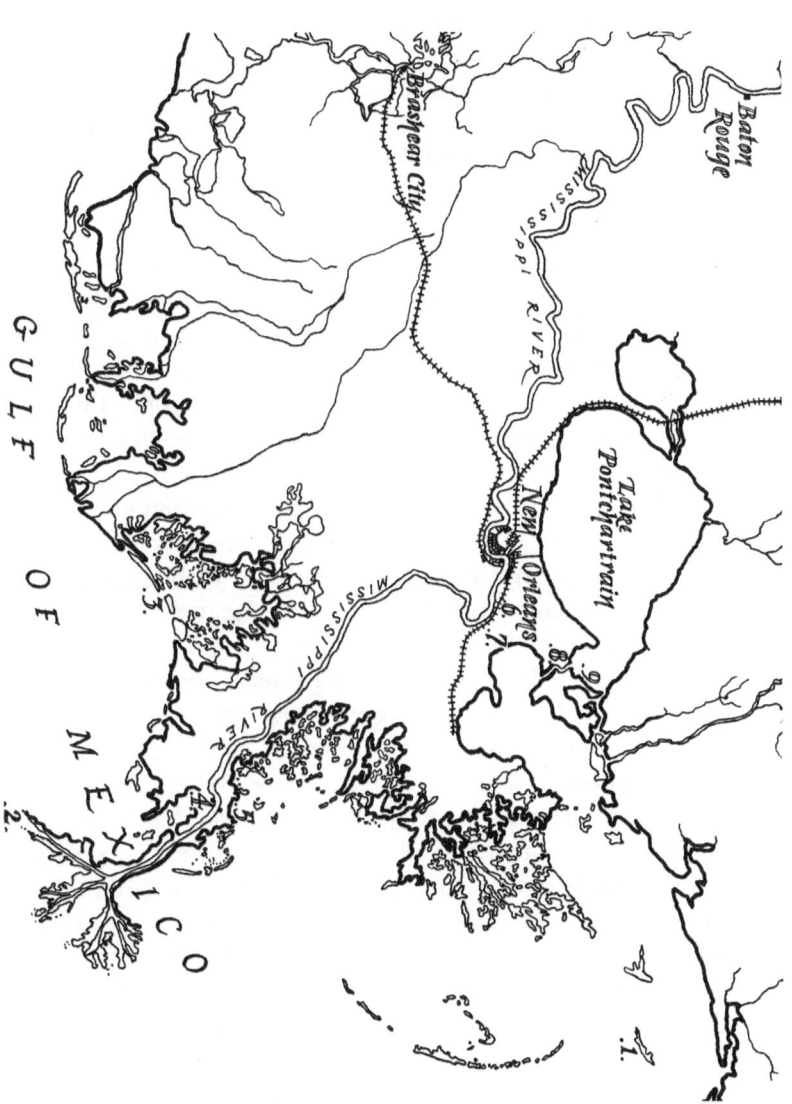

approaches from the seaward. The only real danger we apprehend comes from the Upper Mississippi." And even after news came in March that Farragut was crossing the bar off Southwest Pass, many in command positions still regarded the movement as a feint to induce the recall of military and naval forces recently sent to Tennessee.[6]

On the improbable chance of an advance against the city, in the fall of 1861 the War Department had ordered Lovell to strengthen all local defenses immediately. The new commanding general, a Washington-born West Pointer who had fought in the Mexican War, had resigned his post as deputy street commissioner in New York City soon after the battle of Bull Run to accept his Confederate commission. Though he was personally recommended to Davis by General Joseph E. Johnson, his northern residence caused some misgivings. Lovell had the difficult task of coordinating the defense efforts of the municipality, volunteer citizens' organizations, the state of Louisiana, and the Confederate navy, though he was pointedly informed by the President that the navy was strictly outside his command. For months he struggled against the numerous frustrations of his assignment, receiving commendation from his chief, Benjamin, more than once.[7]

To supplement existing forts, Lovell constructed breastworks completely around the city, heaviest at the old Chalmette battlefield, and sank obstructions in the numerous bayou approaches on the outskirts. He set up several powder mills and a cartridge factory, asking his chief frequently for quantities of saltpeter, and he bought powder from private sources. A careful inspection of the forts, already armed and manned by the state, convinced him that the guns were too small and that many were in poor condition. Their repair was impeded by the fact that many skilled mechanics had departed for service elsewhere in the South. Only a few big

---

[6] *Ibid.*, 644, 651, 658; *Crescent*, Feb. 14, 1862; Jefferson Davis, *The Rise and Fall of the Confederate Government* (New York, 1881), 210ff.
[7] *D.A.B.*, XI, 441-42; *O.R.N.*, Ser. 2, I, 640, 647, 669, 692.

guns had been included in the arsenal at Baton Rouge which Governor Moore had seized the year before. All Lovell could do, therefore, was to keep requesting the War Department for bigger guns which were never sent and to repeat his warnings about the inadequacy of local defenses.[8]

Under the circumstances, Lovell decided that he must resort to some other method of making the fire of the river forts more effective. After consulting rivermen and engineers, he obtained funds from the city council to build a boom across the river between the forts, as General P. G. T. Beauregard had earlier suggested. Consisting of cypress logs sixty feet long chained together by 2½-inch cables, it was anchored at intervals to hold it in place. Since the river was more than a hundred feet deep at the spot and soon in flood stage—the highest within a quarter of a century by the spring of 1862—the rapid rise with its accumulation of driftwood broke this boom in February. Shortly it was replaced by chaining some of the recovered sections to a number of old schooner hulks. The ingenious device, if it held, would double the effectiveness of bombardment from the forts by holding in a terrific crossfire enemy warships attempting to pass.

As usually happens in any area threatened by invasion, pessimism and rumors arose. A minority, including the governor and infirm General Twigg, thought that a fleet might pass the forts on a dark night. General Beauregard, who had years before rebuilt the forts, insisted that a fleet could even pass them in daylight. But competent opinion and most of the public accepted the naval doctrine of the day that guns ashore behind masonry were far superior to guns afloat on wooden ships. If the forts were passed, obviously warships would be necessary to prevent the capture of the city seventy-

[8] This section on the preparations for defense is based upon the *Lovell Correspondence* and the testimony at the court of inquiry and the investigation of the navy. See particularly Lovell's statement in *Court of Inquiry*, 155-64, and also pertinent chapters in Winters, *Civil War*, and John S. Kendall, *History of New Orleans* (Chicago, 1922), I.

five miles upstream. The logical location for such a fleet was just above the forts, so that it could attack the enemy simultaneously. Here the South was at great disadvantage, for it had few shipyards and iron foundries, and most of those along both banks of the river at New Orleans were largely for the repair of vessels. The local Leeds foundry, however, was second in size in the South. Until ships of war could be bought in Europe, towboats, steamboats, and sailing vessels had to be bought and converted for combat purposes.

To solve the problem, the high command in Richmond began the construction in New Orleans of two ironclads—the *Louisiana* and the *Mississippi*—similar to the *Virginia* (ex-*Merrimac*) which had caused so much havoc in Chesapeake Bay. Work on the *Louisiana* under the direction of Commodore George N. Hopkins, who was transferred upriver before the battle, was retarded by various misfortunes, including lack of skilled labor and materials as well as by a three-week strike for higher wages. Her sixteen big guns unmounted and engines malfunctioning, the *Louisiana* had to be towed down to the forts in April, mechanics aboard, in hope that somehow the job would be completed at the last minute. The more formidable *Mississippi,* larger than the *Virginia,* was an armored dreadnought with sixteen engines. Only the Tredegar Works in Richmond could cast so long a driveshaft (which never came), and even night shifts laboring by gaslight failed to get her ready. Launched prematurely by her Georgia contractors in response to public demand, she was still moored when the fighting began. News of the ironclads frightened the Federals, and Lovell and Richmond were repeatedly assured that they would soon be completed. The *Louisiana* would have been ready, had the Federals delayed their attack a few weeks.[9]

Despite their expressed confidence in the sufficiency of

---

[9] The congressional investigation of the navy concentrated on the building of the ironclads. See also John H. Neill, "Shipbuilding in Confederate New Orleans" (M.A. thesis, Tulane University, 1940).

local defenses, both residents and the press constantly complained about the navy's slow progress and the paucity of gunboats. Bombarded by private letters from his friends, Benjamin in December, 1861, ordered Lovell to seize fourteen steamboats in the harbor, crediting his account with $1,000,000 authorized by the Confederate Congress for their conversion and compensation to their owners after an appraisal. (General Leonidas Polk, Episcopal bishop of Louisiana, was the chief advocate of the project.) James E. Montgomery, J. H. Townsend, and John A. Stevenson, steamboat captains put in command of this "riverboat fleet," were assured that they would not be subject to orders from the regular navy. Under their direction the decks were protected by cotton bales, heavy timbers, and iron rails, and the boats were equipped with a few guns and iron prows for ramming. This civilian navy caused trouble from the time of its organization and ultimately proved useless. The governor and the commanding general sent formal complaints to their superiors about its "almost total want of system, vigilance and discipline."[10]

Stevenson was disgruntled because of a sensational incident which had occurred the previous October. With funds provided by citizens and with the approval of Confederate authorities, he had bought an icebreaker in Boston which he converted at the Algiers yards into an iron-prowed ram, renamed the *Manassas*. Several large Federal warships had crossed the bar at the river's mouth and had taken positions at the head of the passes, where they stopped all downriver traffic. The *Manassas* and four gunboats made a surprise attack upon them, but at the last minute Stevenson was replaced as master by a regular navy officer. Upon the attack, the Federals retreated in panic, slightly damaged; so did the Confederates, the *Manassas* having to be towed because of an injury to its engines.[11]

[10] *Lovell Correspondence*, 157.
[11] Kendall, *New Orleans*, I, 246-47.

The local situation underwent an abrupt change in late winter as a result of the Federal advance in Tennessee. Upon the capture of Forts Henry and Donelson and the Confederate defeat at Island Number Ten in the Mississippi, Richmond ordered most of the troops and half of the fleet at New Orleans north to save Memphis and to stop Grant's march which threatened the vital Memphis and Charleston Railroad. Moore and Lovell protested vehemently that this action left the city "about defenseless"; to protect it, only 3,000 ninety-day militia remained, poorly armed and trained. They were told in reply that the forces would be returned in strength as soon as they had assisted in checking the invasion of the middle valley, in ample time to meet an attack from the gulf.[12]

As frequently happens in war, the Confederate high command had to gamble, but it is by no means certain that their decision determined the outcome of the naval operations on the lower river. Placing first priority on stopping McClellan's drive in the Peninsula and the invasion of western Tennessee by land and river, and regarding a full-scale attack from the gulf as uncertain, they took the chance that the forts, the boom, and the ironclads would repel an attack there. There is no way of knowing if a few more inferior gunboats could have stopped Farragut. Certainly, once he trained the big guns of his flotilla on the city from the high river, an army was useless. To prevent a naval bombardment, the defenders would have been forced to evacuate all their troops, regardless of numbers.

LIEUTENANT David D. Porter, on duty with the blockading squadron off the river's mouth, noted with interest the crossing of the bar by the big warships in October, though he regarded their panic during the raid of the *Manassas* as

[12] *O.R.N.*, Ser. 2, I, 896-97, 710; *O.R.*, VI, 869-72.

ridiculous. Having sailed in and out of New Orleans many times, he had become convinced, from talking with pilots and fishermen, that mortar fire could reduce the forts—an opinion confirmed by Lieutenant Godfrey Weitzel, under his command, who had helped Beauregard build them. In November, 1861, he presented his plan to Secretary of the Navy Gideon Welles in Washington. Welles had reached the same conclusion himself and had been pressing it upon the cabinet. Lincoln gave his approval, General McClellan promised to provide 15,000 soldiers under General Benjamin F. Butler, and intensive preparations were begun at once. Assistant Secretary Gustavus V. Fox, given administrative charge of the project, and Porter—now a commander—selected sixty-one-year-old David G. Farragut, then in semiretirement at the Brooklyn Navy Yard, to command the attacking fleet. He too had visited the Louisiana port many times.[13]

Farragut, an adopted son of Porter's father, had fought as a mere lad with the elder Porter on the *Essex* in the war of 1812. He and the younger Porter differed from the outset on the plan of attack. A compromise resulted. First the mortar fleet would throw a barrage against the forts, and if necessary, Butler's army would attack them from the rear. But Porter was confident of reducing the forts by mortar fire alone within forty-eight hours. If they did not surrender but were sufficiently weakened, Farragut would attempt to pass them with his big ships, then cut off their supplies coming down the river, and move on up to attack the city.

Within three months a fleet of more than forty vessels, called by the London *Times* war correspondent the most powerful ever assembled in the United States, sailed from the east coast. The bombardment squadron under Porter consisted of twenty-one schooners and steamers equipped with

[13] Porter's account is in *Battles and Leaders of the Civil War*, R. U. Johnson and C. C. Buel, eds. (New York, 1884), II, 22ff; see also Shelby Foote, *The Civil War, a Narrative* (New York, 1958), I. For the controversy on the authorship of the plan of attack see Dufour, *Night the War was Lost*, 135-42.

thirteen-inch mortars firing a shell weighing two hundred pounds. Farragut's striking force, almost as large, varied from 2,000-ton battleships like the flagships *Hartford* and the *Brooklyn* to much smaller but newly built gunboats and armed steamers. Their total fire power—243 guns according to the most reliable estimate— far exceeded that of the Confederate defenses in the area, ashore and afloat. Forts Jackson and St. Philip, by contrast, had 125 guns and 1,100 men, most of them foreign-born or of northern birth. Butler's army, 18,000 strong as a result of his recent recruiting in Massachusetts, was to follow the flotilla in transports. Naturally every effort was made to maintain secrecy—Farragut did not receive his final orders from Welles until mid-February at Key West—but the arrival of such a huge force at Ship Island must have indicated to the Confederates the imminence of a major operation.

The first job was to get the big warships across the bar at Southwest Pass, the mortars and smaller vessels entering the river by the shallower Pass a l'Outre. When the river pilots, impressed into service, stuck several ships aground, the navy took over the task and accomplished it after three weeks of incessant toil, some of the guns of one big frigate being transferred to the rest. On April 15 the fleet anchored below the forts, mortars in front, Farragut's warships farther down, and army transports in the rear. The Federals intended to concentrate their fire upon Fort Jackson, the larger fort on the west bank, assuming that if it fell, smaller St. Philip across the river would surrender. News of their arrival reached New Orleans at a dark moment. Many of its men were among the casualties at Shiloh, and rumors abounded that sabotage had prevented the completion of the ironclads.

After three days of final preparations the bombardment began on the night before Friday, April 18. The forts stood just above a swift bend in the river, where the woods were cut away in front of Jackson for better vision, but not below the point of the bend. On the basis of a careful survey of depth and distance the mortars were anchored alongshore behind the woods and below the bend, fifteen on the Jackson side and six on the other. Thus neither the forts nor the fleet could see their targets clearly. Sharpshooters sent down from the city to fire on the mortars could not get within range because of the high water.

During the first hours of battle the fire from both sides proved ineffective. Then the Federals zeroed in on Jackson, setting it on fire and forcing its gunners to take refuge in the casements, though the defenders extinguished the blaze after repeated efforts. Most of the Confederate shells fell short, possibly because of inferior powder, and their biggest gun in St. Philip collapsed. Yet only one man was killed in the forts, few guns were hit, and as the Confederates adapted themselves to battle conditions, it seemed likely that the bastions could withstand the attack even if they could not do much damage to the enemy. On the second day, when one mortar schooner was sunk and a shell wounded nine men on the *Oneida,* Confederate General J. K. Duncan, in command of Fort Jackson, sent a confident wire to Lovell in the city.

Duncan had great hope for the fire rafts, which the inefficient river fleet had difficulty getting over the boom. (The general later placed most of the blame for the defeat upon the steamboat captain Stevenson who commanded it.[14]) Loaded with pitch and timber, these rafts at first terrified the enemy, who erroneously thought explosives were on board, but Farragut soon learned that they could be towed ashore by a line and left to burn out harmlessly. He detailed a special patrol for that purpose, but the dispatch of the rafts

[14] This description of the battle is based on the official reports in *O.R.N.,* Ser. 1, XVIII; the accounts of officers on both sides in *Battles and Leaders,* II, 13-102; and *Court of Inquiry.* Foote, Dufour, and Winters all give full accounts. Kendall, *New Orleans,* and James Parton, *General Butler in New Orleans* (New York, 1864), reveal the contrasts in the Union and Confederate versions. A judicious analysis is H. A. Trexler, "The Confederate Navy Department and the Fall of New Orleans," *Southwest Review,* XIX (1933), 88-102.

remained spasmodic. Observing that the boom was imperfect, the Federals inspected it closely when it was left unguarded the second night and cut it with chisels the next, no fire rafts appearing to reveal the attempt to the Confederates.

Belatedly aware of this action, Duncan released a heavy barrage, but the way was now open for Farragut to try his run past the forts. On the fourth day, despite Porter's doubts, he decided to do so and urged that Butler land his troops from the gulf side to join him at the Quarantine Station above the forts. Porter would be left behind with the mortars to continue the attack on the forts. A strong downriver wind, however, caused him to delay his attempt for several days. The firing of 13,000 shells in 96 hours had killed only four gunners in the forts and had disabled only seven guns.

Much encouraged, therefore, Duncan induced Lovell to order Commander John K. Mitchell to tow the ironclad *Louisiana,* on which mechanics were strenuously working, down to the scene of action. Mitchell, who had recently replaced Hopkins in command, took charge of the motley Confederate navy and the fire rafts, but he firmly refused to move his ironclad below the forts to direct a third fire at the Federals, as Duncan insisted. Supported by all of his officers, he argued that the plan was suicidal, since the *Louisiana* could not maneuver under her own power and her guns were not yet in position. It was better, he said, to hold her safely in reserve a few days longer until she was ready. (A court-martial later agreed with him.) To settle the critical dispute, Lovell decided to come down to the forts himself, having first appealed in vain to Mitchell's superior. Knowing nothing of this development, residents in the city remained optimistic as a result of Duncan's earlier wire.[15]

About 2:00 a.m. on the 24th, under the cover of a smoke screen from the mortar steamers which had moved upriver, Farragut ordered his warships into battle position against the

---

[15] Duncan's account of the battle, *Court of Inquiry,* 164-94.

strong current, lining up single file with his own in the middle as his captains insisted. The front group first drew the fire from the forts and engaged the Confederate ships stationed above, but the second and third groups received much heavier bombardment from the shore. The flagship *Hartford* caught fire when the little *Manassas* pushed a raft against it and ran aground briefly, but the flames were soon put out. For a while the outcome was uncertain as ships rammed one another and fired broadsides at ranges sometimes as close as twenty yards.

The Confederates had only seven vessels besides the ineffective steamboats of the "river-defense fleet," whose total fire power was no greater than one of the Federals' bigger ships. Their only chance lay in their initial attack while the enemy remained within reach of the fort guns. The fury of this attack was evident from the casualties suffered by the *Governor Moore*—74 out of a crew of 94—57 of them killed.

In less than two hours the action was over. The southern fleet was sunk or run ashore and abandoned by its crews, except for the *McRae*, which took refuge in front of St. Philip alongside the unscathed ironclad, whose armor at least had fulfilled expectations. Farragut counted 37 dead and 149 wounded, three times the losses in the forts, which otherwise sustained little damage; he had lost only the *Varuna* and three gunboats. Whatever problem remained for Porter in reducing the forts, the Federals had accomplished their immediate mission. Only the small batteries at Chalmette and those directly across the river stood between their still powerful flotilla and the otherwise defenseless city. After resting a day at the Quarantine Station, Farragut knocked these defenses out easily on the morning of the 25th. General Lovell, arriving at the forts by steamer the day before the battle just in time to witness its outcome, had hastened back to face enraged citizens who had already received word of the disaster by telegraph.

Martial law had been declared by the Confederates six weeks before, requiring all white males to register with provost marshals, immigrants from the northern states within the past year to get permits, and aliens to take an oath of allegiance. For months a committee of public safety had been in operation. The blockade had strangled trade, and even imports from upriver had recently declined, causing a shortage of necessities. Two thousand families were still receiving relief from the free market. Union spies had entered the city, though nowhere near as many as was popularly believed. A few farsighted citizens had sent their specie and valuables to safer places, but most had responded to the news of the Federal advance as they had previously to threats of yellow fever—simply by denying the existence of any danger, taking no precautions until it was actually too late to do much of anything. In this instance, however, most Confederate officials had been as confident as the populace. While the battle at the forts was raging, President Davis had wired the governor that he was confident the *Louisiana* would stop the fleet below the town.

When it became certain that the Federal flotilla was approaching, New Orleans panicked. Richmond had just sent a wire (somehow delayed) ordering Lovell to destroy all cotton and tobacco regardless of ownership, but as commanding general he possessed full discretionary powers. All day long on the 24th he and the state officials were busy removing ordnance, stores, and archives to safer points by steamer and by the Jackson railroad, which the military seized. Fifteen thousand bales of cotton were burned on the levee, empty steamboats were set afire to float downstream, and the contents of the customhouse were thrown into a big bonfire on Canal Street.

Many private owners destroyed their own property which might be of use to the enemy; proprietors of the yards in Algiers sank machinery and their big dock in deep water.

The banks sent $6,000,000 in specie out by train under special guard, and foreigners flocked to the offices of their consuls to store their more valuable property. All normal business stopped. Early in the day criminal elements in the city, joined by the poor, looted the warehouses of sugar, molasses, and food. The mob resisted the Foreign Brigade (a military company which European nationals in the city had formed for their own protection) when it attempted to restore order, and called it "Union soldiers in disguise." That night many Confederate and state officials, including the governor, departed by steamer. All of these events embittered the citizenry against the military, particularly those prevented from escaping by the seizure of transportation facilities.[16]

General Lovell was already considering the evacuation of his small force to Camp Moore seventy miles north, and he did so the next day in hope of saving New Orleans from bombardment. Since he believed the forts had fallen (the Federals had cut the telegraph), he had no other choice in view of "the perfect absurdity," as he said later, "of confronting more than 100 guns of the largest caliber, well-manned and served, looking down upon the city, with less than 3,000 militia, mostly armed with indifferent shot-guns."[17] At the same time he ordered the garrisons on the lakes and along the coast west of the river to withdraw. Learning two days later from the *McRae,* which brought up wounded under a flag of truce, that the forts still held out, he tried unsuccessfully to countermand his orders to the outlying defenses. His original decision was correct; Joe Johnson would prove later that at times a general accomplishes more by retreat than by fighting.

---

[16] Eyewitness accounts are George W. Cable in *Battles and Leaders,* II, 14ff; Marion Southwood, *"Beauty and Booty," The Watchword of New Orleans* (New York, 1867), 20-27; and Mrs. Robert Dow Urquhart, *New Orleans Confederate Journal,* Fisk-Urquhart Papers, Tulane Univ.
[17] *Court of Inquiry,* 158.

On the morning of the 25th, just a week after the bombardment began at the forts, smoke filled the air from the smoldering fires of the shocked city. Recovering from their confusion, the mayor and council urged merchants to open their shops. Crowds gathering on the levees to watch the arrival of the victorious fleet were dismayed to see the ironclad *Mississippi* come floating by, set afire because of the impossibility of towing her upstream out of danger. As the Union fleet anchored off the upper part of the town in the midst of a noon rainstorm, shots were fired on the levee— probably at Unionists who cheered or tried to signal. An angry and abusive crowd threatened Captain Theodorus Bailey and another Federal officer, who shortly came ashore, until they were rescued by two prominent citizens and led to the city hall, where Mayor John T. Monroe had just hoisted the Louisiana flag. The mayor was waiting in his office with Pierre Soulé and a few members of the council and the committee on public safety, but soon several Unionists joined them.[18]

In this first of a series of negotiations lasting five days, Bailey presented Farragut's demand for a formal surrender of the city, to be signified by the raising of the United States flag on the mint, the customhouse, and the city hall. Monroe refused, insisting that as a civil magistrate he lacked authority, since martial law had been declared, and that the mint and the customhouse were Confederate property. Appearing in response to a summons, Lovell too refused to surrender but stated that he had removed his troops. Stung by public disapproval, the general that day had advertised for one hundred desperate men to board the ships upon their arrival and destroy them.

In the whole proceedings he, the mayor, and even Farragut

---

[18] Again Kendall and Parton give full accounts. For the correspondence between Farragut and the mayor, see *O.R.N.*, Ser. 1, XVIII, 229-36, and the summary of the mayor's secretary, Marion Baker, in *Battles and Leaders*, II, 95-100.

were trying to save face. At this point Monroe decided to pass the decision to the city council, which he called into session that night, but it adjourned until the next morning without coming to a conclusion. Fearful of offending the Federal commander, the mayor sent his secretary to the *Hartford* on the night of the 25th to explain the delay. The actual wording of the notes from local authorities was the work of former Senator Soulé, who possessed diplomatic experience which they completely lacked.

The situation was ridiculous and somewhat baffling to Farragut—in fact it had many elements of a comic opera, particularly the histrionics of the mayor. Yet the initial positions assumed were based upon realities. When the council finally acted on Saturday morning, it adopted Monroe's suggestion and replied that since it could offer no resistance to occupation, "we yield to physical force alone and we maintain our allegiance to the government of the Confederate States." This answer in effect told the victors to do their own raising of flags. Occupation was not the function of a naval officer, Farragut responded; he had come to New Orleans to restore obedience to the laws of the United States. He repeated his demands of the previous day and urged the mayor to "call upon the good people of New Orleans to return at once to their vocations." Any outrages upon loyal people like the firing on the levee when the fleet arrived, he warned, would be severely punished.

The Union commander had the power to destroy the city with his guns—the mere breaking of the levees would have flooded it—but he lacked sufficient troops to occupy it. That was a job for Butler's soldiers, who could not come up the river in transports as long as the forts held out; an attempt to pass behind them through the bays would take weeks. In time the forts would be starved out; so Farragut could afford to wait, and he was probably willing for negotiations to proceed slowly. His own humanitarian feelings and southern connections disinclined him to a needless attack except under the most extreme provocation. Most of all, if he spent his remaining ammunition by bombardment, he would have none left for the reduction of Baton Rouge and Vicksburg farther north. As long as no overt resistance was offered, he wisely overlooked the mayor's verbal insolence.

Monroe's passive resistance was a clever stratagem, for it put the pressure back on the Federals. Its basic weakness lay in the inability of local authorities to restrain the hysterical populace from bolder acts of defiance which might inadvertently set off a bombardment. Now that the troops had left, the council had only the small European Brigade to enforce its decisions. In a sense, the officials were prisoners of the local mob which could prevent them from yielding any faster. Citizens were divided into three main groups: a minority of Unionists, many of whom for the first time revealed their true sentiments; some Confederate supporters who recognized the futility of resistance and who wanted to take advantage of the fortuitous opportunity to prevent further destruction of property by surrendering; and an irresponsible majority which insisted upon expressing its defiance of the Yankees. This last group soon brought matters to a crisis.

Trouble was barely averted Saturday morning when a shouting crowd surrounded a detail bringing a note from Farragut. The lieutenant in charge ordered his men to draw their arms, but he rescinded the command when the mob shoved women and children to the front. Then a Confederate officer escorted him to the city hall. Later in the day the captain of the *Pensacola*—acting on his own initiative, though Farragut later assumed full responsibility—took a small landing party ashore and raised the United States flag above the mint. Leaving it unguarded, he warned the crowd which had gathered that he had left orders with his men on the ships to fire howitzers loaded with grapeshot if the flag were molested. The captain had hardly left when William B. Mumford, a local gambler, ascended to the roof with three assistants and lowered the flag. At once the *Pensacola* fired one gun, the shot striking a nearby building. According to the northern biographer James Parton, who in 1864 published a history of Butler's occupation, only luck saved the city from a spontaneous, heavy bombardment.[19]

Mumford and his cohorts then dragged their trophy through the streets to Lafayette Square across from the city hall, where they tore it to bits and distributed the pieces as souvenirs to the large mob. Monday morning the *Picayune* reported the incident in full detail, giving the names of the leaders and eulogizing "their patriotic act. New Orleans, in this hour of adversity, by the calm dignity she displays in the presence of the enemy . . . is showing a bright example to her sister cities . . . worthy of the proud position she has achieved."[20]

This was too much. Urged on by General Butler, who had come up for a consultation, Farragut issued what local officials chose to regard as an ultimatum. In view of their refusal to comply with his demands and the danger that a repetition of such incidents might incite retaliation by his men, "it becomes my duty to notify you," he told them, "to remove the women and children from the city within forty-eight hours."[21] The council stood firm, protesting the inhumanity of a bombardment and the impossibility of evacuating citizens in so short a time. The captain of a recently arrived French ship added his formal protest to theirs, demanding at least sixty days for his nationals to remove their property. Farragut denied that he had intended to threaten a bombard-

[19] Parton, *Butler*, 275.
[20] *Picayune*, April 28, 1862.
[21] *O.R.N.*, Ser. 1, XVIII, 232-33.

ment, but drastic action became unnecessary when he shortly received word that the forts had fallen.

Duncan in Fort Jackson and Mitchell on the *Louisiana,* seeing the wreckage floating down the river, had assumed that New Orleans had fallen. For several days after the battle at the forts they had refused Porter's demand for surrender on the grounds that they had received no formal notification of the city's capture. Although the Confederates could prevent the transports from moving upstream, their provisions were running low and they could see preparations for a land attack on their rear. On Sunday evening half of the Jackson garrison spiked their guns, mutinied, and left in small boats. Finding that the remainder favored immediate surrender, Duncan had no choice but to conclude negotiations to that effect with Porter the next morning, forcing St. Philip to do likewise. Mitchell on the *Louisiana* also wanted to continue fighting, but he yielded to the wishes of his officers that the ironclad be set afire and abandoned. Just as this order was given, the chief engineer reported that he had gotten the propeller engines into operation.

The surrender of the forts now gave Farragut absolute command of the situation, since Butler's troops could arrive in a few days. At once he demanded that all state and Confederate flags be replaced. The mayor now agreed through his secretary to permit the raising of the American flag over the city hall. This time the Federals brought along a strong force with two brass howitzers in case of any interference. "Very well, sir, you can do it," Monroe replied to the officer who had come to remove the flag, "but I wish to say that there is not in my entire constituency so wretched a renegade as would be willing to change places with you."[22] Then he dramatically walked out into the street and stood in front of one of the howitzers in case someone fired upon the company. The crowd watched in silence while the flag was hoisted. As

---

[22] Kendall, *New Orleans,* I, 272.

the Federals marched away, it broke into cheers for the popular mayor, who by talking harshly and acting otherwise had done much to save his city from destruction.

THE DEFEAT on the lower river set on a smaller scale the pattern of Confederate failure in the later years of the war. All the breaks had gone against the defenders, particularly the unusual height of the flood which snapped the boom at the forts. They committed tactical errors, chiefly the divided commands which many Union naval officers regarded as the most decisive factor in their victory, but also the failure to guard the boom and light it up at night with fire rafts. New Orleans and the South lacked the technical ability, the materials, and the skilled labor necessary to complete on schedule the ironclads which could probably have stopped Farragut at the forts. Most of all, the high command was forced to neglect one area in order to protect another which it regarded as more vulnerable.

Even if the invaders had been checked at the forts by the retention of local naval forces sent upriver or possibly by reinforcements, the Federals might have captured Memphis sooner. Then, passing the Vicksburg batteries as they did later, they probably could have made a successful attack on New Orleans from its upriver side, because the defenses there were much weaker. For the same reason, had the Confederates repelled the Union advance on the middle river by massing their strength at that point, they might well have recaptured the Louisiana town even though the enemy had seized it. Any criticism of southern strategy in the Mississippi Valley must take into account these probabilities, which were fully considered at the time. The significant fact was the Union victory in both areas and its immediate consequences.

An independent Confederacy could not have become a strong nation without possession of its largest city and control of the lower Mississippi. The agrarian bias of its leaders, if it caused them to underestimate the importance of capital and trade, may have influenced their attitude toward New Orleans. But areas lost in war can be recaptured later, and frequently they are returned by treaty at the end of a war. The outcome of the Civil War was not determined by any one battle, not even Gettysburg, and certainly not the naval engagement at the Louisiana forts.[23] Despite military reverses and the failure of foreign intervention, the South could still have won her independence by inflicting heavy enough casualties upon the invaders to make them give up the attempt. When the Democrats came out for armistice and peace in 1864, both Lincoln and Grant feared that such would be the outcome.

New Orleans, with its Leeds and other smaller foundries, was a potential industrial center whose operations could have been expanded under the necessity of war. But more than its economic value, the psychological effect of the seizure of the Louisiana metropolis motivated the Federal attack upon it in 1862. The blockade was already strangling the port, and the volume of goods (of which salt was all-important) crossing the river there from Louisiana and Texas was small, since the Opelousas Railroad ran only eighty miles west. The Red River, still held by the Confederates, was suitable as an alternate route. In a long war of attrition that volume might have increased, but in that event a southern victory would have required continued operation of the railroads east of the river.

By far the most important consequence of the capture of New Orleans was its effect upon northern morale and upon the attitude of Europe. The largest city in the South had fallen, even if Richmond had not. When the capture of

[23] Dufour, *Night the War Was Lost,* whose contention I reject *in toto,* argues extensively to the contrary. His thesis, it seems to me, is the normal rationalization of an able local historian trying to emphasize the frequently overlooked importance of operations in his own area.

Memphis followed, the western portion of the Confederacy was almost cut off. Starved for victories, northern newspapers in the summer of 1862 began to chant, a bit prematurely it turned out, that the Father of Waters was about to flow to the sea again under the American flag.

THREE ENTER GENERAL BUTLER

*M*ILITARY OCCUPATION of American cities has been rare in our national existence, as no foreign enemy has invaded our mainland since 1815. Yet there are a few notable exceptions: the British held New York during most of the Revolution, and Charleston and Philadelphia for briefer periods; the Federals occupied New Orleans and Memphis for three years during the Civil War. The problems which faced the British in the 1770s were much simpler because of the smaller scale of military operations and the presence of large numbers of Tories or neutrals in the Atlantic ports. In the southern river towns a century later the conquerors had to deal with a citizenry the large majority of whom were actively hostile. As a consequence, the generals who commanded the initial occupation—Butler in New Orleans and Sherman in Memphis—have remained in southern eyes the chief villains of the conflict, though Sherman is remembered more for his later march through Georgia and the Carolinas. They held their occupation commands simultaneously: Butler from May 1, 1862, until he was superseded by General Nathaniel P. Banks the next December; Sherman for five months beginning in July, 1862.

Occupation policies were left largely to the discretion of the commanders, who of course were subject to orders from the War Department. They might use for guidance congressional and executive action in regard to slaves and other rebel property, such as the Confiscation Act of July, 1862, or the Emancipation Proclamation issued the following September, though such action was on the whole confused if not contradictory. Lincoln's primary objective, as he said in his famous reply to Horace Greeley in that year, was to restore the Union. Thus he countermanded orders of Generals John C. Frémont and David Hunter freeing slaves in conquered areas for fear of losing the border states, yet a year later he proclaimed emancipation in areas of resistance to reduce European support of the Confederacy. By contrast, Congress' attitude was mainly punitive, increasingly so as mounting casualties produced greater hatred for the South. By a series of statutes Congress freed fugitive slaves of disloyal masters, slaves fighting in the Union army, and finally, by the stringent Confiscation Act of 1862, all "rebel"-owned slaves. The same measure provided for the forfeiture within sixty days of all property of persons continuing to support the Confederacy.[1]

In April, 1863, the War Department issued General Orders No. 100, outlining in detail the whole area of relations between an invading army and the civilian population in occupied territory.[2] Prior to that date, however, because of the latitude of a general's power which resulted from this lack of a well-defined policy in Washington, his own personality and experience determined the course of action in a particular conquered area. Benjamin Franklin Butler was forty-two when South Carolina seceded. With law offices in Boston and Lowell he had the most lucrative practice in New England, where many considered him the ablest attorney of that region. Reared by a widowed mother in comparative poverty, he attained conspicuous success by combining tremendous energy and thoroughness with shrewd and sometimes unscrupulous methods. Early in his career he

[1] James G. Randall, *The Civil War and Reconstruction* (Boston, 1937), 470-71, 480-82.
[2] Ralph H. Gabriel, "American Experience with Military Occupation," *American Historical Review*, XLIX (1943-44), 630-44.

served as counsel for the factory girls of Lowell and fought in Massachusetts politics for the rights of labor; later his clientele included men of wealth. Like them he invested widely in the lucrative enterprises of New England. A man of contradictions and complex character, he instinctively involved himself in controversies which kept him in the public eye. His friends admired him as a bold fighter, and even his enemies admitted that Ben Butler was likely to succeed in whatever he undertook. Among his many activities he was a colonel in the militia.

Once he had acquired sufficient income from his legal practice, Butler began an active participation in state politics as a Democrat. Though affiliation with that party reduced his chances for national office from Massachusetts, he served in the legislature in the 1850s and ran for governor in 1859 and 1860. He attended all Democratic national conventions after 1848, and in the balloting at Charleston in 1860 he violated his instructions by shifting from Douglas to Jefferson Davis, whom he regarded as a moderate. Though he made his second gubernatorial race as a Breckinridge Democrat, like many northerners in that party he was a Jacksonian Unionist. More intimate with the southerners than many politicians from his section, he nevertheless spurned their enticements and warned them that secession would be crushed by force. From the first he favored harsh treatment of the rebels and pronounced them traitors. In fact, he offered President James Buchanan his services as an experienced criminal lawyer for an attempt to convict the southern commissioners in the capital.[3]

With characteristic energy Butler devoted himself to saving

[3] Robert S. Holzman, *Stormy Ben Butler* (New York, 1954), is an objective but sympathetic biography. Carl Russell Fish's article in the *D.A.B.* is a good short summary. Parton, *Butler*—an apologia by a noted contemporary writer who was paid for the job—has correctly been called "as thorough a job of whitewashing as can be found in American literature." See also Butler's autobiography, *Butler's Book, Autobiography and Personal Reminiscences* (Boston, 1882), and the five volumes of his *Private and Official Correspondence*, Jessie A. Marshall, ed. (Norwood, Mass., 1917).

the Union, but like many other leaders he had political and military ambitions which were consciously supplementary. "In war as in peace," observed a later historian, "he was a P. T. Barnum character. Gross in body, he was unscrupulously clever in mind and incorrigibly political in purpose."[4] No incident reveals his shrewdness more than that by which he acquired the rank of general over several colonels of the Massachusetts militia senior to him. Expecting that state troops would be called to defend Washington, he wired his friend Simon Cameron, secretary of war, suggesting that a brigadier general be called for also. Meanwhile, knowing that the legislature had provided no funds to move the troops, he arranged with a banker to put up the money on the condition that he be placed in command. Under this pressure Governor John A. Andrew yielded to his demand.

General Butler's vigorous action during the first year of the war involved him in constant controversy, but it kept his name in the headlines of the northern press. When a mob in Baltimore attacked his advance regiment, he transported the rest of his troops by ship from Philadelphia to Annapolis, where he soon repaired the railroads cut by the Confederates and lifted the blockade of Washington. Acting without orders, in May he seized Baltimore with a thousand troops, to the dismay of Lincoln and General-in-Chief Winfield Scott, who preferred a conciliatory course to keep the state from seceding. Before they could stop him he stirred up as much trouble as he would later in New Orleans. He issued proclamations, removed the mayor, and threatened the legislature with arrest if they passed an ordinance of secession. He arrested and threatened to hang Ross Winans, a wealthy secessionist, but the President ordered the prisoner's release. Scott wired a formal rebuke and quickly transferred Butler to Fortress Monroe in Virginia. At the same time, to avoid the alienation of a leading Democrat whose rash actions were

[4] George F. Milton, *Conflict* (New York, 1941), 54.

applauded by so large a portion of the northern public, Lincoln offered him a commission as a major general in the volunteers.[5]

Butler precipitated a new crisis when he retained several fugitive slaves who had fled to his lines on the grounds that they were "contraband" of war. The name stuck, and this act won him such acclaim from radical Republicans that Congress quickly confirmed it by statute. His next venture, however, almost ended in disaster. Having decided that Richmond could be taken by way of the James River, without informing Washington of his plans he launched an attack on a Confederate battery at Big Bethel below Yorktown. When his untrained troops were ambushed, they retreated in a rout like the one soon to occur at Manassas, though casualties were not great. As a consequence, the Senate almost rejected confirmation of his new rank, and he was superseded in command by a retired West Pointer.

Butler redeemed himself somewhat by leading the military forces of an amphibious expedition which captured two small forts on Cape Hatteras, where he demanded and received the unconditional surrender of the defenders. Then he induced Lincoln to send him to recruit troops in New England and to create a new department there for him to command. In spite of an acrimonious dispute with Governor Andrew of Massachusetts, backed by Federal authority the general got his recruits. At the end of the year, through his wide political influence in the capital and in face of McClellan's opposition, he received the important appointment of military commander of the expedition against New Orleans.

Though he had caused the administration much trouble and frequently had disobeyed orders, Butler was already the

---

[5] Winfield Scott and a few holdovers from the Mexican War, soon to be retired, were lieutenant generals. Among the new major generals, Butler was appointed on May 16, 1861, Banks and Dix in June, and McClellan and Frémont in July. By the calendar Butler was therefore senior, but government orders were issued later dating their appointments retroactively to make all four outrank him: Holzman, *Butler*, 251n; Parton, *Butler*, 614.

most popular general in the North; he had given the public the dramatic, forceful action for which many clamored. Indeed, he had initiated in the field the policy of revenge upon the rebels favored by the radical Republicans, whose party he joined after the war. In view of the moderation of the President's reconstruction policy later indicated in his "10 percent plan," it seems strange on the surface that Lincoln consented to an occupation post for so vindictive an officer.

Perhaps the President secretly preferred otherwise, but he was to a large degree an opportunist in the early years of the conflict. In a democracy rent by civil war, political considerations must often determine military decisions. He could not afford to make an enemy of so popular and clever a Democrat, particularly one who realized Lincoln's dilemma. According to McClellan's chief of staff, army generals, many of whom he outranked, cooperated in finding "a hole to bury this Yankee elephant in."[6] On the other hand, Butler had shown real administrative ability. He had his own way of getting things done, and done quickly; his unorthodox methods might succeed where those of cautious, well-trained West Pointers failed. Higher authority could always countermand his orders if he went too far, or at worst transfer him. By and large, a political general was better qualified to administer conquered areas than a professional soldier.

For a time luck ran out on Butler. The battle at the forts below New Orleans was exclusively a navy show—all he did was to accept the surrender of the mutineers from Fort Jackson. At once he criticized Porter bitterly, beginning a celebrated feud that was to last thirty years; it was very unmilitary of Farragut, he declared, to steam past forts which had not been reduced. Nor did he have even the satisfaction of receiving the surrender of New Orleans, for Farragut lowered the Confederate flag over the city hall before his

[6] *Butler's Book*, 336.

departure. Robbed of glory, when he took over the difficult task of occupying a defiant city, he was eager to regain the center of the stage. An incorrigible citizenry met the most stubborn military governor who could have been chosen to rule over them.

BUTLER as commander of the new Department of the Gulf brought with him 18,000 troops, mostly infantry but including small cadres of cavalry and artillery. None had been in combat. Most of them were raw New England recruits, but three western regiments—the Twenty-first Indiana, Fourth Wisconsin, and Sixth Michigan—had been on occupation duty in Baltimore. In General Orders No. 20 issued in late February, McClellan suggested to Butler that he occupy only the adjacent towns of Algiers and Carrollton, staying out of the city proper if Union sentiment there appeared sufficient to control it. The mob action against Farragut's men, particularly the Mumford incident, ended this alternative in Butler's opinion. Riled by the hostility and remembering the firing on his troops in Baltimore, he indicated to the secretary of war that he intended to get tough. "I find the city under the dominion of the mob," he informed Edwin M. Stanton. "They have insulted our flag, torn it down with indignity. This outrage will be punished in such manner as in my judgment will caution both the perpetrators and abettors of the act, so that they shall fear the *stripes* if they do not reverence the stars of our banner."[7] One of his first acts was to arrest Mumford, who boasted that the Federals dared not touch him, and arrange for his trial by a military commission.

Though the transports arrived off the city at noon on May 1, Butler delayed landing until after sundown in the belief that a mob was less apt to attack in the dark. That evening

[7] *Butler Correspondence*, I, 428; Parton, *Butler*, 192-94.

he and his staff led several companies to the customhouse, marching behind the drum corps of the Thirty-first Massachusetts as they played *Yankee Doodle*. The soldiers had been given orders to ignore all taunts and to fire only in self-defense, but no forcible resistance was attempted. The crowd that followed contented itself with vile and profane epithets, cheering for Davis and Beauregard, and shouting threats that the yellow jack would soon take care of the invaders. Once the men were bivouacked in the customhouse, Butler returned to his ship and completed his proclamation to the inhabitants. When his officers took the proclamation to the shop of the *True Delta* later that night, the foreman refused to print it, and the next morning the proprietors also refused to do so. Thereupon a detail seized the press and did the job themselves; upon the formal protest of the owners, publication of the paper was suspended until they apologized.[8]

Spending the first night on board ship, on the morning of May 2 Butler seized for his headquarters the St. Charles Hotel, which Lovell had used for the same purpose, despite verbal objections from the proprietor. Then he summoned Mayor Monroe, who at first demanded that the general come to the city hall but changed his mind when the officers bringing the message pointed out that their commander was not a man to trifle with. Cannon had been placed at each corner of the St. Charles, and it was surrounded by several companies of troops. The large crowd which gathered shouted the same sort of insults as those directed at the landing party the night before, constantly interrupting the conversation in the hotel.

As the mob grew more unruly, Parton says that the general gave his men orders to fire, whereupon the mayor asked permission to go out to try to quell the disturbance. Butler

---

[8] Parton, *Butler*, 279-83; W. Hoffman, *Camp, Court, and Siege* (New York, 1877), 26-29.

later claimed that he himself restored order by appearing on the balcony in response to a shout, "Where's old Butler? Let him show himself; let him come out here if he dare."[9] But, as he admitted, it was the charge of the Sixth Maine battery down St. Charles Street from Tivoli (Lee) Circle at full speed with bugles blowing that dispersed the crowd. For the time being the city was so subdued that several days later Butler was able to drive around in a carriage with only a single orderly as an escort. These and similar incidents, about which all contemporary accounts differ,[10] explain Butler's subsequent actions, for they convinced him that boldness backed by force would maintain public order in New Orleans.

The efforts of local officials to continue their policy of passive resistance irritated Butler, though at first he showed unusual patience in dealing with them. In the afternoon conference he told the mayor that he had come to restore the city to the Union and that he intended no interference with private rights or property. Monroe replied that he would give up the administration entirely rather than share it with the conquerors, but agreed to resume the discussion that evening in the presence of the city council. At the second session, also in the St. Charles, Pierre Soulé became the spokesman for the city, presenting in appearance and manner a contrast to the walleyed, stolid Butler which one

---

[9] Parton, *Butler*, 285-89; *Butler's Book*, 376.
[10] It is impossible to resolve the conflicts in contemporary accounts about specific incidents during the occupation. Parton and Butler are naturally biased in favor of the invaders, though the former as a professional writer must be given credit for some objectivity. Local memoirs, like those of Julia Le Grand and Marion Southwood (and most other southern accounts) are even less reliable because they were written by bitter, untrained amateurs who repeated rumors without any effort to check their accuracy. Local newspapers, before their censorship, exhibited such an anti-Yankee bias that their accuracy is equally open to question. Probably the most objective secondary account is Howard P. Johnson, "New Orleans under General Butler," *Louisiana Historical Quarterly*—hereafter cited as *L.H.Q.*, XXIV (1941), 434-536. In general he uses Parton and the local newspapers as his chief sources.

Hereafter, a single footnote will be placed at the end of each paragraph indicating several sources for events described therein, with a comment only when the discrepancies in them are unusual.

observer compared to that of Richard and Saladin in Scott's *Talisman*.[11]

Butler began by reading his proclamation proposing a division of authority between military and civil officials. Denying that New Orleans had been conquered, Soulé audaciously urged the withdrawal of the 2,500 troops stationed in the city proper in order to avoid irritating its "high-spirited" residents, who, he predicted, would not obey the proclamation. If the troops remained, there would be trouble. Butler answered that the time for threats from southern gentlemen had gone forever. "New Orleans is a conquered city. . . . Would you or would you not expel us if you could? New Orleans has been conquered by the forces of the United States, and by the laws of nations lies subject to the will of the conquerors."

Nevertheless, he was willing to let the municipal government continue many of its functions, and once it had demonstrated that it could protect his men from insult and danger, he would gladly remove every soldier. But at the moment "your inability to govern the insulting, irreligious, unwashed mob in your midst has been clearly proved by the insults of your rowdies towards my officers and men this very afternoon, and by the fact that General Lovell was obliged to proclaim martial law while his army occupied the city, to protect the law abiding citizens from the rowdies. . . . I have the power to suppress this unruly element in your midst, and I mean to use it, that in a very short period I shall be able to ride through the entire city, free from insult and danger, or else this metropolis of the South shall be a desert, from the Plains of Chalmette to the outskirts of Carrollton."[12]

According to the proclamation, martial law would be continued. All persons in arms against the United States must at once surrender themselves and their equipment, but the European Brigade was invited to cooperate with the army

[11] *Picayune*, May 3, 1862; Parton, *Butler*, 290-91; Hoffman, *Camp*, 23-32.
[12] Parton, *Butler*, 295-96.

in the preservation of order. Those who wished to renew their oath of allegiance to the United States would be protected in person and property; violation of this oath would be punishable by death. Anyone who continued to give allegiance to the Confederacy would be treated as an enemy. Former adherents, however, who would sever all Confederate connections would "not be disturbed in their persons or property" except as the exigencies of public service might require. The American flag "must be treated with the utmost deference and respect . . . under pain of severe punishment," while all other flags, except those of the consulates, must be suppressed. The killing of an American soldier would be regarded as murder; the house where it occurred would be subject to destruction. Misbehavior by Federal troops, on the other hand, should be immediately reported.

Citizens were urged to go about their business as usual. Shops, amusement places, and churches would be kept open, but saloons and public houses must obtain a license from the provost marshal. All assemblages, by day or night, were forbidden. Only United States taxes and those for streets and sanitation could be collected, and fire companies would continue to operate. Military courts would try those accused of major crimes or of "interfering with forces or laws of the United States"; city authorities, if they wished, could handle minor infractions, and the ordinary courts could try civil suits. Confederate banknotes, but not bonds, could circulate, if anyone was "inconsiderate enough to receive them, until further orders." The press must submit all copy to military censors; articles about movements of Federal troops or in any way disparaging to the United States were forbidden. The army would take over telegraphic communication. In conclusion Butler stated his desire "to exercise this government mildly, and after the usages of the past," but warned that "if necessary it would be rigorously and firmly administered."[13]

[13] Butler's Book, 433-36. For the comments of the local press, see *Picayune*, May 4, 1862; *Bee*, May 5, 1862; and *Delta*, May 6, 1862.

The discussion reached an impasse after Soulé's reply and Butler's response. The general refused to yield on the division of authority, though he promised to issue passes for the immediate importation of supplies and to help care for the poor, who were nearing starvation. When Mayor Monroe said he would suspend the municipal government at once, one councilman objected that so drastic a step should not be taken without further deliberation. In the end it was agreed that the council would confer the next morning (May 3). Later that day a delegation informed Butler of their acceptance of his terms, but persuaded him to remove the troops from the city hall so that it would not appear that they were acting under military dictation.[14]

The division of authority lasted only a month. Within two weeks Butler arrested the mayor and soon after forced the remaining aldermen out of office by requiring that they take the oath of allegiance to the United States. In view of the personalities of the men involved and the many complexities of the New Orleans situation, probably no other outcome was possible. The evidence indicates that the commanding general was willing to give the arrangement a chance to work on his own terms. By intentionally dragging their feet, the city officials forced him to remove them.

The council failed to vote funds to feed the poor or to take any effective steps to clean up the city, which was much dirtier than usual because of neglect during the disruptive events of the past month. Monroe disbanded the European Brigade and hired local thugs, according to Parton, to assist in preserving order. More than that, Butler suspected the officials of complicity in more serious acts of defiance. The safe conduct granted to steamers and to the Opelousas Rail-

[14] Here I am following Parton's account, which *Picayune*, May 4, seems to confirm. Butler states in his autobiography that the council agreed to his terms the night before. The discrepancy, though minor, is typical (see note 10 above). Minor errors of fact occur in the autobiography, obviously due to a slip of memory; e.g., Butler attributed the firing on the mint in April to Farragut's *Hartford* instead of Morris' *Pensacola* (*Butler Book*, 438-39).

road to bring in provisions from Mobile and southern Louisiana was violated by the passage of intelligence to the enemy; some of the food, he believed, was sent to General Lovell at Camp Moore. About the same time he discovered a plot on the part of six paroled soldiers captured at Fort Jackson, who called themselves the "Monroe Guards," to escape to the Confederate lines. Meanwhile, his secret service reported other plots to assassinate him and his men.[15]

Even a milder man than Butler must have been provoked to stringent retaliation for the safety of his troops. Yet he went farther than retaliation, for he used these incidents as an excuse for punishing harshly all expressions of sympathy for the rebel cause; ultimately he demanded from the whole citizenry formal allegiance to the Union. The most publicized of his actions, and in the South the most notorious, were those enforcing a scrupulous respect for the flag and for the soldiers of the United States.

Almost from the day of his arrival he made spectacular examples of certain offenders by sentencing them to prison on Ship Island or at Fort Jackson. To cite only a few cases, one William Benzie was sentenced to life at hard labor for threatening to kill a man who rented his house to the Federals. A bookseller who displayed in his window a skeleton labeled "Chickahominy," supposedly that of a Union soldier slain in that battle, was given two years. Massachusetts-born Judge John A. Andrew was imprisoned for allegedly possessing a small cross made from the bones of a Union soldier. A Mrs. Phillips was banished to Ship Island for laughing when the funeral cortege of a Federal officer passed her residence.[16] But none of these compared, in their national and international repercussions, with Butler's famous "Woman Order" in the middle of May and his execution of Mumford early in June.

[15] Parton, *Butler*, 300-307, 347; *Butler's Book*, 391-96, 440.
[16] Parton, *Butler*, 436-42; *Bee*, May 14, 1862; *Picayune*, July 3, 1862; Johnson, "Butler," *L.H.Q.*, XXIV, 490-91.

BUTLER had been irked a year before when the women of Baltimore had expressed their defiance by wearing Confederate flags on their bosoms. Those of New Orleans went to greater extremes, though not often as far as Mrs. Phillips. Upon meeting Federal soldiers on the streets they would hold their skirts and move off the sidewalks; they would leave streetcars if soldiers got on, and move out of church pews if Federals sat in them. Some were "insultingly and vulgarly demonstrative," frequently resorting to verbal insults as well. One lady fell in a gutter trying to avoid a trooper; when he offered assistance, she told him she would rather lie there than accept help from a Yankee.[17] Public school teachers permitted their students to sing Confederate tunes. The milder expressions of dislike amused Butler, who deliberately refrained from arresting females at first. On one occasion, seeing a group of ladies turn their backs as he rode by, he observed in a loud voice to his aide that "those women evidently know which end of them looks best."[18]

Yet the complaints from his officers and men became insistent, and when one woman spat in the faces of two officers, Butler issued General Orders Number 28 on May 15: "As the officers and soldiers of the United States have been subject to repeated insults from the women (calling themselves ladies) of New Orleans, in return for the most scrupulous noninterference and courtesy on our part, it is ordered that hereafter when any female shall, by word, gesture, or movement, insult or show contempt for any officer or soldier of the United States, she shall be regarded and held liable to be treated as a woman of the town plying her avocation."[19]

Desiring "an order which would execute itself," Butler said that he got the idea from an old English ordinance which he had read somewhere. Though his chief of staff

---

[17] *Butler's Book,* 415-17; Parton, *Butler,* 324-26.
[18] *Butler's Book,* 416.
[19] *Butler Correspondence,* I, 490; Parton, *Butler,* 325. The Howard Tilton Library at Tulane has copies bound by years of the General Orders of the Gulf Department, 1862-65, which can also be found in *OR.*

warned him that his soldiers might misunderstand the wording, which southerners immediately pronounced an open invitation to ravage women of all ranks, such was not the consequence in New Orleans. A gentleman pays no attention to a woman of the streets, the general wrote in letters of explanation to his friends there and in Boston; he leaves her alone unless she persists in annoyance, and then he calls a policeman. The results proved the wisdom of the order, Butler insisted: "Why these she-adders of New Orleans themselves were at once tamed into propriety of conduct . . . and from that day no woman has either insulted or annoyed any live soldier or officer, and of a certainty no soldier has insulted any woman." Thereafter local ladies exercised much more restraint, but they by no means accepted social contact with the Federals and they continued spiritedly to express their devotion to the Confederacy in other ways, such as singing the *Bonnie Blue Flag.* Allegedly prostitutes retaliated by placing Butler's picture "at the bottom of their tinkle-pots."[20]

Though publication of the order created an intense excitement in New Orleans, its muzzled press, except for a guarded comment in the *Delta,* dared not protest. In a brief two weeks Butler had tamed the populace considerably, but not Mayor Monroe, who in view of his recent difficulties with the military may have decided that the occasion was propitious for a dramatic exit. In an impassioned letter to the general he called the edict a license for soldiers to commit outrages upon defenseless women, a "reproach to the civilization not to say the Christianity of the age," and added that he could no longer be responsible for public order. When Butler called him to his headquarters and threatened to send him to Fort Jackson, the mayor signed an apology, upon being assured that the order was not directed against the "virtuous women of the city."

[20] *Butler Correspondence,* I, 581-83, II, 35-36; *Butler's Book,* 417-19; Parton, *Butler,* 332ff; W. C. Corsan, *Two Months in the Confederate States* (London, 1863), 28-29; Herbert Asbury, *The French Quarter* (New York, 1936), 227.

The next day Monroe sought to withdraw the apology, but he changed his mind again when Butler agreed to the publication of the mayor's letter and the apology, along with his own explanation of the order's intent. By this time the escape plot of the paroled Confederates allegedly implicating Monroe had been discovered, so that when the mayor asked a second time to withdraw the apology, Butler called him and a number of his associates in for questioning. Finding them recalcitrant, he ordered the mayor, his secretary, the chief of police, and a judge sent away to prison. General George F. Shepley, whom he at once appointed military commandant of the city, took over Monroe's duties.[21]

Repercussions from the order were immediate throughout the South and abroad. Editorials raved at the outrage in the fair name of womanhood. Governor Moore and General Beauregard answered it in flaming words, calling upon soldiers and civilians alike for greater sacrifices to repel Yankee barbarity. The reaction in Europe, especially in England, was even more serious for the United States. In the House of Commons, Prime Minister Viscount Palmerston called the proclamation so infamous that "an Englishman must blush to think that such an act has been committed by one belonging to the Anglo-Saxon race." To an official protest handed the American minister, Secretary of State William H. Seward replied with an apology for a "phraseology which could be mistaken or perverted."[22]

The hanging of Mumford on June 7, three weeks after the issuance of the Woman Order, produced another furore. A week earlier a military commission had sentenced him to

---

[21] *Delta*, May 16, 1862; *Butler Correspondence*, I, 497-501; Parton, *Butler*, 329-35; Johnson, "Butler," *L.H.Q.*, XXIV, 496-97. Monroe's term was about to expire, and he may have been influenced by the fact that Butler intended to require the oath of allegiance from any officials elected in the future. The general believed that the city council was trying to induce French warships in the gulf to attack the city, and he was incensed that it had formally extended the freedom of the city to the fleet (*Butler's Book*, 64-69; Parton, *Butler*, 329-30). Butler shortly arrested Pierre Soulé also and sent him to Fort Warren in Boston.

[22] Holzman, *Butler*, 86-88; Parton, *Butler*, 339-43.

death because of his part in the flag incident of April 27, an exploit of which he had openly boasted and one which had made him a local hero. The event had taken place before the actual occupation of the city, and there were some discrepancies in the testimony of the three witnesses called by the commission. One testified that Mumford told him that he was the first to put his hand on the flag; another said he saw the accused coming out of the mint with the emblem in his possession. Since criminal elements had threatened to assassinate Butler if he carried out the sentence, he understandably regarded the main issue as law and order versus mob rule. On the day of the order of execution, in fact, he received dozens of threatening letters inscribed with skulls and crossbones, coffins, and pistols. He therefore refused the pleas of the prisoner's wife and local Unionists for clemency. Mumford was hanged in front of the mint, the scene of his crime—in imitation of an old Spanish custom, according to Butler—without any demonstration from the "swearing, whiskey-drinking" crowd which had assembled.[23]

Three days before, in response to the urging of Unionists, Butler had commuted the death sentences of the six paroled Confederates to imprisonment on Ship Island. The commutation doomed Mumford, for in the face of threats from the mob the general could hardly have backed down in both instances, particularly since he and his staff were apprehensive at the moment about rumors of a revolt, supposed to be led by soldiers from Beauregard's army who had entered the city in civilian clothes, and of a possible attack on the city at the same time by a French fleet then in the gulf. Butler had grounds for believing that the execution accomplished its major purpose, for thereafter no general disorder occurred in New Orleans, though there was apprehension again after the battle of Baton Rouge at the end of the summer. The *Picayune* observed in July that never before has the city

[23] *Butler's Book,* 440-43; Parton, *Butler,* 346ff; *Butler Correspondence,* I, 482-83; *Bee,* June 9, 1862; Johnson, "Butler," *L.H.Q.,* XXIV, 488-90.

been "so free from burglars and cutthroats." Fulminations appeared immediately in the southern press. Mumford became one of the Confederacy's first martyrs, and Jefferson Davis made much of the execution when he later proclaimed Butler an outlaw.[24]

Butler controlled his own troops with equal severity. Several days after the execution a group of his own soldiers and some civilians were caught using forged orders to enter a number of houses from which they stole large sums of money and other property. Four of them he hanged at once. A few minor fracases involving Federal soldiers were reported, but critical observers agreed that they were unusually well behaved and orderly. New Orleans did not complain much of misconduct on the part of Butler's men; it directed all its opprobrium against the "Beast" himself.[25]

LIKE SHERMAN'S MARCH through Georgia, Butler's rule in New Orleans is one of the great atrocity stories of the Civil War. Universally in the South, and to some extent in the North, Butler has been condemned on moral grounds. The case against him is based as much upon legend as upon fact. It involves the larger question of the moral justification of the actions of both belligerents in the conflict, which neither historians nor philosophers can settle. Like most northern citizens by 1862, Butler hated the rebels as traitors who began hostilities and wished to punish them for their treason. With equal fervor southerners believed that they had taken up arms to defend their way of life against northern aggression, and many of them justified their action by the natural right of revolution. From one point of view, in exercising this right they exposed themselves to the consequences which rebels who fail have suffered throughout

---

[24] Parton, *Butler*, 348-51, 607-11; *Butler's Book*, 443, 469-70; *Picayune*, July 9, 1862.
[25] Parton, *Butler*, 445-49; Johnson, "Butler," *L.H.Q.*, XXIV, 486-87.

history. Certainly, in comparison with other areas of the South and with subsequent wars, the consequences in New Orleans were not nearly so bad as its residents thought at the time.

The city itself was never subjected to military attack; indeed, if Farragut had bombarded it, Butler probably would have had much less trouble. He gave it in some respects the most efficient municipal administration it had ever had, and the physical comfort of a majority of citizens may have been greater under Federal occupation than in the last weeks of Confederate control. Though some individuals lost their property, the injury done the populace by Butler was chiefly an injury to their pride. In 1769 Spanish Governor Alexander O'Reilly had hanged five men there. Butler hanged only one. During the War of 1812 Andrew Jackson enforced a martial law just as severe as Butler's, but Jackson was not an enemy general. As Butler said in his farewell address, by comparative standards in the history of European warfare his rule was not unduly harsh.[26]

To many New Orleanians, however, pride and feeling mattered almost as much as life itself. What happened in 1862 was simply that a demonstrative and sensitive people clashed with an equally demonstrative general, who bent them to his will by power, craft, and energy. To a considerable degree, both were governed excessively by their emotions. Knowing from the record of the preceding year the attitudes of the man who came to command the occupation, local leaders were incredibly naive in thinking they could continue after the capture to express freely their sympathy for the rebel cause. When they said they would yield to physical force alone, he quickly supplied the force.

Assuming that he was wise in occupying the city, many of Butler's actions were justified by military necessity. "Martial law is the law of military necessity," said Chief Justice Waite

[26] *Butler Correspondence*, II, 554.

for the Supreme Court in 1876, "in the actual presence of war. It is administered by the general of the army, and is, in fact, his will. Of necessity it is arbitrary, but it must be obeyed."[27] Though the resistance of the mayor and council was in part spontaneous, they were deliberately trying to tie down as many Federal troops as possible in New Orleans. By not cleaning the streets, they hoped to hasten the advent of a yellow fever epidemic, which they expected to devastate the enemy. In failing to provide food for the poor, they forced Butler to do so; the fewer the restraints upon the mob and the underworld, the more troops would be required for garrison duty. After all, Butler had stationed only 2,500 of his men in the city proper to control 150,000 people.

The problem of civil disorder was more than one of mere expressions of sympathy for the Confederacy. The criminal element in New Orleans had never been held in check; violence, lawlessness, and municipal corruption had actually increased in the decade before secession because of the extralegal methods of the Know-Nothing party. "For seven years past," said the *True Delta* in comment on Butler's proclamation, "the world knows that this city, in all its departments —judicial, legislative, and executive—has been at the absolute disposal of the most godless, brutal, ignorant, and ruthless ruffianism the world has ever heard of."[28] For the safety of his men, as well as of citizens, Butler had to suppress the mob elements. If he intended to get tough, his initial severity was a wise, economical, and even humane policy. Probably the execution of Mumford saved other lives in the future and reduced the number of prison sentences which otherwise must have been imposed. Butler acted on the basis of the philosophy of total war which Sherman later articulated.

Whether his various actions in New Orleans contributed to the major war objective of the United States—the defeat

[27] *U.S.* v. *Dickelman,* 92 U.S. 520 (1876).
[28] *True Delta,* May 6, 1862.

of the southern rebellion—is open to question. At first Butler was left entirely on his own. As late as the middle of June he had received no directives from the War Department other than his original order from McClellan, which left him wide discretion. It is true that Washington highly approved of his early actions, for Secretary of War Stanton wrote him on June 10, 1862, that "no event during the war has exercised an influence on the public mind so powerful as the capture and occupation of New Orleans. . . . Your vigorous and able administration of that city also received commendation."[29]

It can be argued, however, that Butler might have accomplished more for the Union cause had he never occupied the city proper, since he became so preoccupied with its administration that he was unable to attempt more important military action in the area. The commander of the Gulf Department had other military objectives—Jackson and Vicksburg, Mississippi, and Mobile, Alabama. These he never attempted, so he claimed, because McClellan's Peninsular campaign prevented the sending of reinforcements promised him. New Orleans is an island between the river and the marshes along the arms of the Gulf of Mexico. By keeping his troops on the outskirts to control water approaches and the railroads, he could have prevented it from sending aid to Confederate forces elsewhere—all that really mattered—and left the residents to shift for themselves. Had he done so, he would have avoided the troublesome problems of respect for his troops and the flag, expressions of rebel sympathy, allegiance, and the like.

In the light of psychological warfare, which was practiced extensively in the 1860s though the phrase itself was not used, Butler probably did far more for Confederate than for Federal morale. Whatever support his tough actions won for the Lincoln administration in the North was outweighed

---

[29] *Butler's Book*, 386-87.

by the spectacular "atrocities" he furnished Richmond. Surely the Woman Order was a mistake; his men and officers could have endured feminine unfriendliness. The damage done the American cause in France and England, where the antipathy aroused by his highhanded acts was almost as intense as in the South—at a time when the Confederacy's best chance was foreign recognition—could well have resulted in the defeat of the Union. It was his quarrels with foreign consuls, as we shall see, which led directly to his recall in December, 1862.

For Butler to have followed a policy of restraint would have been out of character. Throughout his long life he was forever dramatizing himself, and he expected the headlines in the press to advance his political career. All his talents lay in administration. At least unconsciously he avoided combat, and his attempts at it before and after 1862 were frequently disastrous.

Though New Orleans was never recaptured, the threat of a Confederate counterattack in the summer of 1862 was real. McClellan's failure in Virginia delayed local reinforcements and increased southern confidence in an early victory. Butler recalled his troops from Baton Rouge in August after a bloody attack upon that city by Confederate forces under General Breckinridge, and it was not reoccupied until after his departure. About the same time Confederate General Richard Taylor was transferred from Virginia to command the District of West Louisiana. After the fall of Memphis, unlike Grant, Butler took no part in the first movements against Vicksburg, though he was planning an expedition against Port Hudson, Mississippi, when he was relieved of command. An expedition led by his protege Godfrey Weitzel defeated the enemy on Bayou Lafourche west of New Orleans in October and seized control of that rich sugar-growing region.

Butler's occupation policy might be compared with that

of Sherman in Memphis in 1862. Both commanders exerted themselves to revive trade and took stringent steps to maintain law and order. But Sherman refused to permit the local municipal government to discontinue its functions, and he did not let verbal expressions of Confederate sympathies by its residents goad him to extreme actions. "If all who are not our friends are expelled from Memphis," he commented, "but few will be left." Though he busied himself in encouraging Union sentiment by various methods, he did not attempt to force oaths of allegiance upon the recalcitrant.[30] Yet he confiscated property belonging to disloyal persons, burned the neighboring town of Randolph when guerrillas fired on troop transports, and took residents hostage to prevent repetition of such incidents. Without question, New Orleans was a much larger city and far more difficult to manage. Only a man of Butler's tremendous will and energy could have borne the strain of its occupation.

It would seem a fair conclusion that Butler's basic errors, understandable though they might be, were psychological and military. The Woman Order and the hanging of Mumford increased hostility in Europe toward the United States and gave the Confederacy atrocity stories which it effectively used to strengthen the morale of its citizens. From a strictly military point of view, his decision to occupy the city, rather than merely to isolate it, tied up troops which could have been used for attacks upon other key objectives in the immediate area. Once he occupied New Orleans, the failure of the War Department to send him the reinforcements which it had promised made such an attack impossible. Having made his initial decision, Butler was eminently successful in its execution.

[30] John B. Walters, "General William T. Sherman and Total War," *J.S.H.,* XIV (1948), 456-66; Capers, *Rivertown,* 157-59.

FOUR THE RULE OF THE BEAST, MAY TO DECEMBER, 1862

*M*ANY OF THE BASIC municipal problems with which the Federals had to cope during the occupation had arisen during the first year of the war, when New Orleans was held by the Confederates. In the early months, before heavy fighting started and while residents were confident of a quick and easy victory, the city in general enthusiastically supported the war effort by volunteering for military service and by financial contributions. Since Lincoln's call for troops after Sumter made the main issue one of defense against invasion, at first all classes responded to the call to arms. While the crack regiments which soon left for Virginia—like the Crescent Rifles, the Louisiana Guards, and the Washington Artillery—were aristocratic in composition, the Louisiana "Tigers" battalion was recruited from the slums and the underworld, the Sixth Louisiana Infantry was composed entirely of Irish laborers, and even the free Negroes formed a regiment whose services were accepted for militia duty only. The city became the recruiting and debarkation center of the state, troops en route to duty elsewhere in the South being quartered at Camp Lewis in Carrollton and Camp Walker on the Metairie Race Course. Apparently the city contributed its quota to the 23,000 men from Louisiana in Confederate service by the fall of 1861, and at least twice that many were enrolled in the state militia.[1]

Enthusiasm waned somewhat as battle casualties and economic depression brought home the grim realities of war. Not until the month in which New Orleans fell did the Confederate Congress pass a conscription bill, but many enlistments, most of them were for twelve months only, were not due simply to a devotion to the southern cause. Growing unemployment in the summer of 1861 forced workingmen to enlist in return for bounties provided by merchants and planters, and social pressure forced some members of all classes into military service. Direct force was also frequently used; the British consul reported to his government in 1861 that he had obtained the release of at least sixty of Her Majesty's subjects shanghaied into local companies. According to British war correspondent William H. Russell, those who expressed northern sympathies, or in some cases mere indifference, were put in jail. Dr. A. P. Dostie and Benjamin Flanders, prominent dissenters, were sent into exile. This stringent action stopped any underground resistance movement, causing those who were secretly Unionist, like Michael Hahn, the future Free-State governor, to hide their true sentiments behind a token conformity.[2]

Though without doubt a majority continued actively to support the rebellion, the merchant aristocracy which had always directed local affairs was definitely the most zealous group. Native and particularly foreign-born laborers were less zealous, as their participation in the civil governments formed during the occupation indicates. Though many of them would fight in defense of their homeland, they were

[1] *O.R.*, Ser. 4, I, 626-33, 747-55; Kendall, *New Orleans*, I, 240; Shugg, *Origins*, 171-72; Winters, *Civil War*, 20-28.
[2] William H. Russell, *My Diary North and South* (Boston, 1863), I, 333; William Muir to Lord John Russell, May 3, 1861, Foreign Office 5, vol. 788, P.R.O., London; Fred H. Harrington, *Fighting Politician* (Philadelphia, 1948), 100—hereafter referred to as *Banks;* Emily H. Reed, *Life of A. P. Dostie* (New York, 1868), 35. See also Ch. Six.

disinclined to sacrifice themselves merely to preserve the institution of slavery.³

The contrasts of selfishness and self-sacrifice in wartime are as old as man, and those who support the popular cause without deep convictions are usually numerous. In early fall New Orleans factors urged Governor Moore to forbid shipments of cotton to the city in order to produce a shortage abroad and in New England. Local bankers complied with his request to suspend specie payment. Yet some of their fellows profiteered when shortages of necessities arose, and others speculated in Confederate bonds and currency. Families with means could pay high prices and contribute to relief without discomfort. But the mass of citizens, unskilled workers or petty clerks who depended upon their weekly pay for subsistence, suffered acutely when their wages failed to keep up with the inflation, and faced starvation when they lost their jobs. Skilled laborers generally fared better because of the demand for their services on local defense projects and elsewhere in the South.

Clara E. Solomon, a young Jewish girl, graphically described the situation in her diary. In the summer of 1861 she recorded the scarcity of clothing and coal in the city. Her diet consisted of okra, soup, figs, and blackberries; meat was scarce, though chicken and seafood were still available. In September she complained of having only bread and molasses for supper, and even bread was exorbitant in price and hard to find, since all flour was imported from the upper valley. Soap was selling for $1.00 a bar, and coffee for $1.25 a pound.⁴

The outbreak of a revolutionary war usually produces severe social and economic dislocations at the local as well as at the national level. These were less noticed and more easily endured in Confederate New Orleans than they were

---

³ Shugg, *Origins,* 145-46, 171, 175-76; *True Delta,* Oct. 13, 1861.
⁴ Clara E. Solomon, *Diary, 1861-1862,* Louisiana State University Library, 7-66, 74, 77-78, 125-32; Winters, *Civil War,* 54-58.

later under the occupation, chiefly because governing bodies —local, state, and national—were nominally of the citizens' own choosing. Steps were taken by these bodies, and frequently by groups of citizens who cooperated with them, to ameliorate conditions. A free market to feed indigent families of absent soldiers, set up in August by voluntary contributions, was soon giving food to 1,350 families and eventually to 2,000. In October, Mayor Monroe issued a schedule fixing the price of bread.[5] Increasing vicissitudes caused no serious crisis because the triumph at Bull Run confirmed the expectation of a quick victory; temporary evils can be borne when their end is in sight. But the hard core of loyalty to the southern cause was so deepseated in New Orleans that it persisted in some instances until the very end of the conflict. Butler silenced it temporarily, and his more tactful successor Banks was never able to eradicate it.

The deepening depression which began in the first summer of hostilities resulted as much from Confederate action as from Federal retaliation. New Orleans was a metropolis whose lifeblood was trade, a distributing point for exports and imports of wide origins. The Union blockade in the gulf cut it off from the sea, and a similar blockade effective in August, 1861, on the river from Cairo south cut it off from the upper valley. Governor Moore's order a month later prohibiting the shipment of cotton to the port was equally ruinous, for that staple was its chief product. Fewer than 5,000 bales were received in the last four months of 1861, in contrast to 187,000 bales during the same period in 1860.[6] It could still receive sugar, molasses, meat, and foodstuffs from areas along the Opelousas and Jackson railroads, the Red River in Louisiana and Texas, and the lower Mississippi,

[5] *Crescent*, Aug. 5, 15, Sept. 11, Oct. 10, 12, Dec. 7, 1861; Southwood, *Beauty and Booty*, 77-82.
[6] *Crescent*, Dec. 19, 1861. Obviously some cotton was smuggled, and Governor Moore licensed some shipments to obtain munitions from abroad (Bragg, *Louisiana*, 79-82).

but where could it sell them? The lack of roads overland put many regions in its geographical hinterland beyond its actual reach, and the Federal advance into Tennessee early in 1862 further reduced its producing area.

In return for imports for its own and for military consumption— a small fraction of its former volume—the city could pay only paper currency of local banks and of the Confederacy, neither backed by gold. Richmond had practically ordered the governor to induce the sound local banks to suspend specie payments in September because of the recent issuance of $100,000,000 in treasury notes.[7] When all but one did so, the currency steadily depreciated. The situation became worse as local firms began to issue their own paper money for small change (shinplasters); even streetcar tickets were used in place of coins. This monetary inflation impeded the little trade that remained and skyrocketed the cost of living. A serious food shortage developed in the spring of 1862 as news spread that the Federal fleet was advancing up the river, causing imports from the adjacent region in Louisiana to dwindle. Supplies were further reduced by the looting during the riot on the eve of Farragut's arrival and by the deliberate destruction carried out by the Confederate military officials. It was estimated at the end of April that the city was only several weeks away from starvation.

Soon after his landing, Butler had taken steps to relieve the shortage by granting free passage to steamers and railroads to bring in food from Mobile, southern Louisiana, and the Red River region. Next, he ordered the sale to civilians of some of the army provisions arriving from the East. At the same time he continued relief for the destitute, using his own and government funds temporarily. Shortly he forced the city council to hire two thousand of the unemployed to clean the city, at a wage of fifty cents a day to be paid by the

[7] *Crescent*, Dec. 20, 1861.

city and a soldier's ration which he furnished from his own commissary. To raise additional funds for relief, later in the summer Butler assessed individuals and firms—who had formerly subscribed more than a million dollars for local defense —one-fourth of the amount contributed, and he made a proportional assessment on the factors who had placed a notice in the newspapers urging planters to withhold their cotton from the market. The $350,000 thus collected was spent, according to his own account, on public works or given to orphanages and the Charity Hospital.[8]

IN THIS DRAMATIC FASHION Butler reduced the problem of food shortages and unemployment, despite resistance from local officials and merchants who were willing to let the poor starve in order to cause the conquerors trouble. Even a man of his energy, however, could not overcome the insurmountable obstacles in the way of an economic revival. Though he opened trade through the lines, contrary to a previous act of Congress, and gave assurances to planters that any sugar or cotton sent to the city would be bought by the United States with specie, little came in. At his urging, Lincoln ordered the lifting of the Federal blockade in May, but it was now the Confederates' turn to blockade New Orleans. Governor Moore answered Butler's overtures by a formal prohibition of commercial intercourse with the city. The *Picayune's* summary of the situation in July was accurate: "We are pressed on both sides; indeed, on all sides. . . . The people with whom the one authority allows us to have commercial intercourse are willing to trade, but the people under the other authority are not permitted to send us the only articles which we might exchange for what the former brings and is ready to sell."[9]

[8] *Butler Correspondence*, II, 242; *O.R.*, XV, 538-42; Parton, *Butler*, 300-19.
[9] *Picayune*, July 2, 1862; *O.R.*, XV, 504-10; Parton, *Butler*, 302-303.

In short, economic recovery depended largely upon sugar and cotton, which had long been the base of local prosperity. But never as long as Butler was in command did the Federals conquer a large enough area of Louisiana or the lower valley from which those products could be brought in any quantity. While northern goods could now enter freely by way of the gulf, the port simply lacked the staples to exchange for them. Summer was expected to be a dull season in New Orleans, but business failed to improve in the fall of 1862. Butler was in no way responsible for the situation, nor could he change it by the most intelligent efforts. Not until the capture of Vicksburg in the summer of 1863 opened up traffic on the Red and Mississippi rivers was substantial recovery possible.

The difference in price of certain items in New York and New Orleans permitted high profits to the lucky few who were able to obtain military permissions. Butler's brother Andrew, who had been with him for a year, was one of those who profited particularly. Local merchants, since most of them refused to take the oath of allegiance, were not allowed to participate in such trade. Yankees indulged in profiteering, as had some Confederates before the capture, but the million dollars Andrew Butler was alleged to have made in cattle, cotton, and sugar was a small sum compared to profits in prewar New Orleans.[10] The general himself was accused of speculation, particularly in two instances when he shipped cotton and sugar back north as ballast in empty transports, but the War Department cleared him after an investigation. He was also charged with being in silent partnership with his brother. This he denied, though he admitted that he had used his own considerable resources to obtain capital for Andrew. The general inherited his brother's fortune when Andrew died some years later.

[10] For a fuller discussion see Ch. Seven. Butler claimed that Andrew's profits were less than $200,000.

The truth of the matter cannot be ascertained, but at least Butler's general policy on trade can be defended, though some of his specific actions cannot. For reasons which will be stated shortly, he deliberately encouraged trade through the enemy lines. He made no effort to check the rampant fraud and corruption indulged in by his staff and by many lesser officers, which Reverdy Johnson, Lincoln's special commissioner who came down in the fall, openly condemned. Butler granted military passes to his brother and allowed him to use army steamboats with the protection of Federal troops.

Though no direct proof exists that the general personally profited from speculation, extensive circumstantial evidence supports the charges against him. Even most Unionists in New Orleans believed them. Local Treasury agent George S. Denison expressed the common view when he wrote to his chief that Butler "is such a smart man, that it would, in any case, be difficult to discover what he wished to conceal." Secretaries Salmon P. Chase and Stanton both warned Butler about the indiscretion of his actions, pointing out that they subjected him to criticism even in the North. The fact that he did not check his brother's operation, but actually assisted him, permanently damaged the general's reputation. His conduct, as the *Nation* said after the war, was clearly not that of "a man of the nicest sense of honor."[11]

On the other hand, no northern general was able completely to rid his department of speculation, and profits of businessmen, legal and illegal, have been high in most American wars. Butler made no attempt to check profits, because he regarded them as an effective means of punishing rebels and of reviving the local economy, though when Unionists complained, he did speak out against "abuses."

[11] *Butler Correspondence*, I, 628, 632, II, 270-71, 320, 355-60, 422-23; Parton, *Butler*, 408-13; *Report of the Special Commission*, New York, Sept, 23, 1865, National Archives, Record Group 94, vol. 737; George S. Denison to Secretary Chase, Sept. 9, Oct. 10, Nov. 14, 1862, "Chase Correspondence," American Historical Association *Annual Report, 1902*, 312ff; Reverdy Johnson's statement, *Delta*, Dec. 17, 18, 1862. Johnson, "Butler," *L.H.Q.*, XXIV, 532-36, and Holzman, *Butler*, 91-95, give detailed analyses.

Apparently he also believed, in contrast to Grant and Sherman, that trade with the enemy aided the Union in defeating the rebellion. Since the South was trying to induce foreign intervention by creating a cotton famine, he sought to block its effort by encouraging shipments of the staple to Europe and to New England. Whether the North would gain more from the cotton than the South would from the gold or munitions it received in exchange was an open question. The congressional statute prohibiting commercial intercourse with the Confederacy permitted it under special presidential license, and Chase's Treasury Department frequently encouraged it. In fact, both belligerents did so throughout the war. Here again Butler initiated a policy in the field which Washington later adopted.

At first Butler permitted the continued circulation of Confederate notes—not bonds—as a necessary evil, but merchants soon began to refuse all local currency even though city officials announced plans to withdraw the shinplasters. To stabilize the currency, on May 27, 1862, Butler ordered the suppression of all Confederate money. When the banks instructed their customers to withdraw such money deposited before that date, he restrained them from passing the loss on to their depositors. Yet he promised the bankers protection if they obtained the return of specie sent out of the city before the capture, as its return would make their own notes sounder and thus check inflation. Richmond vetoed the scheme, however, and the banks proceeded to issue notes on the basis of the absent specie. Thereafter the currency consisted of United States greenbacks, local banknotes, and smaller notes issued by Governor Shepley in the place of the old shinplasters. The press approved of Butler's order preventing the banks from shifting the loss in Confederate money to the public, but by this time the majority of citizens were unwilling to give him credit for anything good.[12]

[12] *Butler's Book*, 507; *Butler Correspondence*, I, 481, 504-505, II, 27-30; Parton, *Butler*, 413-26.

Upon his arrival, residents nicknamed him "Picayune" Butler, the title of a southern popular song about a mythical Butler—a picayune being half a bit (6¼ cents), thus meaning small.[13] This was soon changed to "Butler the Beast," an epithet originated by General Beauregard. Another name by which he was remembered, "Silver Spoon," resulted from one of his most controversial actions, the confiscation of private property. First, Butler sequestered all property belonging to the Confederate government, including funds placed in banks or in the care of foreign consuls. The South had done the same with Federal property after secession. But he also seized private homes for military use, that for instance, of General Twigg, but in most cases the houses were those of residents absent in Confederate military service. His action could be justified by a broad construction of the first congressional Confiscation Act of June, 1862. Congress removed all doubt about the legality of such seizures by the second Confiscation Act of July, 1862, which provided for the immediate forfeiture of property belonging to officers of the Confederate government. The act further imposed the same penalty upon all rebels who persisted in resistance sixty days after its passage. The property of more than three thousand New Orleans residents who had not taken the oath of allegiance by the end of September, as well as of all those who could not take it because they were absent from the city, was legally subject to confiscation.

Real estate and personal effects seized were sold at auction for extremely low prices. The proceeds amounted to a million dollars, according to Parton, an estimate which included the sale of much rebel property brought into the city from the rich Lafourche area west of the river. This is the basis of the "Silver spoon" story, but by enforcing an act of Congress Butler could not fairly be accused of "stealing"

---

[13] Thomas E. Dabney, "The Butler Regime in Louisiana," *L.H.Q.*, XXVII (1944), 495.

private property for his own aggrandizement. However, many Federal officers and northern civilians who had come to the city undoubtedly profited from the sale. Vermonter George S. Denison sent home pistols and shotguns, which he insisted he had paid for, with the repeated admonition to his mother not to mention his purchase.[14]

The wisdom of Butler's various punitive actions as war measures can be debated, but much that was said at the time and later about their legality is beside the point. This was war; more than that, in the opinion of most people in the United States it was a rebellion started by the South. Few of the maxims of European international law were applicable, though prisoners were paroled and exchanged.[15] No American precedents existed, since General Scott's General Orders No. 20 in Mexico in 1846 had applied only to foreign territory. Congress, the courts, and the President in effect made up the law as the conflict continued. These laws could be enforced, however, only in occupied areas of the South. As pointed out above, the Supreme Court later ruled that orders of the commanding general were the law in conquered territory, although during the war such orders could be countermanded by the President and his cabinet. As much as the Confiscation acts of Congress and Lincoln's Emancipation Proclamation of 1862, Butler's punitive acts in the field during the same year were designed to hasten a northern victory by making the penalties for continued resistance increasingly severe. After April, 1863, of course, occupying generals had General Orders No. 100 and a field manual to guide them.

A realistic approach to Butler's regime in New Orleans is to view it as a case of force meeting force in wartime. Many

[14] Parton, *Butler*, 467-77; Johnson, "Butler," *L.H.Q.*, XXIV, 500-502; Randall, *Civil War*, 371-73; "Letters of George S. Denison," *L.H.Q.*, XXIII (1940), 1195.
[15] For a prosouthern discussion see Walters, "Sherman and Total War," *J.S.H.*, XIV, 447-80, particularly note 35.

of his measures, essential for the safety of his troops, were equally beneficial to the populace, yet they were resisted by the majority of residents. Had citizens known at the time that they were to be occupied for the duration of a long war which would end in southern defeat, certainly many would have responded otherwise. But in 1862, Orleanians, including numbers of Unionists, expected the stay of the Federals to be brief.

Most of all, they were confident that yellow fever would soon decimate Butler's army; since it was summer, the odds were that it would. Almost as strongly they believed that their beloved Beauregard would soon recapture the city. Should a Confederate counterattack not succeed, the southern victory which they expected to follow McClellan's defeat in Virginia would soon rid their city of the enemy under the terms of a treaty of peace. The situation being what it was, the risk was certainly worth taking; they could hardly have done less with their sons and brothers dying for the cause on the battlefields. In view of Butler's harsh retaliation and their own growing frustration, it is not surprising that they developed for him the intense hatred recorded in the memoirs of Julia Le Grand and Marion Southwood.[16]

MANY OF BUTLER'S municipal actions were part of an overall plan mutually beneficial to soldiers and civilians. The economic recovery program, designed to restore allegiance to the Union, would make the army's task easier if it succeeded. His precaution against a fever epidemic, primarily for the safety of his troops, also protected local residents.

From the first the Federals regarded yellow fever as their

[16] Southwood's account is confined to the Butler regime. *The Journal of Julia Le Grand*, Kate M. Rowland and Mrs. Morris E. Croxall, eds. (Richmond, 1911) continues into 1863 (see Ch. Nine). Like southern women generally these two New Orleans ladies hated the Yankees much more than southern men.

greatest danger. Since they accepted the local belief that nonresidents would become sure victims because of their lack of immunity, this was Butler's chief morale problem. His officers plied him with requests for transfer, all of which he rejected. His autobiography reveals that he had given the matter much thought. Local doctors would give him no advice; army medics had none to give. Though the germ theory was unknown at the time, his preventive steps kept New Orleans free from the yellow jack during the war and for some years thereafter. Most important of these was a strict enforcement of quarantine regulations by which all infected persons were detained at the mouth of the river—an action officials had formerly refused to take for fear of hurting business. The decline in traffic with the tropics which resulted from the war made his task a bit easier. In the single reported instance when a ship with fever patients aboard reached the city, Butler isolated the sick and burned the objects with which they had come in contact. At the same time, assuming that poor sanitation was a main cause of epidemics, he gave the city the most thorough cleaning it had ever received. Hostile Marion Southwood called him "the best scavenger we ever had among us."[17]

The public works program, like most of Butler's specific measures, had several objectives. Mainly a precaution against an epidemic, it also provided jobs for the unemployed and began a much-needed physical rehabilitation by repairing the levees and rebuilding the wharves burned before the capture. Shepley's new military government which had replaced the city council was in charge of the project. Colonel T. B. Thorpe (a former resident who returned with the Union army) as the new city surveyor directed the work. At the same time Provost Marshal Jonas A. French hired a new and somewhat larger police force which soon included policemen

---

[17] *Butler's Book,* 397ff; *Butler Correspondence,* I, 342; *New Orleans Journal of Medicine, 1870,* 569; Southwood, *Beauty and Booty,* 182; *Picayune,* Nov. 13, 1862.

brought from New York as well as special agents. Many factors accounted for the conspicuous results: more intelligent methods were used, a larger labor force was employed, and disobedience of sanitary regulations was severely punished. The Federals were driven by self-preservation and operated under the advantage of martial law. The accomplishments of the military city-manager system, though exaggerated by Parton and Butler, revealed the inefficiency of municipal government in ante bellum New Orleans.[18]

One of Butler's major endeavors was the encouragement of Unionists and Union sentiment. The establishment of a loyal civil government would ease the task of occupation and gain him much popularity in the North, and he pursued this objective with all the craft and experience of a politician. The economic and relief measures contributed to this end, but in more practical fashion he converted the new government into a "city hall" machine which rewarded the faithful with jobs and other favors. Butler cleverly sought to identify the new party, for such it was, with the native and foreign-born workingmen, who for years before the war had been aware of the class conflict existing between themselves and the merchant groups. Early in May, when he distributed captured rebel supplies among the poor, he appealed to their class interests as a means of stimulating Unionism:

"This hunger does not pinch the wealthy, the influential, the leaders of this rebellion, who have gotten up this war. . . . Striking hands with the vile, the gambler, the idler and ruffian they have destroyed the cotton and sugar, which might have been exchanged for food for the industrious and the good. . . . They have shown themselves incapable of defending the state they had seized upon, although they have forced every poor man's child into their service as soldiers for that purpose, while they made their sons and nephews

[18] Parton, *Butler*, 307-309, 336-37.

officers. . . . They will not feed those whom they are starving. . . . MEN OF LOUISIANA, WORKINGMEN, PROPERTY-HOLDERS, MERCHANTS, AND CITIZENS OF THE UNITED STATES, of whatever nation you may have had birth, how long will you uphold these flagrant wrongs, and by inaction suffer yourselves to be made serfs of these leaders?"[19]

Butler soon strengthened this appeal by his levy on the upper classes to meet the expense of his public works program and by forcing the banks to take the loss resulting from the abolition of Confederate currency. Immediately a Union Association began to hold frequent meetings, supported by publicity and exhortations in the local press. A big rally was held on the Fourth of July, and membership continued to increase throughout the summer, though few of the conservatives, like Roselius, who had opposed secession joined the association. Prominent among the leaders were Michael Hahn, John A. Rozier, Thomas J. Durant, and the exiles Dostie and Flanders, who had returned. The movement did not attain the strength it would later under Banks because members who were secretly loyal refused to risk the retaliation which would follow a Confederate recapture of the city. Though division between moderate and radical factions arose early, it did not produce open dissension until the Congressional election held in the fall. The vote in the election, however, indicated that a large minority favored restoration to the Union, whatever their personal reasons.

To encourage the movement, Lincoln had appointed General Shepley as military governor of Louisiana in June, and in a private letter a month later he expressed his eagerness to have the state take her place again in the Union. Following his orders to "rescue and restore the State," Butler officially gave the election his full support. The occupied parishes were divided into two districts, east and

[19] *Ibid.*, 305-306.

west of a line through the center of New Orleans. Several candidates entered the spirited race; the victors, Flanders and Hahn, were allowed by Congress, after some debate, to take their seats toward the end of the short session of 1863. The total vote of 7,417 was little more than half that cast in the same two districts in 1859.

While encouraging Unionism, Butler continued to punish expressions of sympathy for the rebel cause. With grim humor he had carved on the base of Jackson's statute in the French Quarter Old Hickory's famous toast, "Our Federal Union: it must be preserved." He bore down rigidly on the press by confiscating the *Crescent* and the *Bulletin* because their owners were in the Confederate army, and he converted the *Delta* into his own official organ. Suspensions or warnings soon scared the *Bee,* the *True Delta,* and the *Picayune* into circumspection. An education bureau investigated "treason" in the schools, and the clergy was subjected to even more spectacular discipline.[20]

One of Butler's early orders forbade the observance of fast days ordered by President Davis, as well as prayers for the success of the rebel armies. Some ministers evaded the spirit of the order by calling upon their congregations for a few minutes of silent prayer. When Chief of Staff Major George C. Strong attended an Episcopal church where this practice occurred, he stopped the service and reported the incident to Butler. The minister and two of his colleagues were summoned before the commander and ordered to use the customary service which included a prayer for the President of the United States. Upon their refusal, Butler banished them to New York.[21]

Not content with the suppression of what he considered overt acts of disloyalty, Butler imposed increasingly severe penalties upon residents who refused to take the oath of

---

[20] See Ch. Eight for fuller details.
[21] Parton, *Butler,* 337-38.

allegiance. Certainly he was too intelligent to believe that an oath taken under duress made anyone loyal, for it was common knowledge that many who took it did so with tongue in cheek. The drastic punishment with which he threatened those who violated the oath, however, might well have deterred them from attempting a revolt. Thus in June, when his secret service informed him of an insurrection plot by Beauregard's men, he stipulated that returning Confederate soldiers who failed to take it would be treated as spies, and he forced the resignation of the city council by requiring it of them. To prevent a counterattack on the city after the battle of Baton Rouge in August, he ordered the residents of New Orleans—except proven Unionists—to surrender all arms in private possession. Unquestionably Butler intended the oath mainly as a defense measure, but as such it would be effective only if taken by a majority of citizens.[22]

This was clearly not the case in the summer of 1862. Probably Butler refrained from demanding the oath of everyone for fear that he would thereby actually start an insurrection; instead, he increased the pressure on the nonjurors. His first proclamation promised temporary protection of both person and property to all residents who desisted from disloyal actions, but in June he restricted this to protection from personal violence only. Thereafter, citizens and foreigners alike were required to take the oath in order to receive any privilege or favor under the laws of the United States, to do business, or to take any civil action. Despite these penalties the majority remained steadfast in their refusal. By August, according to official figures, only 12,000 citizens, 5,000 soldiers, and 2,500 foreigners had sworn allegiance. The Confiscation Act passed by Congress in July, however, gave Butler a potent means of enforcement, and the populace surrendered in September at the end of the sixty-day period of grace. Ultimately a total of 68,000

[22] *Ibid.*, 450, 463-66; *Butler's Book*, 64-66. See Ch. Three.

—including aliens, women, and Negroes—took the oath; the more than 3,000 irreconciliables who registered as enemies of the United States were subject to loss of their property but were allowed to leave the city if they chose.[23]

The contention that a milder policy on Butler's part would have encouraged Unionism is refuted by the fact that Banks tried appeasement for several months after his arrival but abandoned it because of the immediate increase in open support for the Confederacy. In one sense, at least, Butler could claim that he had fulfilled his earlier promise to make New Orleans a "Union city or—a home of the alligator." Requiring the oath was in accordance with the trend toward stringent punishment for the rebels which, as pointed out above, both Congress and the President were pursuing during 1862. Lincoln apparently approved of the general's action, for early in the next year he wrote to his secretary of war that he thought "Butler should go to New Orleans again."[24]

WHEREVER the Federals won victories in the South they faced at once the difficult problem of what to do with the Negroes. Being an occupied area, southern Louisiana was exempted from the terms of the Emancipation Proclamation on September 22, 1862, but Butler was handicapped by the failure of authorities in Washington to make any decision on slavery in territories conquered during 1862. According to Parton, the President had told Butler before he left the East that until a decision was made he must "get along" with the problem in the best way he could and try to avoid affront either to northern abolitionists or southern conservatives. To his later requests from New Orleans for specific instructions in dealing with the situation, the War Department, when it replied at all, gave him the same vague

[23] Parton, *Butler*, 450-51, 473-77; Caskey, *Secession*, 58-63.
[24] *Butler Correspondence*, II, 587; "Denison Letters," *L.H.Q.*, XXIII, 1183.

answer. Thus Butler was left on his own in the matter.²⁵

In addition to the slaves and free Negroes resident in the city, after its capture other slaves from the neighboring parishes flocked by the hundreds to New Orleans and the Federal camps in the vicinity. Forbidden by a recent act of Congress from returning them to their owners, Butler tried at first to stop their migration by denying them passes and excluding all unemployed, white or black, from the camps. These efforts checked the influx only slightly. Since he could neither send the Negroes back to the plantations nor let them starve, he put them to work at rough labor, assigned them as servants to his officers, and in other ways found jobs for as many as he could. Sharing the local concern about the danger of an insurrection, to preserve order he continued police regulations like the curfew. His most spectacular step was the formation of several free Negro regiments of militia, a means of strengthening the defenses against a counterattack. By fall, in one way or another he was supporting 10,000 Negroes.²⁶

General John W. Phelps, an abolitionist in command of Camp Parapet above the city, resisted Butler's pragmatic measures and caused him endless troubles. Despite this, the commander treated his subordinate with unusual patience. Phelps first encouraged slaves to come to his camp from the plantations. Then, when Butler stopped this practice, he sent a letter through channels to the President urging the chief executive to abolish slavery immediately under his military powers. The commanding general passed the letter on without prejudice, probably in hope of forcing a top level decision. Waiting a month without an answer, Phelps proceeded to enlist slaves in the army, but Butler rejected his requisition for arms and told him to put the Negroes to

---

²⁵ Parton, *Butler*, 591-92; Johnson, "Butler," *L.H.Q.*, XXIV, 517-18, 522. Later Butler used Negro regiments in the Lafourche expedition (*Butler Correspondence*), II, 448; see also Ch. Ten).
²⁶ Parton, *Butler*, 492-93, 506, 516-18.

work. Phelps replied that he would not become a "slave-driver" for anyone; instead he submitted his resignation, which Washington accepted when Butler failed to dissuade him.[27]

Butler freed slaves belonging to English and French aliens on the grounds that slavery had been abolished in their own nations. He freed others who had been left in jail for safekeeping by masters in the Confederate armies or who had been sent to the city by planters deliberately to burden the Federals with their care. In the first months of the occupation he never seriously considered a general emancipation order, since Lincoln in May had revoked an order of General Hunter's to that effect in South Carolina. Besides, many Unionists and even his own officers had no love for black men. Most of all, as his local followers kept insisting, any drastic change in the prewar relationship of the races would alienate many residents otherwise willing to return their allegiance to the United States. Butler did write in a private letter to Lincoln that experience had convinced him that "slavery is doomed—I have no doubt of it," though he admitted that "it would have been better could this emancipation of slaves be gradual." At the time of his departure he may have been considering, as Parton says, the freeing of thousands of more Negroes under the terms of the Confiscation Act.[28]

Though Butler did not attempt any wholesale change in the legal status of slaves, he granted them certain civil rights previously withheld. He permitted them to testify in court against white men and let them ride on all streetcars. He used them as spies against their masters and stopped jailors from whipping them. His Negro soldiers received the same pay and privileges as the white. In the fall of 1862 he

[27] These letters can be found in vol. II of *Butler Correspondence*, but Parton prints most of them with a commentary that is fair to both.
[28] Parton, *Butler*, 492, 495, 529-31; Caskey, *Secession*, 53-55.

employed hundreds of Negroes on confiscated plantations under a system of free labor. These practices in time would have forced the government to act upon the central question of emancipation itself. As an immediate consequence, colored men began openly to demand more rights, causing comments in the badly frightened local press about their impudence and audacity. On the basis of the record, however, the Negro problem was one which Butler handled astutely and with a consistent caution.[29]

[29] *Butler Correspondence,* II, 447-50; Parton, *Butler,* 493, 522-28; *Bee,* July 2, 1862; *Picayune,* July 22, 1862.

FIVE   CHANGES IN COMMAND, 1862-1865

*B*UTLER'S ATTEMPT to enforce his authority upon the 40,000 foreigners[1] and their consuls in New Orleans proved his undoing. Ironically, the effort was more reasonable on grounds of equity, though not of international law, than some of his other actions. He knew that many of the aliens had actively aided the Confederacy before the capture and that most of them sympathized with it; naturally their protests against almost all of his orders during the occupation produced a violent controversy. From the first they took the position that Butler could not touch them because they were not citizens of the United States. When he uncovered evidence that in some instances they continued to aid and even to trade in contraband with the rebels, he used direct methods to compel their obedience to his will. Unlike native-born residents who felt the brunt of his iron hand, the foreigners had a ready means of appeal: their protests were formally presented through channels by their consuls to the American State Department, which nullified Butler's efforts.

Upon his arrival two incidents aroused Butler's anger. Because the British Guard had sent all its equipment to General Beauregard upon the dissolution of the European Brigade, he ordered its members to leave the city and arrested two men who refused to go. But shortly he complied with Seward's *request* for their release. Then he imprisoned

Charles Heidsieck, head of the French champagne company, for making trips to Mobile on which the Frenchman disguised himself as a ship's bartender and carried letters to the rebels. This time *orders* came for the liberation of the prisoner on parole.[2] In an effort to stop such unneutral acts by aliens, early in June Butler ordered all foreigners to take an oath of allegiance, thereby setting off his first major conflict with the consuls.

Unless they possessed written documentation of the protection of their governments, foreigners who had resided in the United States for five years were required to take the regular oath if they wished to receive more than mere protection from personal violence. All others had to take a special oath that they would not themselves aid or conceal any act "that has been or is about to be done" giving aid to the enemy. In a joint protest the consuls argued that Butler was forcing naturalization and unneutrality upon their nationals, requiring them in effect to become spies. With lawyer's skill the general refuted their contentions at length; his order was not compulsory, and any alien unhappy about the choice of alternatives could avoid them by leaving the country. He denied the right of the consuls as a body to make "argumentative protests" against his orders. Three days later, however, he shifted to surer grounds by substituting for either of the two oaths a third, which simply bound foreigners to support and defend the Constitution of the United States. The wording was identical with the oath of allegiance to the Confederacy formerly taken without protest by the officers of the European Brigade.[3]

After this neat hit, Butler sent copies of the letters to

[1] This was the estimate of the *Bee,* May 3, 1862, of the number left in the city out of a total of 64,000 in 1860.
[2] Parton, *Butler,* 357-63.
[3] The orders and the correspondence with the consuls are included in *Butler Correspondence,* I, 574-604, 619-20. Johnson, "Butler," *L.H.Q.,* XXIV, 507-11, gives the clearest and most judicious account of the controversy.

Secretary Stanton, along with a request that the exquaturs of consuls in the city be withdrawn on grounds of their unneutral conduct. To his surprise, the War Department's reply included a communication from Seward which, though it granted the general's authority under martial law, requested Stanton at the direction of the President to order the discontinuance of oaths for foreigners. Aliens should not be punished by civil or martial law, it stipulated, until they had overtly committed unneutral acts. The polite language of diplomacy could not conceal the fact that Butler had completely lost the fight; even Lincoln agreed that his disregard of international law justified an implicit reprimand.[4]

After this the consuls bedeviled him at every turn. The *Delta* hardly exaggerated when it said "if General Butler rides up Canal Street the consuls are sure to come in a body and 'protest' that he did not ride *down*." Since 90 percent of the residents on relief were foreign-born, consular protests about his assessment of aliens who had previously contributed to local defense particularly infuriated him. They objected again when he ordered the surrender of private arms in August to prevent an attack on the city. Other incidents vexed him also. To avoid confiscation of their property, toward the end of the sixty-day period of grace many citizens made fictitious transfers to the consuls. The Spanish vessel *Cardenas,* arriving from Havana, where yellow fever had broken out, deliberately violated quarantine; the English warship *Rinaldo* raised the Confederate flag and her crew indulged in loud demonstrations of sympathy for the rebels. Washington did not overrule Butler's punishment of the offenders in these instances.[5]

It did overrule him, however, in the more important matter of his seizure and attempts to seize specie in the possession of consuls and contraband goods held by foreign

[4] *Butler Correspondence,* I, 595-96, II, 9-11.
[5] *Ibid.,* II, 188-89, 361-68; Parton, *Butler,* 392-406, 453, 469-70.

business firms. Butler took action on the grounds that the specie actually belonged to the Confederate government and that goods such as sugar and munitions were subject to forfeiture because they were contraband. He produced evidence to indicate the existence of collusion between the consuls and the Confederate officials or local banks to save the specie from the Federals in the event of the city's capture. Many technical points of international law were involved, not the least of which were the legality of commercial transactions before the occupation and the true ownership of the property in question. Some seizures, as in the case of a contraband cargo on the Spanish vessel *Fox* and of three thousand hogsheads of sugar belonging to Greek owners, took place after the occupation began. Like the Irishman in the fight who hit every head he saw, Butler took action of one sort or another whenever the circumstances were suspicious.[6]

The most spectacular instance involved the Dutch consul, Amedie Conturie. Just before the capture of the city, the agent for an Amsterdam banking firm deposited with Conturie for safekeeping $800,000 in silver which the agent had received from the Citizens' Bank of New Orleans supposedly to protect its credit abroad. Hearing rumors of the transfer, Butler sent a detail which forcibly invaded the consulate, took the key to the vault from the irate Conturie, and found there the silver along with engraving plates for printing Confederate bills and notes of the bank. Butler reported the facts at once to the War Department, stating that he was holding the specie subject to orders. Another incident concerned $400,000 in coin held by the French consul, Count Mejan, but supposedly owed to a French house in payment for Confederate uniforms purchased earlier. Butler accepted

[6] Parton, *Butler*, 354-406, gives a full account of the major cases, including reports sent by Butler to the War Department and his correspondence with the consuls. The general summarized his views on the unneutral activities of foreigners and their consuls in a report to Stanton, Oct. 12, 1862, *Butler Correspondence*, II, 361-69; see also I, 490, 577-78.

Mejan's promise not to remove the coin until a thorough investigation could be made.[7]

The Dutch ambassador in Washington delivered a strong protest. Seward repudiated Butler's action, apologized for violations of consular immunity, and sent Reverdy Johnson as a special agent to New Orleans to investigate it and similar cases. Johnson, a Maryland Whig who had turned against secession after some hesitation, was an old foe of the general's, for on a similar mission for Lincoln in 1861 he had obtained the release of the secessionist Winans, whom Butler had arrested in Baltimore.[8] After conducting his inquiry, the commissioner decided against the general in every case pending in New Orleans. Though he admitted that in the conflict with the consuls Butler had acted overzealously out of patriotism, in his report he also strongly condemned the widespread corruption in the Gulf Department.[9] In view of the serious international crisis which the general had created, Seward probably instructed Johnson in advance to render adverse decisions. Yet in no instance had the voluminous evidence presented by Butler *positively* established the guilt of the consuls under international law. Parton, who did his best to justify his friend, admitted as much by saying that "everyone knows the difference that *may* exist between a law case as presented in the law papers, and the known facts of the case. . . . Every one in court may know the fact; yet the papers carry the day."[10]

Butler angrily called Johnson a rank secessionist, but he took his defeat in stride and bore the consuls no malice. Thereafter his relations with them improved, since he attempted no further seizures. To avoid similar trouble in the future, Lincoln established a provisional court in New

---

[7] Parton, *Butler*, 364-82; Johnson, "Butler," *L.H.Q.*, XXIV, 512-16; Manfred C. Vernon, "General Butler and the Dutch Consul," *Civil War History*—hereafter cited as *C.W.H.*, V (1959), 263-75.
[8] See Ch. Three.
[9] *U.S. Senate Documents*, 37 Cong., 3 Sess., No. 16.
[10] Parton, *Butler*, 355-57.

Orleans, with Charles A. Peabody of New York as judge, primarily to settle litigation in which foreign residents were involved.[11]

The prompt repudiation of Butler's highhanded treatment of foreign governments and their nationals could not overcome all the harm done the American cause abroad. European recognition of southern independence in 1862 would probably have resulted in defeat for the Union. Butler committed an error common to generals in magnifying the importance and the problems of his own theater to the injury of the larger war objectives, an injury greater in this instance because he commanded a post where the consequences could well have proven ruinous. No amount of good that he accomplished for the Union in New Orleans could compensate for the risk of international crisis that he provoked so soon after the seizure of Confederate commissioners James M. Mason and John Slidell on the *Trent*. To assuage foreign pride, Butler's recall at an early date was imperative. Washington dared not chance subsequent impetuosity in so critical a command.

In all probability Seward requested Butler's recall, though Lincoln approved it. When Butler asked the President for the reason in January, 1863, he was sent in succession to Stanton, Seward, and General-in-Chief Henry W. Halleck without receiving an answer, but in his own mind he was certain that the secretary of state was responsible. Supposedly the secretary had yielded to pressure from England and France. The French had a particular attachment for New Orleans as well as secret designs on Mexico, and English feeling had been greatly aroused ever since the Woman Order. Butler's military inactivity, speculation in his department, and Lincoln's distrust of his position on slavery may possibly have influenced the decision. Other factors were political in nature; Republican losses in recent congressional

[11] *Ibid.*, 47-72; *Butler's Book*, 522; Caskey, *Secession*, 153-56.

elections suggested the expediency of appointing more generals from the ranks of that party.[12]

Lincoln and Halleck selected as Butler's successor Nathaniel P. Banks, Republican governor of Massachusetts in 1860 and formerly Democratic speaker of the national House of Representatives. Banks was a political general, one of those recently defeated by Stonewall Jackson in Virginia, and the administration may have wished to transfer him from the eastern theater. The President and his close advisers at first concealed the decision to replace Butler, pretending that Banks would lead an expedition against Texas. When the truth leaked out, the radicals forced Lincoln to allow Butler to keep his New Orleans post, with Banks having a field command in Louisiana or Texas. But Butler refused to accept a subordinate assignment.[13]

Butler had heard rumors of his removal as early as August. At first he dismissed them, but evidently he became concerned after Johnson's investigation, for at the end of November he wrote Lincoln a long, unofficial letter spiritedly defending his conduct of the department. He must have been chagrined when Banks arrived on the evening of December 14 with a cryptic order of assignment. Outwardly Butler maintained his composure and treated his successor with courtesy, though he informed the President imperiously that as he had received no orders himself, he was going home to Lowell.

In his final word to his troops before he formally turned command over to Banks, Butler justified himself by praising them. He defended his regime ever more theatrically in a farewell address to the people of New Orleans, issued on Christmas Eve when he sailed with Mrs. Butler for New York.

"I do not feel I have erred in too much harshness. . . . I might have smoked you to death in caverns as were the

---

[12] Holzman, *Butler*, 103-104; Harrington, *Banks*, 85-86; Parton, *Butler*, 593-94, 598-99; *Butler's Book*, 533-37, 549-52.
[13] Harrington, *Banks*, 86-89.

Covenanters of Scotland by a royal British general, or roasted you like the people of Algiers were roasted by the French; your wives and daughters might have been given over to the ravisher as were the dames of Spain in the Peninsular War, and your property turned over to indiscriminate plunder like that of the Chinese when the English captured their capital; you might have been blown from the mouths of cannons as were the sepoys of Delhi, . . . and kept within the rules of civilized war as practiced by the most polished and hypocritical capitals of Europe. But I have not so conducted."[14]

A Polish count working in the State Department thought that "all the hearts in the country resounded with Butler." But a letter the general had received the day before from a woman calling herself "One of the SHE-ADDERS" expressed the feeling of a majority of local residents: "We have always regarded you as a monster in whose composition the lowest of traits was concentrated; and 'Butler the Brute' will be handed down to posterity as a by-word, by which all true Southerners will remember thee monster, thou vilest of scum."[15]

BECAUSE of the high political offices which he had held, Banks brought to his new assignment a greater national prestige than had his predecessor. Just as ambitious as Butler, though quite different in temperament, he was equally conscious of the rewards which would follow a successful military career. Sent to New Orleans to undo the damage that had been done, undoubtedly he had been privately instructed by Seward and Lincoln as to his proper course. In an effort to win over secessionists, conciliation instead of force was to be given a trial.

[14] *Butler Correspondence,* II, 149, 512, 545-49, 554-57; *Butler's Book,* 538-39; Parton, *Butler,* 596-602.
[15] Holzman, *Butler,* 105; *Butler Correspondence,* II, 548-49.

The obvious weakness of this decision lay in its timing. If a policy of mildness had any chance at all, it should have been tried initially; coming after Butler's iron hand, it was regarded as a retreat on the part of the Federals. Once higher authorities made the decision, they selected Banks for the job because he seemed to possess suitable qualities of personality. As a chaplain on his staff well put it, "since Butler had stroked the cat from tail to head, and found her full of yawl and scratch, it was determined to stroke her from head to tail, and see if she would not hide her claws, and commence to purr."[16]

No one could have succeeded in administering the occupation of the Crescent City to the satisfaction both of its residents and of Washington. In contrast to his predecessor, Banks had difficulty in making up his mind. Knowing little about the South firsthand and subject to the usual northern prejudices, he oversimplified the problem by his acceptance of two major delusions. The question of the Negro, he predicted shortly after his arrival, was as simple as "choosing white or black beans for bean soup." Planters and merchants, he was convinced, had forced secession upon the masses; "a clear majority of the people . . . were opposed to the war and could you remove from the control of public opinion one or two thousand in each of these states . . . you would have a population . . . loyal and true to the Government." Yet at the moment he fully agreed with Washington about the wisdom of a conciliatory policy and exerted himself to carry it out. Louisianians were naturally sympathetic with the Confederacy, he admitted, but fair treatment would soon dissuade them from supporting a "long, bloody and doubtful war."[17]

[16] George H. Hepworth, *The Whip, Hoe, and Sword* (Boston, 1864), 27-28.
[17] *Congressional Globe*, 39 Cong, 1 Sess, 2532-33, 2 Sess, 174-76; New Orleans *Times*, Sept. 24, 1864; Harrington, *Banks*, 104, 140. This biography traces the evolution of Unionism in considerable detail, and it is the best analysis of the subject that exists.

He made the new tack clear in his first proclamation by promising equal treatment for all. He asked for full cooperation in the effort to eliminate public and private suffering. Louisiana was "not in rebellion" against the United States, since she was at the time represented in Congress, and all loyal men could expect compensation "for losses by acts of the United States, including slaves." The object of the war was preservation of the Union, not the "overthrow of slavery." Lincoln's proclamation being a "declaration of purpose only," slaves would not be encouraged to desert plantations.[18] These words alone would hardly have convinced anyone, since the new general hedged or contradicted them in subsequent statements, but they were followed by formal orders which repealed many of Butler's harsher policies.

On Christmas Eve the Episcopal churches closed by Butler for refusing to pray for the President were reopened. All sales of property under the Confiscation Act were suspended, as well as the recently ordered second levy on private citizens for relief. Registered enemies were permitted to leave if they wished, but they were given a second chance to take the oath of allegiance. More than one hundred political prisoners were immediately released. Federal officers were forced to return private houses which they had seized, and owners were promised payment for any required for military use in the future. Promising to investigate extortions and condemning "the ignoble army of speculators, confiscators, and devastators," Banks announced that he would grant no permits for trade or travel beyond the lines. He continued relief with funds from sequestered property, though he was soon forced to collect the second special levy for that purpose ordered by Butler in December, and opened new jobs for the unemployed on government projects.

Police began to clamp down on Negroes, enforcing the

[18] *O.R.*, XV, 651-54; *Picayune*, Dec. 17, 18, 20, 1862; New York *Herald*, Jan. 3, 1863.

curfew and the prohibition of assemblies; in some instances planters were aided in catching runaways. Lesser military authorities, such as those in the provost courts, took the cue and began to treat citizens with leniency and consideration. With the cooperation of his wife, who joined him later, the new commander invited the social elite to balls, concerts, and receptions in an effort to "dance the fair creoles to loyalty." He was equally cordial in his relations with foreign consuls.[19]

The press applauded the reversal of the Butler program. "The course of Major General Banks and his subordinates is eliciting the approbation of our citizens," observed the *Picayune* on December 28; "People begin to breathe more freely." Taken in by such mild commendations, the general wrote privately that the streets were filled with cheerful women and children and that more stores were opening every day: "Everyone says if I could have been here earlier the State would have been for the Union. It will be now."[20]

Yet he soon learned that he was badly mistaken. Diarist Julia Le Grand, who refused to take the oath, expressed the true sentiment of rebel sympathizers when she noted that "there is a difference even among devils, it seems, as some of Bank's people do try to be kind to us, while Butler's were just the reverse." Regarding the new accent on leniency as a sign of weakness, the populace responded with wholesale manifestations of disloyalty. In the winter of 1862-63 Treasury agent George S. Denison repeatedly complained to Secretary Chase that New Orleans was "less a Union city now than when General Banks came here. . . . The policy of conciliation, in whatever form, is useless, absurd, and hurtful."[21]

The facts supported his criticism. Once again local ladies

[19] *Picayune*, Dec. 28, 1862, Jan. 16, 1863; Gaskey, *Secession*, 70-71; Harrington, *Banks*, 92-95; Southwood, *Beauty and Booty*, 244, 267-69; "Chase Correspondence," 340.
[20] Banks to his wife, Jan. 11, 30, 1863, *Banks MSS*, Essex Institute, Salem, Mass.
[21] *Picayune*, Dec. 28, 1862; *Journal of Julia Le Grand*, 55-56, 77; "Chase Correspondence," 362.

began to insult Union soldiers as "Lincoln's hirelings," openly wore Confederate colors, and even smuggled medicine and intelligence through the lines. Led by their teachers, children in the schools sang *Dixie* and the *Marseillaise*. Drunks shouted "three cheers for Jeff Davis" and "to Hell with Butler." Refusing to publish matter submitted by the military authorities, newspapers defiantly played up Federal defeats. Secessionists even demanded the playing of southern tunes at theaters. After a riot in the spring at the Varieties between rebels and a group of Unionists led by the ubiquitous Dr. Dostie, the provost marshal ordered the manager thereafter to play only national airs. Ministers ignored a prayer-and-fasting proclamation or read it to their congregations with an apology. Local bankers refused Union greenbacks, though they accepted their own and city notes at par, and used their power in various ways to hinder the Federals.[22]

The most spectacular incident occurred on February 20 in the so-called "Battle of the Handkerchiefs." A crowd of ten thousand, mostly women, assembled on the riverfront to cheer as southern officers who had been captured and imprisoned by the Federals left the city to be exchanged. Discovering contraband on the persons of the Confederates and disturbed at the hostility of the women, who shouted epithets and waved their handkerchiefs, Union officers called for reinforcements to disperse the spectators. No fatalities resulted, but the melee convinced many soldiers that New Orleans remained "rebel from center to circumference."[23]

Nevertheless Banks, recalling his predecessor's fate and the fondness in Washington for conciliation, hesitated for some time to use harsh measures. Instead he merely forbade

---

[22] Harrington, *Banks*, 94-97; Bragg, *Louisiana*, 277; *Bee*, Dec. 19, 23, 1862; *Delta*, Dec. 27, 1862; New York *Herald*, Jan. 14, 1863; New York *Tribune*, April 2, 1863.
[23] *Journal of Julia Le Grand*, 137-44; Captain John G. Palfrey to his family, April 5, 1863, *Palfrey Papers*, Houghton Library, Harvard; O. S. Clark, *The 116th Regiment of New York Volunteers* (Buffalo, 1868), 49; John C. Gray, *War Letters* (New York, 1927), 354.

"offensive" attacks on the Union, issued reprimands to the press, and censored it more closely. The provost courts began to issue light fines. Some registered enemies were shipped out, and talk arose of confiscating the property of absent Confederate leaders like Slidell and Benjamin. A new school board under Dostie, Hahn, and Flanders fired a number of principals and teachers for encouraging treason, but at one point half of the city's students left class rather than obey an order requiring the singing of Union songs. Since many enthusiastic rebels were willing to pay the penalties, suppression failed almost as completely as conciliation.[24]

What was worse, both attempts alienated and disgusted the Unionist minority whose support was essential to success of the occupation. George Denison's confidential letters to his chief, Secretary of the Treasury Chase in Washington, reflected their reaction to the course of events. Though he highly approved of Butler's other actions, the Treasury agent had been so disturbed by the volume of trade with the enemy that at first he was optimistic about the change in command. Yet within a few weeks he was writing that Banks was afraid of responsibilities, lacking in decision, and a poor judge of men. By March, Denison became convinced that the deterioration was critical. Disloyalty and corruption, in his opinion, were greater than in any previous period of the occupation. "And the reason is that no punishment, or insufficient punishment, follows offenses. . . . I now regard this failure as complete and impossible to be retrieved by the present Commanding General. . . . General Benjamin F. Butler is the man, and the only one. In two weeks he could restore everything."[25]

Finally in early spring General Banks yielded to the

[24] Reed, *Dostie*, 47-50; New York *Tribune*, May 8, 23, 1863; Harrington, *Banks*, 94-95.
[25] "Chase Correspondence," 340, 358-60, 362, 372-74. When Denison later learned that Banks was to stay in New Orleans, he sought to retract some of his criticism (*ibid.*, 379-80).

pressure from Unionists and his own officers; abruptly he changed his tactics. In view of the open resistance in the city and his approaching departure on the Vicksburg-Port Hudson campaign, he was more than a little concerned with the possibility of a revolt during his absence. In late April, therefore, he issued a series of severe orders giving registered enemies fifteen days to leave the Gulf Department, requiring the oath of allegiance from all remaining residents, and decreeing the death penalty for those who furnished supplies to the Confederate army. Learning that Lincoln had decided to recruit Negro slaves, Banks began to enlist them in a "Corps d'Afrique," which by summer would include twenty regiments. He refused to permit the three pastors banished by Butler to reenter the city, and he sent to the Confederate lines another who had held secret services for rebel sympathizers. Heavy fines and in some instances imprisonments were imposed for various expressions of disloyalty; the *Picayune, National Advocate, Estafette du Sud, Courier Francaise,* and *Southern Pilot* were all suppressed.[26]

Intended primarily as military preparations for the attack on Vicksburg, the stern measures indicated that Banks had abandoned conciliation and that he was now seeking a closer rapprochement with the Unionists. From then on he expressed his acute irritation by increasingly stringent penalties upon the recalcitrant. His experiences of the first four months evidently convinced him that the control and restoration of New Orleans could be accomplished only with the support of its workingmen. The matter was not that simple, however, for the city's Unionists had split into three factions: conservative, moderate, and radical. Nor was it certain at the time how strongly Lincoln would back the Seward moderates in the capital against Chase and the congressional

[26] *Ibid.,* 382; *Picayune,* May 1, 1863; *True Delta,* May 14, 1863; *O.R.,* XV, 710, 716; Caskey, *Secession,* 71-72; Harrington, *Banks,* 96-97; New York *Tribune,* May 8, 1863.

radicals in the fight over reconstruction policies. Banks was caught between two fires: developments in Washington and the situation in New Orleans.

Alliance with local conservatives, who wished to maintain prewar social institutions, was inexpedient among other reasons because they were lukewarm to political action. The radicals, on the other hand, were actively anti-Banks and even anti-Lincoln. Butler's officers and civilian appointees, under the leadership of city surveyor Thorpe and Military Governor Shepley, had joined Chase's Treasury agents and were after the spoils of office. They used every opportunity to make trouble for the new commander and opposed much of his program even after he cracked down on the rebels. Under the circumstances he had no choice other than to ally himself with the moderates led by Michael Hahn, an alliance which proved advantageous to both and for some time successful because by the end of 1863 their position on reconstruction coincided with that of Lincoln.

Until the end of the war this triple division of New Orleans Unionists remained the major obstacle to the restoration of civil government in Louisiana, though Banks strove against it with a wisdom acquired from long experience in politics. In this struggle he was constantly handicapped by his extended absences in the field and by Chase's adroit use of the power of a cabinet post to sabotage his program. Considering these difficulties, as his biographer Fred Harrington says, Bank's accomplishments in administration were by no means inconsiderable.

SINCE SUBSEQUENT CHAPTERS will deal topically with urban life during the occupation, a brief summary of military action in the lower valley after the capture is necessary as a general background. New Orleans was a garrison city from the start of the war. Though it was never attacked or recaptured, it lay within a combat area where heavy fighting occurred at intervals and lesser skirmishing was frequent. Contrary to general impression, hostilities did not end in the Southwest with the surrender of Vicksburg on July 4, 1863. The bloodiest fighting in Louisiana came in April, 1864, when Generals Richard Taylor and Kirby Smith checked Banks' expedition against Shreveport in the battles of Mansfield and Pleasant Hill.

From 1862 until the war's end two civil governments and two armies existed in the state. As a matter of fact, Louisiana suffered almost as much as Virginia and Georgia from the campaigns of the rival armies, and from depradations of numerous bands of guerrillas as well.[27] Like the British during the American Revolution, the Federals captured the ports accessible by water (river towns) but failed in their attempts to conquer the interior region. Though they inflicted much damage by their raids into the center of the state, they subjugated only the southeastern section of Louisiana along the river. The direct and indirect consequences of this military action affected every aspect of life in New Orleans, economic, social, and political.

For some months after the capture, lack of reinforcements exposed the Federals to the threat of a Confederate counterattack supported by an internal revolt in the city. Thus many of Butler's measures, such as the execution of Mumford, loyalty oaths, and the restriction of assemblages and private arms, were dictated by actual military necessity. When the Confederates attacked Baton Rouge in August, 1862, Butler withdrew his troops south to New Orleans to strengthen its defenses. For the time being, a real military weakness made movements against distant points like Mobile or Vicksburg impossible; Weitzel's conquest of the Lafourche region immediately to the west was the only extension of the occupied area in 1862. Nevertheless, Butler retained possession of

[27] Shugg, *Origins*, 191.

New Orleans in the critical early months of the occupation. By subduing its defiant residents and taking other steps to insure the safety of Federal troops, he made possible the combat missions of his successor in 1863.

Like Butler, Banks was a political general who proved incompetent in the field. In both instances a lack of professional training and experience was probably the basic cause, though possibly the War Department assigned them officers and men inferior to those in the more crucial eastern theater. On the other hand, regular officers like Grant, Sherman, and Farragut won their first victories in the West. Banks was extremely critical of his predecessor, whom he accused of "neglect not only discreditable but almost treasonable."[28] Yet he was soon to learn for himself how stupendous was the dual job of occupying the city and fulfilling the command functions of the Gulf Department, for in early spring he left on his first expedition into the field. Thanks to the improvement of the Union position in the East when Robert E. Lee's invasion of Maryland was checked at Antietam, Banks now had 30,000 troops, twice as many as Butler had had.

Soon after the fall of New Orleans and Memphis, the Confederates planned a counteroffensive in the West, using the armies of Sterling Price and Earl Van Dorn in Mississippi and of Taylor in Louisiana. The new southern war secretary, George Randolph, at once ordered Taylor, appointed to command the District of West Louisiana in midsummer of 1862, to begin preparations for an attack on the Crescent City. During the year following the capture the actual military situation on the lower river was a stalemate. The Union fleet of Farragut and Porter prevented the Confederates from shipping supplies across the river, but at the

[28] Banks to his wife, Jan. 22, 24, Feb. 5, March 14, 1863, Banks *MSS*. Captain (later General) John G. Palfrey of Boston considered the officers in the department poor (letter to his family, Aug. 15, 1864, *Palfrey Papers*).

same time the southern batteries at Vicksburg and Port Hudson kept all commercial traffic from moving up or down the Mississippi. The economic effect of this Confederate blockade from the north on New Orleans was even more drastic than the earlier Union blockade from the gulf.

The southern attack in the West never materialized. On the contrary, in the first months of 1863 the rebel armies in the area—those east of the river now commanded by Generals John C. Pemberton and Joseph E. Johnson—were forced to fight a purely defensive action. For more than six months Grant and Sherman, assisted by the Federal fleet, tried various stratagems against Vicksburg without success. As a general plan of attack upon the two Mississippi forts, Lincoln had earlier decided upon a pincers movement: Grant to move down from Memphis and Banks up from New Orleans, the two to cooperate or to combine under the latter as the ranking general. Instead they went separate ways, Banks never getting above Port Hudson, which he might have taken easily had he attacked it in late winter. After spending several months getting his raw troops ready, he led them first on a march up the Red River against Alexandria, supposedly to prevent Taylor from attacking New Orleans in his absence.

Meanwhile, in May Grant moved into the interior below Vicksburg, defeated Pemberton in a series of brilliant victories, and bottled him up in the bastion. At this point Banks, yielding to the stern insistence of his superiors in Washington, finally reached Port Hudson, which the Confederates had meanwhile reinforced. When attacks on May 27 and June 14 were repelled with heavy casualties, he decided to starve the defenders out by siege. They surrendered on July 9, five days after Grant had taken Vicksburg. In these operations the commander of the Gulf Department proved himself deficient both in strategy and in tactics.[29]

[29] A thorough recent account is Winters, *Civil War,* 221-84. See also Harrington, *Banks,* 117-39, 151-62.

Still bent on glory, Banks chose Mobile as his next military objective on the grounds that the trans-Mississippi region was of no strategic importance now that it was cut off by the fall of Vicksburg. Grant confirmed this view when he replaced Halleck as general-in-chief in 1864. Instead, Lincoln and Halleck decided to send Banks on a campaign against Texas in order to check French designs on Mexico and to close the southwestern ports through which, after the capture of New Orleans, a heavy southern trade with Mexico and Europe was carried on. His advance force failed to recapture Galveston in September, but later Banks occupied several other passes into the gulf. However, despite his announced intentions of conquering the interior of Texas as well as all its coastal passes, he returned to Louisiana leaving Houston, Galveston, and Sabine in Confederate possession.

IN THE SPRING of 1864 Banks left on his second Red River campaign, which ended in a disaster that caused his removal from military command. His enemies falsely charged that he initiated the march as a cotton raid; on the contrary, again he acted under orders from Halleck. The expedition was planned in Washington by army men, mainly to capture Shreveport, the Confederate capital of Louisiana and headquarters of the Trans-Mississippi Department, which could then be used as a base for a drive into Texas. The President and his advisers, however, were quite aware that the resulting acquisition of cotton would hasten a northern victory.

According to the plan, Generals Frederick Steele from Arkansas and A. J. Smith from Sherman's Army of the Tennessee were to converge with Banks against the objective, assisted by Porter's navy coming up the Red River. Again there was little cooperation, and as usual the gulf commander was slow. Early in April, Taylor attacked the Union advance guard at Mansfield, driving it into panic-stricken retreat; the next day the Confederates defeated the Federals in the bloody battle of Pleasant Hill twenty miles to the south. Instead of advancing at once against Shreveport, Banks listened to his generals, who overestimated Taylor's strength, and ordered a retreat which soon became a rout. Though his forces were larger than those of the enemy, he withdrew in such haste that he left his wounded on the battlefield at Mansfield. His alibis were unconvincing; "his own report," Grant wrote Halleck, ". . . show[s] all his disasters to be attributable to his own incompetency."[30] On his way back to New Orleans in May, Banks learned that General E. R. S. Canby, heading a new Trans-Mississippi Department, was to take over his field functions, leaving him as commander of the Gulf Department with only civil duties.

In this capacity Banks extended himself during the summer of 1864 to complete the civil restoration of the state and succeeded in obtaining ratification by the voters of the new constitution finished by a convention in July. A governor and other executive officers had been elected the previous winter and, upon the adoption of the constitution, state legislators and congressmen were chosen. Chafing under his reduced powers, with Canby's consent, in September Banks went on leave to Washington for a consultation with the President. There he remained for the next six months at Lincoln's suggestion, trying in vain to induce Congress to recognize the Free-State government which he had set up in Louisiana. During his absence General Stephen A. Hurlburt took over his duties in New Orleans.

Though skirmishing continued during the last year of the war, no major engagement was fought in the lower valley. Hurlburt, Illinois lawyer and politician, had served under Grant in the West since the beginning of the war. For his

[30] *O.R.*, XXIV, pt. 3, 279. Ludwell H. Johnson, *Red River Campaign: Politics and Cotton in the Civil War* (Baltimore, 1958), is a detailed account.

meritorious service in the Union victory at Shiloh he had been promoted from brigadier to major general. Probably his assignment as substitute for Banks in New Orleans was due to the fact that he had previously been in command at Memphis after Sherman's departure.

In his new post Hurlburt at once cracked down on gambling, and he incurred displeasure on all sides by closing amusement places and theaters on Sundays. He constantly clashed with Governor Hahn and the legislature, whom more than once he threatened to remove from office. When Madison Wells became governor in March, 1865, upon Hahn's resignation, one of his first acts was to oust from office the entire Banks' municipal regime. But Hurlburt's most serious clash was with a military commission headed by General William F. Smith sent down by the inspector general's department in the spring of 1865 to investigate corruption during the occupation. Smith arrested Colonel Robinson, Hurlburt's provost marshal, who resigned to avoid court martial, and recommended similar action against the general himself on grounds of drunkenness and corruption.[31]

Strictly speaking, the commission was concerned with violation of army regulations, but it dug into a variety of subjects: cotton permits, the conflict between the Treasury Department and the commanding general, the gubernatorial election, the constitutional convention of 1864, and the trading activities of big operators like Andrew J. Butler, Dr. Issachar Zacherie, and the local banker Jacob Barker. It called as witnesses Banks' former provost marshal, Treasury agent Benjamin Flanders, a detective, Alan Pinkerton, who had been hired by the commission, and a number of individuals whose testimony in many instances was either prejudiced or based on hearsay. The commission properly concluded that

[31] *Report of the Special Commission,* New York, Sept. 23, 1865, 1-213, National Archives, Old Army Records, Record Group 94, vol. 737—hereafter cited as *Smith-Brady Report. Crescent,* May 17, 1868, published a part of this report.

the Gulf Department had been riddled by "oppression, peculation, and graft," and formally presented its findings to Secretary of War Stanton as the "Report of the Special Commission," New York, September 23, 1865. The secretary, however, decided against its publication as contrary to the public interest.[32]

Throughout the war the response of New Orleans residents to Federal occupation policies was conditioned fundamentally by the military situation in the immediate area. As long as the Confederates kept the city cut off from the river and the adjacent valley to the north, Unionization progressed slowly and rebel sympathizers continued their passive resistance. The fall of Vicksburg, however, brought economic recovery and convinced many of the skeptical that Federal control of the region would be permanent. More citizens began to cooperate with the effort to establish a civil government; 11,000 of them voted in the gubernatorial campaign of February, 1864.

But Banks' defeat in the Red River campaign injured his prestige as well as his restoration program. It was opposed by both radical and conservative Unionists, and voting in subsequent elections declined sharply. This Federal setback in Louisiana in 1864, coinciding with the peace platform of the northern Democrats in the presidential election of the same year, revived the hopes of local rebels for a southern victory and hardened resistance to restoration efforts. Had Union forces conquered the entire state in 1862 instead of merely a few parishes, in all probability the course of the occupation in New Orleans would have been considerably different.

[32] *Smith-Brady Report;* Elizabeth J. Doyle, "Civilian Life in Occupied New Orleans" (Ph.D. dissertation, Louisiana State University, 1955), 313-14.

SIX   UNIONIST POLITICS
         AND RECONSTRUCTION
         GOVERNMENT

OF NECESSITY the government established in Federal Louisiana was in essense a *military* government, set up in an occupied area under the war powers of the President through the agency of his generals. It was called a *civil* government at the time because elections were held in which a portion of the populace was permitted to vote for state but not municipal officials, for a constitutional convention, for congressmen, and for a legislature. But to a considerable extent the commanding general influenced the outcome of these elections and thereby the choice of officials, whose action he had the power to curtail and overrule. The government represented only a minority of the citizens. It was rejected outright by Congress after 1862, and most of the formal actions taken—like the constitution of 1864—were repudiated by the electorate of the state after the war. How much it contributed to the victory of the United States at Appomattox, if at all, cannot be determined.

Reconstruction in Louisiana began when Butler's troops occupied New Orleans on May 1, 1862. After the overthrow of the existing municipal government a month later, Federal officers, most of whom had previous legal experience, were appointed to serve as "military" mayors, provost judges, and provost marshals for the duration of the war. Not until the spring of 1866 did the city again elect its own officials. Since civil law, not English common law, existed in Louisiana and litigation continued to arise, Butler and Governor Shepley soon set up several inferior district courts under Unionist civilian judges. Later in the year Lincoln established Judge Peabody's special court to deal with cases which had come within Federal jurisdiction before secession. In 1863 Banks restored United States district and circuit courts.[1]

Formerly the capital of Confederate Louisiana, New Orleans after 1862 was the *de facto* capital of Federal Louisiana. Sixty percent of the total population of 309,000 in the thirteen occupied parishes exempted from the Emancipation Proclamation lived in the city, and three-fourths of the total white population of 203,000. It was the headquarters of the commanding general of the Gulf Department, as well as of officials of the several executive departments of the national government. It was the residence of the military governor and the meeting place of civil bodies like the constitutional convention and the legislature of 1864. Inevitably the city became a center of the intrigue that accompanies wartime politics.

Great confusion resulted from the problems of occupation and the necessity of improvisation. Executive departments in Washington, not just those of War and the Navy, sent representatives to the city. To enforce trade regulations, collect duties, and handle confiscated properties, the Treasury soon had a large staff at work. In some matters the Justice and State departments were involved; Seward, for example, sent Reverdy Johnson as special commissioner to deal with the property of foreigners seized by Butler. From the first, Lincoln kept in close touch with the situation in Louisiana, frequently instructing the commanding general and the

[1] Kendall, *New Orleans*, I, 289-99, gives the names of the military mayors and a brief description of their administrations. Most of them served a short time only, but Captain J. F. Miller served from November, 1862, to July, 1864. For a discussion of the courts see Caskey, *Secession*, 153-56, and Doyle, "Civilian Life," ch. XII.

military governor on specific policies. These two officials, whose authority and function overlapped, shared the immediate responsibility for the restoration of the state.

Holding that the southern states were constitutionally still in the Union but out of their normal relationship to it, the President was eager for an early reestablishment of civil government in Louisiana. He hoped thereby to induce other states, especially Mississippi, Arkansas, and Texas, to cease their resistance. Informed of his wishes, Butler and Banks encouraged local Unionists to move in this direction long before the moderate, presidential "10 percent" plan was proclaimed in December, 1863. Under this plan, if as many as 10 percent of the voters in the presidential election of 1860 would take a loyalty oath, they could set up a civil government.

Success in this objective depended immediately upon the response of citizens of occupied Louisiana, but ultimately upon recognition of the local civil government by Congress. Prospects seemed promising with the admission of Representatives Hahn and Flanders to the short congressional session in the spring of 1863. During the next two years residents of the occupied area elected other congressmen and senators, a governor and a legislature, and delegates to a convention which drew up a new constitution abolishing slavery. Before the end of the war, therefore, all the requirements of the presidential plan of reconstruction had been met. Yet, to a greater degree perhaps than in the period after 1867, this civil government was subordinate to the military authorities and lacked the support of a majority of citizens.

Obviously there were enough Unionists for the restoration of civil government, most of them in New Orleans, where the white population of the occupied parishes was concentrated. But the votes in elections hardly supported the belief of the Federals that, because of the large number of residents of northern or foreign birth, a majority had been loyal at the outbreak of the war. It was true that the 7,400 votes from thirteen parishes in the congressional election of 1862 was more than half the total of 13,000 from the same area (two districts) in 1859, and that many former voters were absent in military service. Much was made of the fact that the 1862 vote in the districts exceeded the average of that cast in the last five municipal elections. These figures cannot be taken at face value, however, since the city vote had declined sharply after 1855 because of intimidation by the Know-Nothing party; in 1862 no such intimidation existed.

More to the point, by August, 1862, only 20,000 had taken Butler's oath of allegiance, fewer than a third of the total of 67,000 who ultimately took it. On the basis of these more pertinent statistics, two out of three residents still seemed to sympathize with the Confederacy in the fall of 1862. Undoubtedly some were afraid to declare their Unionism at the time. But Unionist voters did not increase greatly during the remainder of the war, for the largest vote—11,355 in the gubernatorial race of 1864—was only one-third more than that in 1862.[2]

Because of the insistence of Unionists, Butler and Banks believed that a majority of citizens had been loyal in 1861; Congressman Hahn said so several times in speeches to eastern audiences. In view of later divisions among the Unionists, the question was more than academic. Whether wishful thinking or deliberate misrepresentation, Hahn's statement was simply not true. The close vote on secession in January, 1861, indicated strong opposition to withdrawal *at that time*, but many of the defeated cooperationists were not Unionists. Like moderates in Virginia, North Carolina, Tennessee, and Arkansas, which did not secede until after Sumter, they supported secession later in defense of their section.

Original opponents of secession like Christian Roselius

[2] See Ch. Four; *Delta*, Dec. 4, 10, 1862; Caskey, *Secession*, 65, 107.

and John A. Rozier openly gave their allegiance to the Confederacy when hostilities commenced. Even the Germans in New Orleans furnished the Confederacy with hundreds of soldiers and two generals. Repressive measures, such as the exile of Benjamin Flanders and Dr. A. P. Dostie and jail sentences for other dissenters, subdued the minority of genuinely loyal men in the first year of the war. Expecting a southern victory, they kept their private views to themselves and avoided trouble by token gestures like Hahn's acceptance of a notary's commission from Governor Moore. In many cases the original Unionists secretly knew each other's identity.[3]

When the Federals captured New Orleans, some of these secret Unionists immediately took the oath of allegiance and began to participate actively in politics. As the danger of Confederate recapture declined with the passing of time, others from this group and even some secessionists joined the Unionist clubs, mainly to gain favor with the conquerors or to hasten the restoration of civil government. Recrimination subsequently arose between individuals over the date the oath was taken. In 1864 Dr. Dostie publicly accused former secessionist Jacob Barker, head of the Commercial Bank and later a conservative Unionist, of taking it only ten minutes before the deadline in September, 1862. Barker denied the charge in the press and produced an affidavit stating that he had sworn allegiance two months earlier.[4]

Far more pertinent was the date of membership in the Unionist clubs. Those who joined during 1862 when the personal risks were great, regarding themselves as "Simon Pure" Unionists, were often scornful of the many who delayed their participation until the hold of the Federals on the city was more secure. The majority of the populace took

[3] See Ch. One and Four; Robert T. Clark, "The German Colony in New Orleans during the Civil War," *L.H.Q.*, XX (1937), 997ff; New Orleans *Times*, Feb. 1, 1864.
[4] Reed, *Dostie*, 136-54.

the oath only to protect their property and never voted in any of the elections during the occupation. Had this group voted, the conservative Unionists might have controlled the local government—a danger of which Lincoln and Banks were quite aware.[5]

Since the President and his generals were in haste to set up a civil government and to get out as large a vote as possible, local Unionists were in a strong position to demand concessions. They soon weakened their position somewhat by splitting into three factions, a development which forced Lincoln and Banks to back the moderates when it became evident that they were the most numerous, though the Federal leaders advocated compromise on certain matters in hope of retaining conservative and radical support. The stand of the moderates in most instances coincided with their own views. "If the policy proposed," Banks observed, "is too Conservative or too Radical it will bring a *Counter Revolution.*"[6]

Unionists divided on basic issues, chiefly slavery and the status of the Negro, but also on the conduct of the war and the struggle of the common man to wrest political power from the merchant-planter oligarchy. Conservatives wanted to retain the aristocratic constitution of 1852 intact, hoping at worst for compensated emancipation. The other two groups, at first united in what was called the Free-State party, wanted a new constitution but differed on the degree of change. Both supported the rights of labor and emancipation. The moderates, however, opposed political and social equality for Negroes, to which white urban workers objected almost as much as small farmers in rural areas. The radicals, on the contrary, would move farther in this direction, and they also favored harsher war measures like confiscation of the property of Confederates and the recruiting of Negroes.

[5] "Chase Correspondence," 334; Harrington, *Banks,* 100.
[6] Banks to Lincoln, Dec. 21, 1863, *Banks MSS.*

WITH MOST prewar leaders absent in Confederate service or disqualified, a new group of politicians arose during the occupation from the Louisiana middle class. Most successful of them was Michael Hahn, who was brought as a child by his parents from Bavaria and practiced law after graduating from the University of Louisiana in 1851. Except for Roselius and Rozier, who had been delegates to the secession convention in 1861, the new group had little experience in politics. Most of them had been residents before the war, though like their prewar predecessors many were born outside the state. On the whole they seem to have been motivated as much by a desire for personal advancement as by positive convictions. Those who held such convictions tried to gain a large following in order to exercise pressure on the Federal authorities. To obtain votes, others simply identified themselves with what they thought was the position of the majority, the laboring class in particular.[7]

Personal views and economic interests did not always determine political affiliation. Thomas J. Durant, secessionist and successful lawyer, became a prominent radical, while Dr. Dostie, who held extreme views on the status of the Negro, followed Hahn's moderates and received as a reward the post of state auditor. With public opinion so divided and in a constant state of flux due to the impact of war, and with the future so uncertain, sustained political success was far more difficult than in peacetime.

The immediate political plums were administrative jobs in control of the army and other Federal departments, since elective offices would not be available until a civil government was established. Flanders, M. F. Bonzano, and Cuthbert Bullitt, for example, got top posts with the Treasury. In fact Bullitt, a conservative who later joined the Banks-Hahn moderates, went to Washington in 1862 and induced Chase to appoint him collector of customs on the grounds

[7] New York *Herald*, Aug. 8, 1863, Mar. 24, Oct. 1, 1864.

that Union interests would be best served if a loyal resident were assigned to so important a position. The incumbent George Denison, a Vermonter who had moved to the South in the 1850s, was named collector of internal revenue.

As the upper classes were either absent on Confederate service or refused to vote, Unionist leaders knew that the war had increased the proportion of laborers in the electorate.[8] But the bid for the labor vote by Butler, Banks, and Hahn was no Yankee innovation. The last two prewar mayors, Gerard Stith, a printer, and John Monroe, a stevedore, had attained office as a result of the strength of labor in New Orleans. After the breakup of the Whigs, American merchants had used the nativist Know-Nothing party to take local power away from the Latin Creoles who controlled the municipality briefly after the consolidation of the city in 1852 by a coalition with German and Irish immigrants. The Know-Nothings stopped the voting of immigrants by an outright use of force and won support for their own candidates by appealing to the prejudices of native workers. Then, when labor realized its numerical strength and took over the party, wealthier members withdrew and formed an independent group. With the merchant class divided by the Creole-American conflict, labor leaders insured their power by courting the previously rejected immigrant workers.[9]

In March, 1861, the New Orleans correspondent of the New York *Tribune* reported that "Secessionists are afraid of New Orleans." If they pressed too hard, he said, they would drive the Union party into a "Free Labor Party," and he predicted that within five years there would be an avowed Free Soil party in the Crescent City. In regard to current local depression he observed laconically that "cotton cannot be eaten."[10]

During the war the rival politicos, too numerous to identify

[8] "Chase Correspondence," 333, 354-57.
[9] Soule, *Know Nothing Party*, gives a full discussion.
[10] New York *Tribune*, Mar. 29, April 2, 1861.

by name, jockeyed for the favor of the commanding general and even of the President himself, both of whom used their power to influence the outcome of elections by direct and indirect methods in order to encourage the adoption of policies which they desired. Old hands themselves in practical politics, Lincoln and Banks knew the risks they ran in permitting elections, which were only nominally free as long as the city remained occupied. Michael Hahn won his seat in Congress on his own popularity, but he owed his subsequent election as governor as much to the strong backing he received from General Banks as to his support from labor and his fellow Germans.

Roselius, on the contrary, refused appointment as chief justice of the state supreme court, as well as the conservative nomination for governor in 1864, because he disliked subservience to military power as much as he had secession. Devoid of political ambition, he clung to his consuming admiration of the civil law. But even Roselius could change his mind. He worked with the Confederates in 1862 to preserve the old order, and two years later he cooperated with the conservative Unionists, though he made a devastating attack upon slavery at one of their meetings. His objective is so doing seems to have been partly to rid the city of military government, and for this reason he accepted election to the constitutional convention in March, 1864, but soon resigned in disgust.[11]

THOUGH the three factions among the Unionists did not formally oppose one another until each nominated a candidate for governor in February, 1864, the congressional election of December, 1862, clearly revealed their existence. Butler and his civilian lieutenants had used a ward-politics technique in encouraging loyal citizens to join Unionist

[11] Clark, "German Colony," 1009-10.

clubs, which sponsored reading rooms, women's auxiliaries, and other social activities. Over them was a central committee that allied itself with the Butler-Shepley-Thorpe city hall machine in dispensing patronage.

These two groups were the "bosses" who selected Benjamin F. Flanders and Edward H. Durell as their candidates for Congress. Rejecting dictation from the top, however, the rank and file of the clubs backed Hahn, who defeated Durell in the second district by several hundred votes. Conservative candidates who ran independently in each district received a small vote.[12] Durell's defeat was a rebuff to Butler and the machine. The victors Hahn and Flanders actually represented rival Unionist factions, and they were chosen as the respective nominees of the moderates and radicals in the governor's race a year later.

Banks' arrival heightened the conflict between the two liberal blocs, particularly since he was sent to New Orleans to reverse the policy of his predecessor. As soon as he began to do so, he met with resistance from Butler's friends, entrenched in power both in the army and outside. The rumors which persisted for several months that Butler might return, and the letters which he wrote from the North encouraged them in their refusal to cooperate with the new commander, who naturally wished to appoint his own subordinates. General Weitzel in the army, Governor Shepley through his judges and provost marshals, and surveyor Thorpe with his city officials made things difficult for Banks in countless ways.

To check their interference, therefore, the new commander used the Hahn moderates in the Union associations to create what was actually a new machine. In short order he took patronage away from the central committee, made Shepley surrender to him the control of the provost marshals, city police, and the Home Guard, and transferred many of

[12] *Picayune,* Dec. 10, 11, 1862; *Delta,* Dec. 4, 10, 1862; Caskey, *Secession,* 64-65.

Butler's officers out of the department. He took over the pro-Butler *Delta* and made it his own journal, renaming it the *Era*. As a result of these actions the Banks-Hahn group soon became the leading Unionist faction.[13]

But the radicals by no means ceased to fight. They still controlled the courts, and they started their own paper, the New Orleans *Times*. Treasury agents in the city under Flanders and Denison had considerable patronage at their disposal; backed by Chase, they demanded exclusive administration of sequestered plantations, trade, confiscation, and taxation. Believing that an act of Congress required him to do so, Banks yielded somewhat on the issue. He knew that he could not rely too strongly on Lincoln's support in the matter, as the President was anxious to keep the Treasury chief in the cabinet. Yet he retained the bulk of his powers.[14]

This conflict between the two liberal wings of New Orleans Unionists resembled that in Washington between the Seward moderates and the Chase-congressional radicals. At the local as well as the national level it involved policy no less than power, even though Banks and Hahn ran their machine in their personal interests. Developments at one level influenced those at the other. As sincere moderates, Lincoln and Banks favored conciliation rather than a fight to the finish, but if they were to succeed in the task ahead of them, neither could afford to alienate the radicals completely. Anxious for all the support he could get, Banks was disinclined to force an internecine fight upon his opponents. They in turn, knowing the extent of his powers as military commander, dared not break with him openly and worked against him by indirection.

Encouraged by the division in the Free State party, local

[13] Harrington, *Banks*, 101-103. Caskey, *Secession*, replaces the older work on the early history of reconstruction in Louisiana by John R. Ficklin in 1910. Caskey deals extensively with political developments down to 1868, whereas Shugg, *Origins*, stresses economic and social matters. Harrington, *Banks*, as observed above, is the best analysis of Unionist politics.
[14] Harrington, *Banks*, 100-102.

conservatives made a bold bid for power during 1863. Strong in the parishes but weak in the city, they first tried direct pressure when a planters' conference in February unsuccessfully demanded that elections be held at once under the constitution of 1852 to replace the appointees of the commanding general and the military governor. Then in June they sent a delegation headed by Dr. Thomas Cottman to Lincoln, asking him to direct Banks to hold a congressional election in the fall.

Firmly but politely the President refused the request. Nevertheless, at the end of October the conservatives called for such an election and announced their candidates, apparently hoping to catch the liberal Unionists off guard. The Free State central committe refused to participate, and when Shepley forbade the election, the conservatives called it off, but not in time to stop a hundred or so votes from being cast in the parishes. Two of the candidates, Cottman and A. P. Field, went to Washington and claimed seats on this basis. After admitting them temporarily, Congress later declared their election invalid.[15]

Much disturbed at the attempted coup, in November Lincoln wrote Banks to "go to work, and give me a tangible nucleus which the remainder of the State may rally around as fast as it can, and which I can at once recognize and sustain. . . . Time is important. There is danger, even now, that the adverse element seeks insidiously to preoccupy the ground. If a few professedly loyal men shall draw the disloyal around them, and colorably set up a State government, repudiating the Emancipation Proclamation, I cannot recognize, or sustain their work."[16]

Meanwhile, in the spring of 1863 the moderates and radicals, who, whatever the differences between them, equally

[15] Lincoln to the Committee, June 19, 1863, J. G. Nicolay and John Hay, eds., *Abraham Lincoln* (New York, 1894), VIII, 420; Caskey, *Secession*, 80-86.
[16] Lincoln to Banks, Nov. 5, 1863, Nicolay and Hay, *Lincoln*, VIII, 423; New York, *Tribune*, April 2, 22, 1863.

opposed a return of the conservatives to power, had started a movement for a constitutional convention. Learning in a letter from Hahn that Lincoln had promised to instruct the military authorities to cooperate, in March the Union Association by a close vote passed a motion to that effect at one of its weekly meetings in Lyceum Hall. Though action was delayed in hope that Banks' campaign against Vicksburg would also conquer a large portion of Louisiana, in June a radical-dominated committee asked Shepley to start registration of loyal free white voters for an election of delegates. It proposed a strict, "ironclad" oath as a requirement and suggested as a basis for representation one delegate for every 2,500 white persons, thus giving New Orleans 60 out of an estimated total of 148 delegates for the state.

The military governor at once put Durant in charge of the registration, but it proceeded slowly because the terms of the oath were so stringent that few Unionists could meet them. Even Hahn, it was charged, could not honestly comply because of the notary's commission he had held under the Confederates. When the registration revealed to the radicals that they could not defeat either the moderates or the conservatives, they secretly postponed its completion.[17]

BANKS WAS unwilling to throw out the constitution of 1852 entirely, for in so doing he would support the "state-suicide" theory—in his opinion "a national crime." The radicals argued on the contrary that secession had invalidated it. Yet he publicly backed registration for a convention, partly to appease the radicals and chiefly because Lincoln instructed him to push it. The President was eager for resumption of

[17] *O.R.*, XXVI, pt. 1, 694-95; Harrington, *Banks*, 142; Caskey, *Secession*, 77-79. Firsthand accounts of wartime politics by active participants can be found in Reed, *Dostie*, which includes many of the doctor's letters and speeches, and in Denison's confidential letters to Chase. Both were radical in their views on major issues, though Dostie acted politically with the moderates.

civil government but insisted upon the abolition of slavery in Federal Louisiana, which he himself had exempted from his proclamation. Banks had already set up a free labor system on sequestered plantations.

Actually the general was too busy with his military campaigns during the spring and summer to give much time to the project, and he may have viewed a convention with skepticism. It would take too much time and increase strife among all factions, and its work would have to be approved by Congress. Since a token civil government would serve his purposes just as well, Banks preferred simply an election of a governor and other state officials. But Shepley and his radical cohorts refused to cooperate, for a civil administration would displace them from office.[18]

In his November letter quoted above, Lincoln expressed acute disappointment that registration had not succeeded. Yet shortly he sensed the predicament of the general, who shrewdly suggested that he be given exclusive control over reconstruction. Soon after the announcement of the "10 percent plan" in December, the President informed Banks that he had "supreme and undivided authority" in his department and was *"Master . . .* in regard to organizing a State government." Shepley and other Federal officials were "not to thwart him or act independently of him." He was to "take the case as you find it, and give us a free-state reorganization of Louisiana, in the shortest possible time."[19]

Thus encouraged, Banks issued a series of proclamations, supplementary to the more general one already announced by the President, calling for two elections: the first to be held on February 22, 1864, for state officials, and a second on March 28 for delegates to a constitutional convention. In addition to this basic compromise, he offered other concessions by which he hoped to induce the participation of all

[18] Harrington, *Banks,* 141-43; Banks to Lincoln, Oct. 23, 1863, Lincoln to Banks, Aug. 5, 1863, Nicolay and Hay, *Lincoln,* VIII, 423-24.
[19] Lincoln to Banks, Dec. 24, 1863, Nicolay and Hay, *Lincoln,* VIII, 427-28.

three Unionist factions. He recognized the constitution of 1852 except for its slavery provisions, extended the franchise to all white males, and changed the rules on representation in favor of New Orleans.[20] Partial acceptance of the old constitution pleased the conservatives; abolition of slavery and extension of the suffrage pleased the two liberal factions. On most points Banks followed the wishes of the moderates, mainly in his complete rejection of Negro suffrage, but radicals offended thereby would have the opportunity of presenting counterproposals in the convention.

The recent presidential proclamation which barred certain classes of Confederate officials from voting and required a special oath of other citizens made the task of restoration more difficult than it appeared on the surface. Ten percent of the vote cast by the whole state in the presidential election of 1860 was required, yet less than half of Louisiana was actually occupied by the Federals—twenty parishes in 1864. Since the vote in 1860 had been roughly 50,000, a minimum of 5,000 was now necessary. Conservatives who had taken the original loyalty oath of 1862 objected to taking the presidential oath in addition, especially because the latter imposed acceptance of all acts of Congress regarding slavery. Lincoln may have devised this strategy to prevent a conservative victory, and Banks planned to cancel the election of 1864 if disloyal men should win.[21]

At any rate the conservatives were encouraged by the revival of the old 1862 division between their opponents at the Unionist convention of February 1, where the central committee again found itself unable to control a majority of delegates. Still in control of the committee, the radicals adjourned the session and reconvened elsewhere to nominate a ticket headed by Flanders. Six executive officials other

---

[20] *O.R.*, Ser. 3, IV, 22-23, 96-98.
[21] *Picayune*, Feb. 16, 17, 1864; Caskey, *Secession*, 94-97, 103. Denison ("Chase Correspondence," 431) thought the conservatives would have won the election had the proclamation oath not been required.

than governor were being chosen; the moderates, remaining in Lyceum Hall, proceeded to nominate a slate headed by the popular Hahn. Both liberal factions selected as their candidate for lieutenant governor J. Madison Wells, a Unionist planter who had opposed secession, hoping this would win some upper class votes. Later in the month the conservative Unionists announced a ticket headed by J. Q. A. Fellows. Attention centered mainly on the gubernatorial contest.

For some time registration was so slight that it seemed the presidential terms would not be met, only 1,500 having registered three weeks before the election, according to the *Times*. Then Banks, an old campaigner, stepped up his effort to get out the vote by entreaties and threats. Voting, he said, was a "solemn duty," indifference would "be treated as a crime, . . . and men who refuse to defend their country with the ballot-box or cartridge-box" could expect no favors from him. He saw to it that all Louisiana soldiers in Union service cast ballots, and he exerted pressure on civilian employees of the army. Although the general was officially neutral in the campaign, his preference for Hahn was no secret. Army bands played only at the latter's rallies, and the military carefully watched ballot boxes on election day. As a result, Fellows received only one vote out of the 800 cast at army camps, while Flanders got a little more than 10 percent.[22]

Ablest and most popular of local politicians, Hahn might have won without the soldier vote and Banks' influence. To aid his own cause he bought the *True Delta* in January, 1864. Appealing to the workers' dislike of Negroes, he accused Flanders of advocating social and political equality of the races, the chief issue in the campaign. His opponent's denial of the charge proved ineffective, for Negroes had regularly

[22] New Orleans *Times*, May 2, 3, 6, Aug. 20, Nov. 15, 1864, May 23, 1865; Caskey, *Secession*, 111-14, 172; *Smith-Brady Report*, 1-13.

attended radical meetings and the extreme views of many leaders in that faction were well known. The *Times,* which supported the radical ticket at the start but shifted at the last minute to Hahn, constantly warned the two liberal factions of the folly of their split. Seeing that the cards were stacked against them, Denison and a number of other radicals went over to the moderates early in the campaign. Out of a total vote of over 11,000 (5,771 in Orleans Parish) Hahn received 6,171, Fellows 2,959, and Flanders 2,225.[23]

As in prewar contests, both of the losing factions immediately protested the legality of the election. The radical Durell, president of the Union Association, charged in letters to Lincoln and Thaddeus Stevens that in calling the election Banks had violated the state constitution of 1852 in numerous ways and that he had rigged the voting. Renewed publicity was given to the fact that Hahn had served as a notary under the Confederates, and the President was asked to punish him for perjury in taking the oath as a prize commissioner in 1863. Fellows and Flanders, the defeated candidates, submitted reports, published in full by the *Times* and the *Picayune,* alleging that the moderates had used state funds for electioneering expenses. Washington ignored these protests, but the Federal commission under General William F. Smith which investigated the Gulf Department in 1865 pronounced half of the registrations fraudulent.[24]

The victor was destined to be overshadowed by Banks. At the inaugural ceremonies on March 4—an occasion which had all of the trimmings of Mardi Gras, including floats, music, fireworks, and a ball—the crowd of 20,000 seemed to cheer the general much more than the new governor. Lincoln formally recognized Hahn as chief executive under

[23] New Orleans *Times,* Jan. 27, 1864; Harrington, *Banks,* 144-45; *O.R.,* XXXIV, pt. 2, 230-31. During the months before the election the *Times* gave full accounts of the latest developments in almost every issue.
[24] *Picayune,* Feb. 21, 1864; New Orleans *Times,* Feb. 20, 1864; Caskey, *Secession,* 104-106; "Chase Correspondence," 433-34.

the old constitution, investing him also with the military powers which Shepley had been exercising. At last Louisiana had a civil government of sorts, however limited its functions.[25]

ELATED at the outcome, Banks and Hahn forgot their recent fears of a conservative victory. Yet the election clearly revealed the strength of the rightwing faction, for heavy support in plantation districts placed them second in the contest. If the Federals captured more parishes in their imminent Red River campaign, and if the many Confederate sympathizers in the city should decide to vote, the conservatives could win the next election despite the moderates' power in New Orleans. Almost certainly the ending of the war would produce such a consequence. The proper strategy for the moderates at this point was a strenuous effort to close ranks with the radicals, who were already embittered by the events of the campaign. Instead, the victors widened the split by depriving them of patronage and by opposing all their candidates for the constitutional convention.

Thereafter the other two Unionist factions fought every move of the moderates with increasing intensity, immediately evident in the light vote for delegates to the convention at the end of March—6,300, two-thirds of which were cast in the city. Durant and Rozier, as spokesmen for each, challenged the legality of the proceedings. Chosen by an exclusively white electorate, delegates were not carpetbaggers or scalawags, as sometimes charged; sixty-three came from the city, thirty-five from the parishes. Since conservatives had opposed a convention all along and since most radical candidates had been defeated, the assembly on the whole represented only one of the three Unionist factions, a clear minority of the citizenry.

[25] Harrington, *Banks*, 146-47; Caskey, *Secession*, 110.

As a group the delegates lacked prominence if not ability and, most of all, political experience. Many of them were laborers—steamboatman Benjamin Orr, for example—"men of the people," Banks called them. The few capable of leadership, conservatives like Roselius and Edmund Abell and radicals like Judges Edward Durell and R. K. Howell, were able to exert little influence upon such a motley body of delegates. Most of the conservatives soon resigned in protest against a resolution requiring delegates to take the ironclad oath.[26]

Banks' defeat by the Confederates in May and his removal from command further reduced the prestige of the convention; for some time, in fact, the city itself expected a Confederate attack. But the main handicap under which the assembly worked was its own limitations as a deliberative body. Reflecting the wartime spirit of corruption, its members voted themselves a *per diem* of ten dollars and spent public funds lavishly for their own convenience. Frequently drunk and disorderly, they often absented themselves to prevent a quorum and thus extended the session almost four months, from April 6 to July 25. Hahn's *True Delta* was alleged to have received more than $100,000 under its contract for the public printing of the convention. Mounting hostility from the press and citizens, who referred to delegates as "creatures of Banks," might have forced a discontinuance, had it not been for the protection of the military.[27]

Nevertheless, members of the convention knew what they wanted. Despite public repudiation and other vicissitudes they drew up a document that made significant changes in the organic law of the state, which for more than a decade had been the planters' constitution of 1852. As might be expected

[26] Caskey, *Secession,* 116-20; Harrington, *Banks,* 147-48; Shugg, *Origins,* 199ff.
[27] Caskey, *Secession,* 120-23, 135-37; New Orleans *Times,* April 13, 1864; "Chase Correspondence," 439.

under the circumstances, most of the changes upon analysis were "progressive" only to the extent that New Orleans labor was progressive. Prominent among them was a nine-hour day and a minimum wage of two dollars a day on public works, the removal of property qualifications for holding office, and the extension of the franchise to all white men who had lived in the state one year. Slavery was abolished, but a memorial was sent to Congress requesting compensations for loyal slaveowners. Separate schools were established for the children of both races, to be supported by public taxation. To reduce the planters' power, representation in the legislature was to be based upon the "voting population" instead of total population as before.[28]

Had they remained in force, these new provisions would have brought about a political revolution in Louisiana of tremendous proportions. The old planter-merchant oligarchy would have been overthrown, and the white majority of urban workers and rural farmers, unless they divided, would in time have controlled the state government. But on the race question the delegates of 1864 were as conservative as the planters. They persistently refused to grant suffrage to Negroes; even the clause providing free education for the blacks was blocked for some time by a strong opposition.

Hahn and Banks knew that Lincoln was considering a limited extension of the franchise to Negroes—the President had written the governor a personal letter about it—and that without it radicals in Congress would oppose the new constitution. Consequently they exerted strong pressure on the delegates for some concession, but all they could get was an article *permitting* the legislature to enfranchise *other* persons

[28] The chief primary source here is *Debates in the Convention for the Revision and Amendment of the Constitution* (New Orleans, 1864). In refuting the older biased account of Ficklin, Shugg in his *Origins* overstresses somewhat the liberal features of the new constitution, but on the whole his discussion is not uncritical. Caskey's chapter on the convention is fuller but less incisive.

later on grounds of military service, education, or taxation.[29] Banks wildly called the constitution the "best that this country has ever produced." With more objectivity Lincoln said that though "it was only to what it should be as the egg is to the fowl, we shall sooner have the fowl by hatching the egg than by smashing it."[30]

Two steps were required to put it into effect: ratification by the voters on the first Monday in September, a month after the close of the convention, and recognition by Congress. Residents of Federal Louisiana, had they been allowed to vote freely on adoption, might have defeated it, since both conservatives and radicals objected to many of its provisions. In view of the local political situation in 1864, the two factions were also inclined to reject it simply because it was the work of the moderates. Even in an election under military control, ratification seemed doubtful for a time, as indicated by a spectacular incident at the end of the session. The convention sentenced editor Thomas P. Mays of the *Times* to ten days in jail for publishing a story about the drunkenness of its members. Though Banks upheld the sentence, his superior, Canby, set it aside.[31]

Judging by the eight-to-one affirmative vote in the city, it would appear that the support of labor was the decisive factor. Again Banks called out the soldier vote and exerted heavy pressure on the numerous civilian employees of the army. Hahn and state officials used their patronage and spoke to mass meetings in favor of adoption; later it was charged that large sums were spent in outright fraud. Lincoln too applied pressure, sending Banks a letter directing him to inform all civil officers that the President was "anxious" for adoption. "Let me know at once," his letter concluded, "who

---

[29] *Constitution of 1864*, Art. 15; Shugg, *Origins*, 206; Caskey, *Secession*, 130-31; see Ch. Ten.

[30] Nicolay and Hay, *Lincoln*, VIII, 435-36; *Collected Works of Abraham Lincoln*, R. P. Basler ed. (New Brunswick, N.J., 1953), II, 675.

[31] *Debates in the Convention*, 598-600; New Orleans *Times*, July 22, 1864.

of them openly declares for the Constitution, and who of them, if any, declines to so declare."[32]

Though the voting was almost as light as it had been for the earlier choice of delegates, the constitution was ratified on September 5 by a four-to-one margin.[33] At the same time, congressmen and state legislators were also elected. Called at once into special session, the legislature chose two senators for the unexpired terms of Slidell and Benjamin, and presidential electors as well.

IN DECIDING whether to accept or reject these various representatives from Louisiana, Congress had to pass on the new constitution as the basis of civil government in the state. Before the end of September, Banks went to Washington to aid Lincoln in the fight for congressional approval of their handiwork. In close contact with the President at all times, he became an energetic lobbyist, writing letters and pamphlets, appearing before committees, making numerous speeches, and talking privately to his congressmen friends. Louisiana was a test case, one of the first presented to Congress, which —like the Unionists in New Orleans—was divided into three groups; conservatives (Democrats), moderate Republicans who supported the President, and radical Republicans. Led by Charles Sumner, Benjamin F. Wade, and Thaddeus Stevens, the radicals had already expressed their objections to Lincoln's mild terms of reconstruction by the Wade-Davis bill of July, 1864, to which he gave a pocket veto.

Probably they would have opposed any civil government set up by the President in the South, whatever its nature, on the grounds that he had violated the Constitution by failing to consult Congress on its establishment. The Durant-

[32] Caskey, *Secession*, 137-38, 140; *Picayune*, Sept. 6, 1864; New Orleans *Times*, Sept. 6, 7, 1864.
[33] Harrington's statement that the margin was only two-to-one (*Banks*, 149) is incorrect according to his own figures (note 99).

Flanders faction in New Orleans supplied them with ample evidence to discredit the Louisiana experiment, which actually had not completely satisfied Lincoln. The new constitution failed to give even a limited franchise to Negroes, and the legislature did not use its power thereafter to grant it.

The Free State government was not only corrupt, the congressional radicals charged, but "monarchial and anti-American" because it had been set up by military power; both the presidential oath and Banks' pressure on citizens to vote were unconstitutional. Sumner condensed their objections in calling the "pretended State Government of Louisiana . . . a seven months abortion, begotten by the bayonet in criminal conjunction with the spirit of caste and born before its time." Though a majority of the Senate favored a resolution recognizing it, reported by the Judiciary Committee in February, 1865, the radicals blocked the measure by threatening a filibuster. A resolution in the lower house to seat the congressmen from the state met a similar fate, and Louisiana's electoral votes for Lincoln were rejected.[34]

The President, regarding this defeat as only the first round of a battle which he had every intention of continuing, sent Banks back to Louisiana in April. During the general's absence the position of the moderates in New Orleans had deteriorated badly. His substitute, General Hurlburt, had attacked the governor and legislature as creatures of "Executive power" and called their Free State government "an experiment liable to be cut short at any time by military orders." Hurlburt and Canby, it turned out, were partial to the conservatives.[35]

The legislature, which met for six months in a special and then a regular session, proved as disorderly and as extravagant as the convention which called it into existence.

[34] *Cong. Globe,* 38 Cong. 2 Sess., 1107-108, 1128; Caskey, *Secession,* 158-59; Harrington, *Banks,* 164-65.
[35] *O.R.,* XLI, pt. 4, 412-13; Caskey, *Secession,* 145-52, 157.

Though it ratified the thirteenth amendment, it took almost no action on the many pressing matters facing the state. Showing its independence and allegedly as a result of bribery, it chose two unknowns for the unexpired Senate terms, R. King Cutler and Charles Smith. Later it elected Governor Hahn for the new Senate term beginning March 4, 1865.[36]

The worst blow came when Hahn, evidently seeing how the political winds were blowing, resigned the governorship to go to Washington as senator. Equally opportunistic, J. Madison Wells who as lieutenant governor now became the chief executive, broke with the moderate and radical factions that had put him in office and went completely over to the conservatives, who were soon strengthened by the return of Confederate veterans and planters from parishes beyond the Union lines. At once Wells ousted Banks' appointees from municipal and state office, including the mayor, Stephen Hoyt, and the city auditor, Dr. Dostie, and replaced them with secession sympathizers like Hugh Kennedy and Glendy Burke. The changeover went all the way down the line to the police force and civilian employees.[37] Regardless of the somewhat fortuitous nature of these developments in Louisiana, the ending of the war and Lincoln's sudden death would have doomed the moderates' shaky regime in any event.

When Banks arrived in New Orleans, he used his military power to put his own appointees back in office briefly. Wells fought back and soon emerged as victor in the struggle, for in May, 1865, Andrew Johnson recognized the governor's civil regime by removing the general from his command. The President's action left the moderates no choice but to join forces with their radical opponents on the latters' terms;

[36] Denison ("Chase Correspondence," 453) said that Hahn favored Judge Durell and Cuthbert Bullitt for the unexpired terms. If so, the governor was trying to work out a compromise to strengthen his moderate regime, for Durell was a radical and Bullitt a conservative.

[37] Harrington, *Banks*, 166-67.

even Hahn, denied his seat by the Senate, went over to them. This move of the liberal Unionists came too late, however. Early in 1866 John Monroe was again elected mayor of the city, and another ex-Confederate was elected sheriff in a parish election. Moreover, congressional reconstruction in Louisiana, which began the next year, was not directed by resident Unionist leaders of the occupation period, but by new figures like the carpetbagger Henry C. Warmoth and the mulatto P. B. S. Pinchback.[38]

Considering the ease with which former Mayor Monroe and other Confederates returned to power, it is doubtful that occupation politics would have had any permanent effect upon the city but for the decade of congressional reconstruction which followed. The introduction of the question of Negro suffrage during the war, it is true, led to the bloody riot of 1866 in which many Negroes and a few whites, including Dr. Dostie, were killed. But it is equally clear that suffrage for the blacks was rejected by an overwhelming majority of the Unionists.

Elections during the occupation were by no means as violent and as fraudulent as those in prewar New Orleans. Certainly the Yankees could not be accused of bringing corruption to a pure city—if anything, the reverse was true. As Governor Warmoth said later, "Why damn it, everybody is demoralizing down here. Corruption is the fashion."[39]

[38] *Ibid.,* 167-69; Caskey, *Secession,* 220.
[39] *U.S. House Reports,* 43 Cong. 2 Sess., No. 261, p. 973.

SEVEN THE ECONOMY OF A CONQUERED METROPOLIS

BOTH BELLIGERENTS suffered certain immediate economic losses during the American Civil War. The most obvious of these was the physical destruction of property in the South, where almost all of the major battles were fought in the course of four years of hostilities. Many southern areas sustained inestimable damage from military campaigns, like Sherman's march to the sea, the objective of which was the economic destruction of interior regions supplying the Confederate armies. The United States early imposed an increasingly effective blockade of southern ports which slowly strangled the South's agrarian economy. On the other hand, the diversified North, after a brief depression in 1861, entered a boom period as production of farms and factories was stepped up to provide material for the war effort.[1]

The South's chief vulnerability was its highly specialized economy and its extreme reliance upon external markets. Concentrating upon the production of cotton, sugar, tobacco, and other staples which it had long exported to Europe and to the North in exchange for capital, manufactured goods, and even food, it depended both for its income and for its comfort upon uninterrupted access to these customary markets. Cut off from them, despite heroic efforts the Confederacy could not continue for four years to equip its military forces sufficiently, even for a defensive war, or to provide its soldiers and civilians with many of the necessities of life. The blockade hindered the importation of foreign goods and also reduced the main source of capital with which such goods might have been purchased. To repel invasion, therefore, the South tried to convert as rapidly as possible to a self-sufficient economy. With the decline of foreign trade, depression developed early in its cities, along with a gnawing inflation as the government issued ever greater quantities of paper money.

The different areas of a nation and its cities do not suffer equally in wartime, though all are indirectly affected by the broader economic consequences. Remaining in Confederate possession only during the first year of hostilities, New Orleans was spared much of the physical damage inflicted upon the South at large, for it was never under attack. The only local destruction of property, in fact, came at the hands of its own citizens and Confederate officials when Farragut's fleet approached the city. Yet as the largest southern city, dependent to so great an extent upon the production of cotton and sugar and upon foreign and domestic trade, it inevitably experienced a severe economic decline during the first two years as a result of military actions by both belligerents. By the end of 1861 the Union blockade had cut exports to a trickle. Though the blockade from the gulf was lifted after the city's capture in the spring of 1862, the situation worsened during the next year because the Confederates then imposed a similar blockade from the north.

A decided recovery began, however, with the resumption of downriver traffic after the fall of Vicksburg in the summer of 1863, and conditions improved rapidly. The value of imports in 1864-65 ($111,000,000) was almost four times that

[1] For a good recent discussion, see David Donald, ed., *Why the North Won the Civil War* (Baton Rouge, 1960).

in 1862-63 ($30,000,000); twice as great as in 1861-62 ($51,000,000), when the Confederates held the city; but still only two-thirds of the total for 1860-61 ($155,000,000). This recovery, ignored by embittered Orleanians who did not share in the profits, was more extensive than might have been expected under the circumstances. If the entire four years of the war are considered, not just 1862, the alleged devastation of New Orleans throughout the period of Federal occupation is clearly a myth fostered by its upper classes because of their own heavy losses.

The evolution of the city's economy during the war years is evident from the following summary of January, 1866, in *De Bow's Review,* the famous local journal which specialized in statistics for the ante bellum period:[2]

	ARRIVALS IN PORT		VALUE OF IMPORTS
	Western Steamers	Sea Vessels	
1860-61	3,171	1,579	$155,863,000
61-62	1,436	241	51,510,000
62-63	655	2,045	29,766,000
63-64	1,414	2,891	72,233,000
64-65	1,481	1,449	111,013,000

	COTTON TRADE		
	Bales	Average Price	Value
1860-61	1,849,312	$ 50.00	$92,000,000
61-62	38,380	45.50	
62-63	22,078	231.32	
63-64	131,044	356.20	46,000,000
64-65	271,015	270.54	73,000,000

[2] *De Bow's Review,* n.s., I (1866), 48-50. De Bow got these figures from the New Orleans *Price Current.*

	SUGAR Hogsheads	Value
1861	459,110	$25,095,000
62	87,231	7,749,000
63	76,801	13,801,000
64	9,800	1,994,000

On the basis of these figures the initial depression and the subsequent period of recovery can be analyzed in more detail. As observed in an earlier chapter, the decline of 1861-1863 resulted from the isolation of the metropolis from its normal markets and producing areas. The Union blockade of the river from the gulf north and from Cairo south reduced the arrival of sea vessels from 1,579 to 241 in 1860-61, but arrival of western steamers declined only 50 percent (3,171 to 1,436 in 1861-62), since the Confederacy still held the lower Mississippi and its important tributaries like the Red River. Cut off from trade with Europe and the United States, New Orleans in 1861 retained contact with its southern hinterland, though the southern cotton embargo reduced receipts of that staple to a mere fraction of the former volume. As a consequence, the value of imports was cut in third.

The capture reversed the trade pattern but not the economic decline. With the lifting of the gulf blockade, arrivals of sea vessels rose from their prewar figure (241 in 1861-62 to 2,045 in 1862-63), but many of these were military ships bringing in men and provisions. Yet in the same year arrivals of western steamers and receipts of cotton dropped another 50 percent (1,436 in 1861-62 to 655 in 1862-63, and 38,000 bales to 22,000). The Confederates held the valley above the city, cutting off trade with Texas, Mississippi, and most of Louisiana, and their batteries at Vicksburg and Port Hudson kept Union commercial traffic out of the lower river. Economically New Orleans lost far more than she gained by the occupation, and imports dropped another 40 percent. The restoration of access by sea to northern and foreign markets did little good as long as the port received few staples to exchange for imports. Revival of trade was not possible, wrote Bank's confidante, Dr. Issachar Zacherie, until "the country now regained by the General throws off its commercial shackles and is again opened to the commercial world."[3]

IN 1860 New Orleans was probably the most commercial and the least industrial of the larger cities of the nation. It had no rice mill, no flour mill, and only one small sugar refinery. It claimed to manufacture shoes, but these were only cheap brogans. Low transportation rates caused it to import most of its manufactured goods in order to concentrate upon the marketing of staples. Though it had iron foundries and shipyards, these were mainly for the repair of ships and the port actually built very few vessels. The foundries and the shipyards were largely destroyed by their owners or the military upon the approach of Farragut's fleet in the spring of 1862. Private industry, therefore, such as it was, ceased to exist with the capture. Just as the Confederates had set up powder mills to meet the needs of war in 1861, later the Federals were forced by military necessity into superficial manufacturing. At the most, "industry" during the occupation was either government operated or government sponsored.

Excluded from trading because of their resistance to Federal authorities, most of the older commercial houses had gone out of business by 1863, leaving the remaining commerce largely to northern merchants who had arrived since the capture. Comments in the older anti-Federal newspapers naturally emphasized the current economic stagnation. On "the great centrality of trade, Carondelet Street," said the

[3] Zacherie to Banks, April 23, 1863, *Banks MSS;* Elizabeth J. Doyle, "Greenbacks, Car Tickets, and a Pot of Gold," *C.W.H.,* V (1959), 352.

Picayune in April, 1863, ". . . the devotees of cotton, sugar, tobacco . . . have been gradually diminishing and now seldom half a dozen individuals are seen together at one or two corners." On Poydras, Tchoupitoulas, and New Levee streets "scarcely a dozen of the old Western merchants and dealers . . . are to be met with. Rows of vacant stores and warehouses" could be seen everywhere, and the same was true of the wholesale grocery area on Common and Gravier.[4] General Banks' *Era,* on the contrary, saw indications of a "perceptible revival," but unlike the *Picayune* it did not remember the prewar activity. Even the profits of the new merchants would remain limited until the former markets were restored.

The sweeping dislocations of commerce imposed extreme hardships on the middle and lower classes no less than on the merchant oligarchy. On the eve of the conflict two-thirds of the city's freemen were employed in trade and transportation; the other third performed the various services required by the whole populace. With the constant curtailment of exports and imports the first group found itself increasingly without employment, and the general drop in purchasing power similarly affected the service group. Shopkeepers and grocers sold fewer and fewer goods; carpenters and domestic servants lost their jobs. In the months preceding and following the capture thousands faced sheer starvation, and a large majority had to content themselves with a bare existence.

For many in Confederate as well as in occupied New Orleans, only relief, military spending, and military service made survival possible. Men without work joined the army, their small soldier's pay being supplemented by relief for their families. According to one estimate, 10,000 Louisianians volunteered or were drafted in the Union army. When conditions began to improve in 1863, General Banks offered bounties, handsome uniforms, and other inducements to recruit skilled laborers for various jobs. The Federals con-

[4] *Picayune,* April 19, 1863.

tinued the direct food relief for the poor provided earlier by the "free market," and they launched an extensive public works program which employed hundreds of the jobless. By these means Butler was caring for 40,000 citizens by the end of 1862, one-fourth of the total population; a year later Banks reported that 24,000 were still being supported in the same manner. As Federal operations in the lower Mississippi Valley expanded, the army and other departments hired larger and larger numbers of local residents, leading one Unionist to assert that "the commissary department has kept for nearly three years two thirds of the people from starvation."[5]

Unlike peacetime depressions, which are accompanied by deflation, the economic decline in New Orleans coincided with a rapid rise in all prices that further reduced the general standard of living. This inflation was partly the result of the overissuance of Confederate money and bonds, but the basic cause was the severe shortage of goods that arose when military action cut off contact with the regions which usually supplied them. Since the city imported so much of its food and manufactured goods from distant areas, the local cost of living before the war had been the highest in the South.

Confederate control of the lower valley after the capture stopped the importation of western flour, Texas meat, and even Louisiana foodstuffs, for the southern parishes seized by the Federals concentrated on the production of sugar and hardly raised enough food for their own needs. The shipment of such necessities by sea from the Northeast meant higher transportation costs, causing a greater increase in the price of food than of clothing, for example, which had always been imported by the sea route. Meals of ordinary quality rose to six dollars a day. At the same time the heavy demand for housing from northern businessmen arriving in the city and

[5] *Debates in the Convention,* 298; *Louisiana House Debates, 1864,* 89; *Picayune,* Dec. 19, 1862; Shugg, *Origins,* 187-91.

from military and government personnel made rents rise precipitously. Though the Federals arbitrarily fixed the price of flour and prevented poor Unionist renters from being evicted, citizens constantly had to spend more for the bare necessities—whether they were living on savings or on salaries.[6]

The economic revival which followed the fall of Vicksburg, however, was as extensive as the decline which preceded it. During 1863-64, arrivals of western steamers jumped from 655 to 1,414, and of sea vessels from 2,045 to 2,891. Cotton receipts rose from 22,000 bales in 1863 to 271,000 in 1865, and the value of imports in the same two-year period rose from $29,766,000 to $111,013,000. Thus the economic activity of the port was several times greater than it had been during the year before the capture.

Fundamentally this recovery resulted from the restoration of contact with the upper valley and parts of the lower. Workers were reemployed and new businesses were formed— such as the First National Bank, incorporated by a group of Unionists led by George Denison and Federal Marshal James B. Graham. Both profits and wages rose, causing a rapid increase in local purchasing power and greatly stimulating retail trade. The local Treasury office reported in the fall of 1863 that it had recently collected one million dollars in duties. Consumers got further relief from a drop in prices when western foodstuffs were once again imported freely, though all shortages did not end at once and in some instances speculators kept prices from dropping appreciatively.[7]

The increase in the volume of external trade was the primary factor in the upswing, but military expenditures and the labor policy of the Federals greatly accelerated it. Skilled labor in New Orleans before the war received an average wage of two dollars a day, unskilled one dollar—the

[6] Shugg, *Origins*, 113; George N. Gordon, *A War Diary of Events in the War of the Great Rebellion* (Boston, 1882), 307; Captain John G. Palfrey to his family, April 4, 1863, *Palfrey Papers*. Doyle, "Civilian Life," 29-55, traces the variation in prices of various products in great detail.

[7] Doyle, "Civilian Life," 38; "Chase Correspondence," 400-16, 423-25, 436.

highest rates in the South. As preparations for the Red River campaign got underway, the government paid first-class mechanics and locomotive engineers $3.25 a day and unskilled workers $1.25. New unions were started in addition to those already in existence; a baker's union, formed in 1864, soon announced the cessation of Sunday work. But the Federals refused to permit strikes—a group of coopers on government contract who struck for higher wages in the same year were sentenced to jail. The higher government rates undoubtedly produced some rise in wages of those in nonmilitary employment, though not enough in most cases to offset the higher cost of living after 1864.[8]

As long as hostilities continued in Louisiana, the return of prewar prosperity was impossible in New Orleans. By comparison with the first years of the war the extent of the recovery beginning in 1863 was considerable, yet inevitably there were limitations upon it. The total shipping of the port equaled that of 1860, but much of it was engaged in military rather than commercial service. The value of imports must be discounted, since it was expressed in an inflated dollar, and the price of the basic commodities—cotton and sugar—had risen several times as much as the general price level. As excessive profits went to the speculators, the city's income was even more unequally distributed among its populace than before the war. Due to the failure of the Federals to conquer central Louisiana and the Red River, the wholesale grocery trade with the hinterland was not restored and imports from the upper valley, therefore, remained below normal.

As a result of the destruction of farming areas which

[8] *Era,* Jan. 3, 31, 1864; Shugg, *Origins,* 189-90; Doyle, "Greenbacks," *C.W.H.,* V, 352-54. Shugg thinks the average worker enjoyed higher wages at the end of the war than he did in 1860; Doyle violently disagrees. Statistics are insufficient for any certainty on this point, but no doubt exists about the improvement in 1864. Having cited figures to this effect, Doyle adds the amazing nonsequitur that the "improvement was purely relative." All economic changes, of course, are by definition relative. What she is trying to say is that prewar levels of trade were not attained, an established fact.

produced the staples, only one-seventh as much cotton and an even smaller percentage of sugar was received in 1865 as in prewar years. Fewer workers were required, and unemployment would have remained more serious had not the military demand for labor partly filled the gap. Despite a sharp new rise in prices toward the end of 1864—apparently the result of the general wartime inflation throughout the whole United States—residents of New Orleans were much better off than their brethren in southern cities behind the Confederate lines. Those in the lower income brackets, because of the high cost of living, were probably in worse economic straits than at the beginning of the war, but so were the urban masses of the North.[9]

THE MERCHANTS of New Orleans, like the propertied classes of any nation defeated in a long, bloody war, suffered heavy financial losses by their support of the struggle for southern independence. The local tradition, however, that these losses were largely the result of arbitrary Federal confiscation is fictitious. As younger businessmen left the city for service in the Confederate army, many of those who were too old for military duty made liberal contributions to the war effort. Among them were the million dollars for local defense, the funds for the operation of the Free Market, and the bounties to encourage enlistment. Previously two-fifths ($6,000,000) of the first Confedrate domestic loan in February, 1861, was subscribed in New Orleans.[10]

Though such actions were taken in enlightened self-interest and in confidence of an early southern success, merchants thereby reduced their capital in the year before the capture. Their assets were further contracted by the severe decline in trade and their encouragement of the cotton embargo. Even

---

[9] For the effect of the war on northern labor, see H. U. Faulkner, *American Economic History*, 7th ed. (New York, 1954), 332-34.
[10] Randall, *Civil War*, 350.

THE ECONOMY

had they not subsequently been restrained from trading by the Federals, many of them would have lacked sufficient funds for a resumption of commercial operations when opportunities for profit returned in the summer of 1863.

British Consul William Mure, formerly an affluent cotton factor himself, reported to his government in December, 1860, before Louisiana seceded, that a severe panic had already begun and that within a fortnight more than thirty local factorage houses had "suspended, . . . whose aggregate liabilities amount to over 30 Millions of Dollars."[11] From this figure one can estimate the tremendous losses of New Orleans businessmen in the ensuing sixteen months before the capture when the Federal blockade became effective.

A considerable amount of real property, such as ships, docks, cotton, and other provisions, was destroyed on the eve of Farragut's arrival by military authorities or private owners to prevent it from falling into the hand of the enemy. During the riot which preceded the capture, the mob looted quantities of food supplies from the warehouses, and fires caused heavy damage to buildings and other personal possessions. Though the banks sent their gold out by train just prior to the capture, the cessation of specie payment months before prevented individuals from converting their holdings into gold and arranging for its safe deposit.

The defeat at the forts, in fact, came so unexpectedly and transportation facilities were so limited that few citizens were able to remove real property from the city. As an alternative, both foreigners and natives placed their valuables in the care of foreign consuls for safekeeping. All these losses prior to the capture resulted from direct, voluntary support of the rebellion by the mercantile community or from the misfortunes of war.[12]

Butler's prohibition of the circulation of Confederate

[11] William Mure to the Foreign Minister, Dec. 13, 1860, F.O. 5, vol. 744, P.R.O. London.
[12] See Ch. Two.

bonds and paper money was the main punitive measure of the Federals, but it could hardly be called confiscation, for it was not necessarily irretrievable; the South would probably have redeemed its obligations had it won the war, though their actual value would have been reduced by inflation. The 25 percent tax on contributors to the defense fund and on the factors who had publicly sponsored the cotton embargo, however, *was* arbitrary and *ex post facto*. Yet it could be regarded as a form of progressive taxation, as the proceeds were spent on poor relief and public works.

Just prior to his removal from command, Butler ordered a second levy on the same groups. At first Banks postponed it; then he collected it in January, 1863. In October, 1864, he ordered a third levy, but those who had not been exiled as registered enemies lacked funds with which to pay it. In the first two instances, whatever the justification, the immediate effect was a serious financial loss to New Orleans businessmen.[13]

The various other penalties which the Federals imposed on residents, it should be emphasized, were in retaliation for resistance to the occupation measures of the conquerors. These measures had a military objective—victory of the United States in the war. Confederate sympathizers in New Orleans resorted to resistance of their own volition in order to prevent that victory. Citizens who were willing to cooperate fully with Federal policies incurred none of these penalties. However courageous their action, those who chose instead to persist in a devious or open opposition knew the risks they ran, certainly after the first month of the Butler regime. Naturally they resented the punishment, but it was no less justifiable than the resistance which provoked it, and the Federals could not fairly be accused of indiscriminate mistreatment of an innocent population. Many Orleanians

[13] *O.R.* XV, 538, 607, XLI, 574-75. See Ch. Four.

were partisan, not neutral, and even neutrality is rarely permitted citizens in a combat area in any war.

A case in point is the exaggerated and much-publicized confiscation of property of those who refused to take the oath of allegiance before the deadline in the fall of 1862. Butler's purpose in requiring the oath, it will be recalled, was to lessen the danger of a recapture of the city and to make more troops available for field duty. Residents were warned months in advance of the penalty for refusal, as the act of Congress in July had been specific on that point, and they well knew that the general usually carried out his threats. Many, in fact, transferred their property to foreign consuls as a precaution, but most residents took the oath in the end. The several thousand who registered as enemies could have saved their property by taking the oath. Sold at auction at prices far below actual value, the seizures produced revenues of less than a million dollars. The amount of private property confiscated after 1862 was small, for Banks discontinued his predecessor's practice of taking private residences for military use.

As onerous to the older merchants as their capital and property losses were the restrictions placed upon their participation in trade in the staples, but here again they brought their fate upon themselves by their refusal to cooperate with the Federals. Most trade was through enemy lines, since the area subjugated by Union forces was so small. It required a pass from the commanding general or a license from the Treasury officials, the obvious purpose being to prevent military information from reaching the enemy and to insure the collection of taxes. Banks discontinued this practice, as he was opposed to all trade with the enemy.

Native merchants were denied licenses in 1862 because of their refusal to take the oath and later, after most of them had taken it, because of their refusal to join the Unionist clubs and to vote in elections. The situation would have been different had they given positive proof of loyalty by becoming active Unionists at once; but since they did not, the Federals would have been foolish to permit them to trade when preparations for combat operations against Vicksburg were being made.

Many rebel merchants would have refrained from contraband trade of their own volition in 1862, as most of them were still anxious to maintain the cotton famine in order to encourage foreign intervention. When Confederate policy changed later, had it been in their power to do so they would have attempted to furnish the Confederacy with military supplies in exchange for cotton. At any rate, northern speculators took their places and the new arrivals banded together against the few older merchants who had the capital and the license necessary to compete with them. "There is no chance for a man here now," wrote stationer Thomas Shield to his partner, "unless he is identified with the Yankees and the Bostonians." Resident Unionists did engage in speculation —among them Thomas P. May, the young planter-editor of the radical *Times,* and the aged conservative Jacob Barker, whose *National Advocate* was suppressed by Banks because of its strong southern sympathies. Barker formed a partnership with Bostonian A. L. Mansfield, a man of considerable means, and the two received a permit from General Banks himself.[14]

Economic conditions were so bad during the year after the capture that few of the Yankees made large profits until late in 1863. By that date many of the older firms had disappeared, and by 1864 names new to the city predominated in the reorganized Chamber of Commerce. Resident businessmen, however, still controlled some concerns like banks and

[14] Thomas H. Shields to Arthur W. Hyatt, Aug. 15, 1863, *Hyatt Collection,* I, Louisiana State University Archives; Reed, *Dostie,* 137-45; Harrington, *Banks,* 148-49. The *Smith-Brady Report,* 57ff, gives the details of the Barker-Mansfield dealings, which had been investigated by special detective Alan Pinkerton.

utilities whose operations were confined to the city. Secretly sympathetic to the Confederacy, they incurred Banks' hostility by rebuffing his initial conciliatory policy. When local banks discounted United States Treasury notes (greenbacks) in favor of their own notes, he approved a provost marshal order placing the Bank of Louisiana and the Louisiana State Bank in receivership and issued a general order forbidding the practice.

Apparently the other banks refused to obey the order, justifying their action on the grounds that greenbacks were not redeemable in gold, whereupon Banks decided to destroy them for their defiance. In March, 1864, he appointed a five-man commission to examine all private banks and other businesses in New Orleans, and in June he ordered all local firms with specie in their vaults to deposit it in the new National Bank established in 1863. The commission was to check on the capital, liabilities, and assets of each company; the relation of the directors to their own institution; the character and influence of the stockholders; and the status of both directors and stockholders "in relation to the Government of the United States." The broad scope of the investigation indicated that Banks' patience with all southern businessmen was at an end.[15]

By a three-to-two vote the handpicked commission recommended immediate liquidation of the offending banks. In a minority report the two conservative members, Creoles Aristide Miltenberger and F. J. Ducourge, protested strongly that most of the banks were sound and that it was unfair to penalize "the present loyal Directors and Stockholders" for actions before the capture like the suspension of specie payment. On the basis of the commission's recommendation Banks had state auditor A. P. Dostie check the state banking law and start liquidation proceedings against them.

[15] "Chase Correspondence," 441; *True Delta,* Aug. 22, 1864; Doyle, "Greenbacks," *C.W.H.,* V, 357-58, 360-62.

Evidently the case was a weak one, for General Hurlburt suspended legal action after Banks left for Washington in September, and probably the courts would have rejected the suit for reasons advanced in the minority report. Hostile to Banks' Free State government, Hurlburt reversed many of his predecessor's policies and even gave official support to local banks in their successful fight to collect a million dollars in accumulated interest on municipal bonds which they had deposited with the state auditor in 1861. In the suit, which resulted from the city's refusal to pay the interest, Provisional Court Judge Peabody ruled in favor of the banks.[16]

Though it condemned the banks, the commission attested to the stability of other businesses like the Commercial Water Works, the Gas Light Company, and the City Railroad. Dissatisfied with this verdict, Banks appointed a second commission, headed by his stanch supporter Cuthbert Bullitt, to reexamine the matter. All the new body could uncover were rumors about "treasonable" activities of the companies and their former directors prior to the capture, for which by its own admission it could find no confirmation. The complete failure of Banks' attack upon the local businesses shows that Federal observance of civil procedures gave citizens considerable protection, even from the wrath of the commanding general himself, in cases where the charges against them were too sweeping and in part dubious.[17]

Besides his order against the discounting of greenbacks, Banks took other action in regard to local currency, intended not as a punitive measure but to check inflation. This did little good, since shortages were the main cause of high

[16] "Chase Correspondence," 457.
[17] Doyle, "Greenbacks," C.W.H., V, 361 and note 39. The reports of the two commissions are filed in Letters Received (Civil), 1864, in the National Archives. On this and many other points Miss Doyle has unearthed much evidence which she often misinterprets. In this instance, for example, her account gives the reader the clear impression that Banks was successful in his effort to liquidate the banks, but she relegates to a footnote the all-important fact that his suit against them was later suspended. Then she adds the erroneous statement that the Bullitt report on the utilities "would have given Banks sufficient grounds *for liquidating these firms too.*"

THE ECONOMY 161

prices. With the disappearance of gold and silver and silver coins the Confederates had permitted the use of shinplasters for small change—railroad and streetcar tickets as well as notes issued by private firms and by the city itself. Soon after the capture Butler ordered the issuing companies to redeem their notes upon demand in specie or Treasury notes. At the same time the city redeemed and canceled most of its notes.

In the fall of 1862, because of public demand the city reissued the canceled notes, but meanwhile counterfeiters had put quantities of bogus shinplasters into circulation. When the City Railroad announced in December that for this reason it would no longer redeem its "blue tickets," Banks countermanded the repudiation and remained adamant in the face of railroad officials' protests. In the summer of 1864 the city had to issue $150,000 more small notes. Because the continued activity of counterfeiters made the cost of redemption so heavy, Banks stopped the circulation of all shinplasters, both city and private.[18]

AFTER THE CAPTURE Yankee "speculators" flocked to New Orleans in expectation of quick and easy profits, as they did to Memphis up the river and to other areas of the South occupied by the Federals. This migration to the Louisiana metropolis was hardly surprising in view of the fact that it was the largest southern city and the largest cotton market in the world. For half a century northerners had been arriving there in a steady stream, and many of them, like impecunious James Robb, had made fortunes in trade.

With local merchants denied commercial privileges, once news spread about Andrew Butler's profits in "contraband" and General Butler's sale of confiscated property, a tremendous influx set in. "They have continued to arrive and every steamer brings an addition to their number," wrote

[18] Doyle, "Greenbacks," *C.W.H.*, V, 355-57.

Treasury agent Denison satirically, "Each expects to be a millionaire in six months. They have few scruples about the means of satisfying their cupidity." The next year he recorded that "a host of speculators, Jews and campfollowers, came hither in the track of Banks' expedition."[19]

All Confederates and many Federals voiced their condemnation of the new arrivals and their activities. For the southerners it was enough that they were Yankees and took over the economic functions which formerly belonged to residents. Federal critics disapproved for a number of reasons, chiefly because they thought trade with the enemy was beneficial to the Confederacy. Union soldiers regarded speculators as northern draftdodgers, and General Banks instituted conscription soon after he took command of the Gulf Department. Decrying the "ignoble army of speculators, confiscators, and devastators," in his first proclamation the general announced the discontinuance of trade and travel beyond the Union lines.[20]

However reprehensible the motives and actions of these traders, the case against them has been exaggerated and theirs was by no means the sole responsibility for trade with the enemy. All businessmen who deal in commodities in the market, during war or peace, are by definition speculators, and the New Orleans traders were not the only northerners who made profit out of the war. Cornelius Vanderbilt was selling rotting ships to the government on fat contracts; John D. Rockefeller was acquiring his initial capital as a commission merchant in Cleveland. Nor were they alone in avoiding military service by the hiring of substitutes as the law permitted—even future President Grover Cleveland did so.

The conduct of traders in New Orleans was worse in the eyes of the northern public because they operated for profit in a combat area where their fellow Americans were dying in

[19] "Chase Correspondence," 353, 359-60.
[20] See Ch. Five.

battle to save the Union and because they supplied the enemy with munitions which increased the casualties. But trade across the lines was not necessarily illegal. Actually it was sanctioned by the United States government as an effective war measure. Without publicizing the fact, both belligerents secretly encouraged trade with the enemy during the war. The Nonintercourse Act of Congress in 1861 permitted it under license from the President—a power which Lincoln sometimes used directly but one which he usually transferred to the Treasury Department. The Federal objective was to obtain cotton for foreign mills to prevent European recognition of the Confederacy and for northern mills to induce support of the war and the program of the administration. Conversely the South, when it became apparent that the cotton embargo was not accomplishing its purpose, began to exchange the staple for military necessities like munitions, medicine, gold, and essential commodities such as salt.

Though the crop was greatly reduced as a result of the diversification to foodstuffs and of the physical destruction of plantations in military campaigns, the southern government obtained possession of much cotton through produce loans, impressment, and taxes in kind. To prevent the Federal army from seizing it—a major objective of Banks' several campaigns in Louisiana—the Confederates usually burned it upon the approach of the enemy. Both governments therefore resorted to the services of traders as the most effective means of accomplishing their respective purposes. Since neither planters nor the Confederate government would accept greenbacks, gold or critical military supplies had to be given in exchange for cotton unless it was captured before it could be burned.[21]

[21] This complex subject is discussed in A. S. Roberts, "The Federal Government and Confederate Cotton," *American Historical Review*, XXXII (1926-27), 262-75; E. M. Coulter, "Commercial Intercourse with the Confederacy in the Mississippi Valley, 1861-1865," *Mississippi Valley Historical Review*, V (1918-19) 378ff; and Johnson, *Red River Campaign*, which is largely a study of cotton and politics.

Disloyal individuals on both sides, traders and planters, indulged in contraband trade for their own aggrandizement regardless of its effect upon the war aims of their governments. Yankee speculators obtained the necessary license by bribing Treasury agents, or by the same method induced Federal officers to permit passage through the lines. Military personnel of all ranks speculated on their own or formed partnerships with traders; cotton, said Louisiana General Dick Taylor, made "more damn rascals on both sides than everything else." The practice was so easily arranged and so widespread that it would have been difficult to stamp out in any event. But it seems certain that the President and his top advisers desired the continuance of trade with the enemy, though for fear of public reaction they could not openly restrain the commanders in the field from attempts to check it. In 1862 Lincoln did countermand an order of Grant's expelling all Jewish traders from his department.[22]

In view of the clandestine nature of the trade, the lack of reliable records, and the prevalence of wild rumors in contemporary accounts, it is impossible to ascertain most of the true facts about the situation in New Orleans during the occupation. The report of the official investigation into corruption made in 1865 by General Smith often accepted local rumors at face value. Closer to the truth, perhaps, were the confidential letters of agent Denison to Secretary Chase, since his official position gave him access to information withheld from the public. Even his testimony must be discounted because of his opposition to trade with the enemy and his obvious desire to confirm the preconceived beliefs of his chief. Some tentative conclusions, however, appear substantiated by the evidence.[23]

Throughout the occupation the Treasury Department con-

[22] New York *Herald*, June 11, 1864; *O.R.*, XVII, pt. 2, 158. An excellent case study is Joseph H. Parks, "A Confederate Trade Center under Federal Occupation: Memphis, 1862 to 1865," *J.S.H.*, VII (1941), 289-314.
[23] See Ch. Five.

stantly fought the commanding general for control of trade and sequestered property in the Gulf Department. Since Butler and Military Governor Shepley gave passes and active assistance to northern speculators, at first Chase's local agents attempted to check trade with the enemy. In this effort they received the support of Admiral Farragut, who protested to the general by letter and, according to the Smith-Brady report, arrested his brother Andrew. Acting under orders in October, 1862, Denison complained to Butler about the violation of departmental regulations. The General convinced the agent of his own compliance but apparently made no effort to suppress the bribery that was rife among his officers. Reverdy Johnson, sent down as special agent of the State Department to referee Butler's disputes with foreign consuls, reported the existence of a "state of fraud and corruption . . . without parallel in the history of the country."[24]

The struggle for control shifted after Banks' arrival, and the position of the contestants changed completely. The new general disapproved of trade with the enemy, but the Treasury now began secretly to encourage it. Rejecting a bribe offer of $100,000 early in 1863, Banks officially forbade trade across the lines; to check corruption among his officers he promised protection to planters in occupied Louisiana if they would send their cotton directly to the city. In view of Butler's recent difficulties with the consuls, however, Banks dared not stop aliens from bringing in southern cotton under the protection of their governments.

Though Andrew Butler and a few other operators soon left, large numbers of new speculators arrived. In the city they were so far accepted as to attend Mrs. Banks' balls, but the general tried to keep private merchants off his marches into the field. He was well aware of the prevalence of bribery in the army and also of the necessity of the acquisition of cotton, yet he was reluctant to swap critical supplies to the

[24] "Chase Correspondence," 320-29, 338-42; *Delta*, Dec. 17, 18, 1862.

Confederates in exchange. At least twice he formally suggested to Washington plans by which Union officials would withhold part of the sales price of cotton received from planters behind the enemy lines as a guarantee that the Confederacy would not benefit from the deal. Evidently Chase was able to prevent acceptance of these plans.[25]

Some months before the attempt to bribe Banks, Denison reported that he had received an offer of $50,000 for his "cooperation." As early as the summer of 1863 Banks complained that his failure to prevent the passage of munitions to the enemy was caused by the fact that the War Department had transferred to Treasury agents almost unlimited power over trade. Commodore Porter wrote General Sherman about the same time that assignment of the task of enforcing the regulations to Treasury aids was "very much like setting a rat to watch the cheese to see that the mice don't get at it." Banks voiced his disapproval officially, but he did not press his attack on bribery too hard because, as an adroit politician, he knew that the President supported Chase's policy of acquiring cotton by the most practical means.

Hundreds of lesser officials, therefore, in the army and navy as well as the Treasury, were approached by traders with impunity and with success. Numerous other methods were used to cover up illegal activities. Aliens were cut in on the profits in return for bringing cotton into New Orleans. Journalists' passes on the Red River expedition sold for $2,500 each. Among the several traders who accompanied the troops, Kentuckian Samuel L. Casey had a pass from Lincoln himself and William Halliday received naval protection. Dr. Issachar Zacherie, secret agent for both the President and Banks, indulged in speculation while on official missions. Even George Denison was not above suspicion, in view of the large sums of money he invested in the new

[25] "Chase Correspondence," 341, 348-49, 355, 359-60; Harrington, *Banks*, 135-38.

National Bank and in the purchase of local newspapers. In fact, the Smith-Brady report charged him with accepting a bribe.[26]

PHYSICAL ACCESS to the cotton producing regions, not official policy, was the key factor which determined the volume of trade. For this reason, as the statistics listed earlier in this chapter show, five times as much cotton came in during 1863-64 as in the first year of the occupation. But in 1860 sugar was the main crop in the area of Louisiana conquered by the Federals.

After the capture of New Orleans, planters in the central and northern portions of the state, as well as those in Texas, sent their crops overland and out through the Texas ports. Under Confederate sanction a booming trade with Mexico sprang up, the disruption of which was the main objective of Banks' Texas expedition, and northern traders from Memphis up the river competed with those in the Crescent City. Much more trade passed through Memphis prior to the fall of Vicksburg, since it was closer to Confederate lines and easy to reach by river from the upper valley. So much, in fact, that Chase and Lincoln by formal orders cut it off from all imports when the siege of Vicksburg began in the spring of 1863.[27]

A flurry of local trade occurred immediately after the capture of New Orleans, chiefly because the blockade had built up a surplus of cotton during the preceding year but had also caused an acute shortage of other products, causing a reverse situation in the East. Turpentine, for example, brought $3.00 a barrel in New Orleans but $38.00 in New

[26] Harrington, *Banks,* 160-62; "Chase Correspondence," 336, 353-55, 359-60, 375-76, 378, 415; Gordon, *War Diary,* 32; *O.R.,* XXXI, pt. 1, 780-81; *Smith-Brady Report,* 57-80; Johnson, *Red River Campaign.*
[27] "Chase Correspondence," 348, 353, 427-31; Parks, "Confederate Trade Center," *J.S.H.,* VII, 304.

York, while flour sold locally for $24.00 a barrel but for only $6.00 in the northeastern port. In the region north of the city still held by the Confederates prices were much higher. In Confederate currency flour sold there for $100.00 a barrel in March, 1863; beef or pork for $80.00 a barrel; salt for $30.00 to $100.00 a sack (four bushels); whisky for $1,000.00 to $2,000.00 a barrel; and calico for $2.00 a yard.

Profits were therefore high in the legitimate trade between New Orleans and New York, and much higher in the contraband trade between the city and the adjacent enemy areas, reached by river steamers on the Mississippi and its tributaries and by schooners on Lake Pontchartrain. Denison reported to Chase in great detail about the heavy traffic across the lake, in which quantities of salt were exchanged for Confederate cotton with the approval of high officials on both sides. A sack of salt, bought in the city for $1.25, would sell across the lake for from $60.00 to $100.00; cotton bought with the proceeds on the north shore at 10 cents a pound would be sold in New Orleans for 60 cents. With a few thousand dollars invested in one cargo a man could quickly make a fortune of several hundred thousand dollars.[28]

Andrew Butler's exceptional profits were the result of his large operating capital and his brother's aid in providing passes, government ships, and soldiers for the necessary labor and protection. But most speculators were not so fortunate, and the total imports were comparatively small in 1862-63. As more and more goods moved through the port, the disparity between local and eastern prices was soon reduced. And for a few months, at least, the combined efforts of Denison, Farragut, and Banks made it difficult for traders to obtain passes beyond the lines.

The surrender of Vicksburg opened traffic on the river and contact with plantations on both banks, and the military

---

[28] "Chase Correspondence," 336-40, 348, 375-76; Parton, *Butler*, 411; *Smith-Brady Report*, 145-59.

campaigns which began in the region in the spring of 1863 greatly extended physical access to the cotton areas. Though some private trading was carried on at all times, private operators obtained the greatest quantities whenever the army moved into the interior. In cases of direct military seizure the army confiscated Confederate government cotton, but it made compensation later to Unionist planters.

Banks' expedition up the Red River into the Teche country before the siege of Port Hudson seized three million dollars of spoils, including livestock, sugar, molasses, and ten thousand bales of cotton. His quartermaster arranged for the disposal, but Union General George H. Gordon recorded in his diary that speculators made a killing: "under threats of destruction of cotton and sugar, these products were transferred in immense quantities to New Orleans, where a low price was offered the unfortunate owner, with a choice of acceptance or confiscation for disloyalty. I withhold the names of prominent officers whose fortunes were made." On the march against Alexandria and Shreveport a year later Banks cut military personnel out of fraudulent profits by transferring the booty to the Treasury Department.[29]

Though the big money went into cotton and sugar, northern businessmen who had come to the city bought and sold all kinds of products in response to variations in current supplies and prices. It is unnecessary to trace these activities in any detail, for the pattern remained the same as it was in 1862, but commercial operations were gradually extended over a much wider area. The main exports to the Confederacy during the occupation were gold, munitions, medicine, salt, and sometimes foodstuffs. As for the distribution of products acquired from the outlying areas, merchants usually sold provisions in the local market or to the army and shipped staples to the Northeast. More cautious northerners were often content with a smaller profit and a quicker turnover;

[29] Harrington, *Banks*, 119-20; Gordon, *War Diary*, 325-26.

when conditions improved during 1863, some of them began to invest their capital in various businesses within the city.

Unquestionably the total volume of trade was greatest during the last year of hostilities. The production of sugar, confined to a small area ravaged by military operations, dwindled to almost nothing because of the disruption of the labor force; but receipts of cotton were twice that of 1863-64, since it came in from the entire lower valley, now within easy access. So much gold and silver were passing through the city to finance commercial operations with the enemy that the provost marshal general in June, 1864, prohibited all shipments of specie and ordered a rigid search of all vessels clearing the port. With the end of the war in sight, however, either as a result of a Federal military victory or a negotiated peace, speculators were restive and the volume of trade varied greatly from month to month. "Everything seems waiting," wrote southern observer Gus Mandeville to his sister, "for the result of the struggle between Grant & Lee and Johnston & Sherman."[30]

The condemnation of the activities of northern merchants, both by Federals and Confederates, has usually been accepted at face value. Whatever the effect upon the outcome of the war, these activities were highly beneficial to the economy of the city and therefore to the whole populace. Since resident merchants had lost their capital or were restrained from trading by Federal authorities, the economic recovery of 1863 would hardly have come about had not Yankee businessmen spent the funds they brought with them in quest of profits. Speculators injured the community only to the extent that they kept food prices high, as their southern predecessors had done before the capture. In both instances inflation was an inevitable byproduct of the war.

The new arrivals, in short, assumed the essential economic

---

[30] "Chase Correspondence," 441; Doyle, "Greenbacks," *C.W.H.*, V, 353, 358; *Picayune*, Oct. 23, Nov. 27, 1864.

functions of the former merchants. Despite the hostile attitude of military men and of residents, they were the entrepreneurs who supplied the capital and directed the customary business operations. The movement of contraband goods created jobs for workers and a demand for the services of ships, banks, docks, and warehouses to the profit of their owners. The legality of the trade did not matter as long as part of the profit was reinvested locally. However selfish their motives, the Yankee speculators should be given much credit for starting the chain reaction which brought New Orleans out of the earlier depression.

EIGHT PRESS, CHURCH, AND SCHOOL

$S_{EEN\ FROM}$ the longer experience of the midtwentieth century, the complexities of the problem of military occupation are more apparent than they were to Americans of the Civil War era. An occupied population, in fact, has certain advantages over its conquerors—even in wartime. From a mere military point of view the simplest method for the conquerors to achieve security is a stern one backed by the threat of severe punishment or execution for disobedience, like that of Butler in New Orleans or the Germans in France during World War II. Even this method has its limitations, for as the Germans discovered, a desperate population can form an underground, turn to sabotage, and fight terror with terror.

Actually, however, for a conquered nation a nonresistance or token resistance policy is more effective. It involves the conqueror with numerous difficulties of administration and supply, and it gradually saps the morale of the occupying forces. Regardless of the determination of the commanding general or the general staff, regulations must be enforced by the lesser members of the military hierachy—the lieutenants, sergeants, and privates. They can hardly shoot down an unresisting citizenry, least of all women and children. Far away from home in a strange land, sooner or later they begin to fraternize. Since Yankees and Orleanians in 1862 had a common language and on the whole a common cultural and national heritage, the human problem of occupying the Louisiana metropolis presented more than the usual difficulties for the invaders.

It must be kept in mind, however, that the objective of the Federals in taking New Orleans was a military one, a step toward victory in the war. They were not there to improve or clean up the city. From it they planned to launch military campaigns toward the east, north, and west. Since for three years it was a command headquarters in a combat zone, military security was the first essential. To prevent vital information from reaching the enemy the press must be closely censored, and conceivably for similar reasons certain restrictions could be placed upon other institutions like the schools and churches. Nor should it be forgotten that a Confederate counterattack was always a possibility of which both Federals and citizens were ever aware, particularly when troops departed on the drive against Vicksburg in 1863 or up the Red River the following year.

After taking the initial steps toward military security such as precautions against insurrection and a yellow fever epidemic, the Federals might simply have left local residents to shift for themselves as best they could, regardless of the misery and hardship that resulted. Had such a course been followed, life for the average citizen during the war would have been far worse than it actually was. Instead, the Federals assumed responsibility for the administration of the city and thus involved themselves in endless troubles of a nonmilitary nature.

That they did so was not due merely to the personality of Ben Butler, who after all was there only seven months. Fundamentally the responsibility was Lincoln's, for it was he who decided to make Louisiana the model restored southern state. Regardless of the wisdom of the decision, it saddled the conquerors with various administrative problems and immeasurably increased the burdens of the commanding general of the Gulf Department. To win the necessary votes the Federals had to woo the citizenry. As a result, whether they realized it or not, life for the ordinary Orleanian was much freer and in many material aspects better than that of most conquered populations in wartime. It was not so, of course, to the few who had rather been "dead than red."

Certain factors alluded to above, which made the occupation less onerous to the civilians, should at this point be reviewed. Butler thoroughly tamed the city in the course of 1862, and there was every indication that it would have remained quiescent had he continued to receive stanch support from Washington. But the Lincoln administration realized that victory for the United States at that moment depended even more upon the attitude of Europe than upon success in the field. New Orleans was extremely fortunate that its commercial ties with England and its cultural ties with France focused European attention upon it more than upon any American city. The severe European disapproval of some of Butler's much-publicized and dramatic actions forced his removal from command and the shift to the mild, conciliatory policy of Banks.

Lincoln frequently gave advice and issued orders to the commanding general, as did the several executive departments. But they were far away in Washington, and the general was present on the scene. At all times the personality of the general influenced the treatment of citizens and set the overall tone of the occupation. His subordinate officers soon responded accordingly. Thus when Banks came in, as Julia Le Grand noted, citizens immediately sensed the milder attitude of the military hierarchy.[1] But Banks was so frequently absent upon field duty that it was impossible for him to supervise his local military administrators as closely as Butler had. Consequently, when he attempted to clamp down

[1] *Journal of Julia Le Grand*, 55-56.

before he departed on the Vicksburg campaign and again in the summer of 1864, he was far less successful than his predecessor.

The political ambitions of both generals, who were young enough to anticipate a long career in public office after the war, always exercised a cogent influence upon the occupation. However sound Butler's harsh policy was on military grounds, he was consciously seeking popularity with the radicals and with a northern public which increasingly demanded punishment of the rebels. Banks was ever cognizant of the prestige he would gain should he succeed in making New Orleans a Unionist town. He even hoped for the Republican nomination over Lincoln in 1864. When Seward praised "the great and brilliant military results and the eminently successful civil administration" in the Gulf Department, Banks wrote his wife in September, 1863, "I begin to think I may be somebody by and by."[2] Yet northern criticism and fear of unpopularity sometimes kept him from pressing intelligent programs he had initiated, notably in regard to Negroes and to trade in cotton. The President himself was subject to similar pressures and equally sensitive to public opinion.

Generals, trained to think and act with a sense of detachment, will sometimes yield to their feelings. Butler and Banks both regarded southerners as traitors who had started the war, and the Beast hated them with fervor. It is not surprising that he became enraged when ministers continued to pray for the enemy or when schoolteachers led their children in singing "Dixie." It would have required unusual self-restraint for a man of his temperament, possessing the power he did, not to retaliate—though he was also conscious that retaliation would gain a favorable press in the North. Equally understandable was Banks' loss of patience when residents so openly rejected his olive branch, and he might have reverted to severity in the spring of 1863 even if military

[2] Banks to his wife, Sept. 15, 1863, *Banks MSS.*

security and political considerations had not required it. Certainly his attacks upon southern businessmen in the summer of 1864 were in part motivated by pique at his recent removal from military command.

There can be no question that strict censorship of the press was mandatory in a combat zone. But it is at least questionable that the restrictions attempted by both generals on schools and churches could be amply justified on grounds of military security. In view of what they actually accomplished, it can be safely said that the baneful effect of such restrictions in New Orleans has been greatly exaggerated.

MORE THAN a score of newspapers were published locally during the 1850s, three of them in both French and English. Some of the dailies also printed weekly, semiweekly, and "California" editions. Several catered to special ethnic groups, but as elsewhere in the nation all except the *Price Current* and the *Picayune* had distinct political affiliations. With the disruption of the Whigs, the rise of the Know-Nothings, and the split of local Democrats into Soulé (Douglas) and Slidell (Buchanan) factions, the decade proved journalistically chaotic. The *Bulletin* remained old-line Whig, but the *Crescent* shifted to the new American party, and even the *Bee* did so until the municipal election of 1858. The *True Delta,* second largest in circulation, spoke especially for the Irish and was therefore inclined toward the Democrats. The Democratic *Courier,* founded in 1807, was purchased by Slidell in 1859 but discontinued publication within two years. Its uptown Democratic rival, the *Delta,* supported Soulé. The *Picayune,* largest of all in 1860 with 12,600 subscribers, usually followed rather than led public opinion. Founded in 1837 by Yankee George W. Kendall, it was the most independent in politics (its competitors would have said opportunistic), but even it flirted with the Know-Nothings at the height of their popularity. Only the *True Delta* persisted longer in opposition to secession. By contrast, in the crisis of 1860-61 the *Delta* and the *Crescent* became rabidly secessionist.[3]

Butler dealt harshly with the local press, not for divulging military information but simply for expressions of hostility to the Federal occupation. After he seized the presses of the *True Delta* for refusing to set type on his proclamation and suspended its publication until owner John McGinnis apologized, the other eleven newspapers in New Orleans printed the proclamation in full. When McGinnis offended again in an editorial on May 11, 1860, defending the burning of cotton prior to the capture, Butler warned him that such language was "inadmissible." Thereafter the *True Delta* ceased to indulge in even the mildest criticism of the Federal program.[4]

About the same time the *Bee* and the *Delta* were suspended for similarly offensive editorials. Because the *Crescent's* owner, T. O. Nixon, was absent in the Confederate army, Butler confiscated its plant and sold it to the local banker Jacob Barker, who republished it under the name of the *Advocate*. But the following November the General suspended it for what he regarded as obnoxious reporting. On May 29 the *Bee* was allowed to resume publication after a formal apology, but it continued to be more cautiously critical of Federal actions than any other local paper. When the *Bulletin* printed a eulogy on its owner, Colonel Isaac Seymour, who had recently been killed in battle, Butler sequestered it and jailed its editor. About the same time the *Picayune* was suspended, and the French literary sheet *La Renaissance* was required to furnish the provost marshal in advance with an English translation of all its copy.[5]

[3] Separate histories of early New Orleans newspapers, Charles Youngman, ed., 1938, can be found in typescript in the New Orleans Public Library.
[4] General Orders 17, New Orleans; *True Delta,* May 11, 1862.
[5] *Bulletin,* June 5, 27, 1862; *O.R.,* XV, 533; *Delta,* May 16, 1862.

Needing a local paper as his semiofficial spokesman, Butler ousted the editors of the *Delta,* which had been strongly pro-southern, and appointed in their places two of his officers, Captain John Clark, formerly of the Boston *Courier* and Lieutenant Colonel E. M. Brown, a Vermonter. In retaliation, employers of other local papers blacklisted the fifty printers on the *Delta* as Yankee stooges.[6]

In the first six months of Federal occupation, therefore, the *Crescent* and the *Bulletin* disappeared. Barker's *Advocate,* using the *Crescent's* plant, was suspended. The *Bee* and the *Picayune,* much chastened, resumed publication after doing penance but were forced to print mostly court news in order to avoid offense to the commanding general. Advertising dwindled to almost nothing because of the depression. The *Delta* became a Federal organ, and the frightened *True Delta* largely its echo. But the very real danger of an insurrection at the time might be considered a justification for such strict repression of hostility in the press.

Banks brought with him three eastern correspondents, A. C. Hill of the New York *Herald,* A. G. Hill of the Boston *Traveller,* and a member of the staff of *Leslie's Illustrated Weekly.* To combat the Butler crowd he sequestered the *Delta,* renamed it *Era,* and appointed the two Hills as its editors. Thus the *Era* became his semiofficial organ as much as the *Delta* had been Butler's. About the same time the radical Unionists, mostly followers of Secretary Chase, started the *Times.*[7]

Straddling the fence in order to avoid internecine conflict among the Unionist factions, the new commanding general divided a subsidy of $800 a month between his own *Era,* the radicals' *Times,* and the *True Delta.* But when Barker petitioned for reinstatement of his *Advocate* as a journal catering to the women of the city, Banks apparently denied the re-

---
[6] Special Orders 37, 39, New Orleans, May 13, 1862; Parton, *Butler,* 312; *Journal of Julia Le Grand,* 131.
[7] *Era,* Feb. 14, 15, 1863.

quest, for Barker shortly asked for permission to sell it. In line with a stricter surveillance policy on the eve of the Vicksburg campaign, in April the general suspended the French *L'Estafette du Sud* and the Catholic *Southern Pilot* for "obnoxious articles."[8]

In Banks' absence on the Vicksburg campaign, General Thomas W. Sherman took over command of the city. John E. Hayes, correspondent for the Boston *Traveller,* sent his paper an article pointing out the weakness of the city's defenses. Enraged, Sherman put him in jail and then banished him and A. C. Hill from the department. Evidently Banks interceded for Hill, for he was soon back at his job on the *Era.* Actually northern correspondents, who enjoyed greater license, were more of a threat to military security than the local journalists, who had to be more circumspect.[9]

Naturally censorship of the press was greatest prior to the military campaigns of 1863 and 1864. It varied, however, from week to week and month to month. The relations of the commanding general with the press were usually much more influenced by political than by military considerations. To some extent under Butler but much more under Banks, a favorable press was essential to the whole Unionization program. The *Delta* and its successor the *Era* were, so to speak, the administration organ, yet the opposition could not be too openly muzzled. The *Bee* and the more cautious *Picayune* spoke for the old southern conservatives, the *Times* for the radical Unionists and the Chase coterie.

In June, 1863, upon the death of McGinnis, a local conservative, Dr. Hugh Kennedy, later appointed mayor by General Hurlburt, bought the *True Delta.* This action aroused Treasury agent George Denison, who wrote his chief that Kennedy "was always in opposition to those in authority, unless he can make personal gain by being otherwise, and is fond of abusive language which he uses on all occasions.

[8] *Ibid.,* April 24, 1863.
[9] *Ibid.,* May 6, 9, 1863.

What else can be expected of an Irishman (as Kennedy is) with red hair?" Denison, who owned a one-sixth interest in the *Times* and was able to influence its policy by friendship with the other owners, told Chase that to offset the conservative threat he was seeking to get control of at least three other local papers. His main target was the *Era*.[10]

Obviously the key to New Orleans journalism during the occupation was the infighting between the rival Unionist factions and their relations with the commanding general. Denison, at heart a radical Unionist, opportunistically joined the Banks-Hahn moderates, and the outcome of his attempted coup is not clear. On January 1, 1864, prior to the gubernatorial race, Hahn bought the *True Delta* from Kennedy and used it as his own organ, allegedly receiving more than $100,000 for printing the records of the constitutional convention in that year. Upon his election he turned the editorship over to W. R. Fish. In April local Negroes started the *Tribune,* the first successful Negro daily in the United States. It succeeded the weekly *L'Union,* begun in 1862 and edited by a native colored teacher, Paul Trevigne. According to the Tribune's publisher, Paris-educated Dr. Louis Roudanes, it lost $35,000 within a few months. Its tone was generally vitriolic, and by and large it presented the viewpoint of the educated free Negroes still resident in the city. Meanwhile, when the editors of the *Era* started fighting among themselves, Banks threw them out and appointed new ones.[11]

Prior to his departure for the Red River, Banks decided that a crackdown on the press was essential to military security. On June 1 he sent the editor of the *Picayune* beyond the lines and temporarily suspended its publication. The semiofficial *Era* was caustic in its comment; the *Picayune,*

[10] Denison to Chase, "Chase Correspondence," Oct. 10, 1863.
[11] See Ch. Six: Charles B. Rousseve, *The Negro in Louisiana* (New Orleans, 1937), 118-21.

it said, had "done more than all other influences combined to keep alive the secession feeling and to fan secession hopes in New Orleans." In August, 1864, General Canby ordered the New York *Herald* and *Tribune* correspondents to leave the department.[12]

During the economic recovery of 1863-64 newspapers doubled their size. Before its demise the *Era* claimed the largest circulation in the city, 17,000 to 20,000. With the late summer inflation of 1864 all papers announced a 100 percent increase in subscription rates. In August General Canby banished the editor of the *Tribune* and suspended its publication. On January 1, 1865, the *Era* folded, urging its patrons to transfer their subscription to the *True Delta*. Otherwise, with the end of the war in sight and the political future uncertain, the journalistic situation in New Orleans was at least temporarily more stabilized than it had been since the beginning of the occupation.[13]

By the time of secession the major Protestant denominations, with the exception of the Episcopalians, had split into northern and southern branches. Many of the Protestant clergy in New Orleans became chaplains in the Confederate army in 1861, notably the Presbyterian divine, Dr. Benjamin Palmer, who had delivered the fiery sermon in support of secession shortly after Lincoln's election.[14]

Soon after his arrival Butler encountered as much opposition from the local clergy as he did from the local press. Since President Davis had set May 16, 1862 as a day for southern prayer and fasting, the general forthwith forbade its observance and the churches complied. When at the end

[12] *Era*, May 28, 1864; Provost Marshal Order, May 25, 1864, National Archives.
[13] New Orleans *Tribune*, Aug. 25, 1864; *Bee*, Aug. 29, 1864; *Era*, Jan. 1, 1865.
[14] *D.A.B.*, XIV, 175-76; see Ch. Two.

of May his officers complained that they were being forced to hear prayers for southern military success and for the Confederate President, Butler peremptorily forbade that practice. For several months ministers avoided further offense by substituting a period of silent prayer in the service.[15]

In September, Military Governor Shepley issued a special order stating that "omission in the service of the Protestant Episcopal Churches in New Orleans of the prayer for the President of the United States and others in authority, will be considered as evidence of hostility to the Government of the United States." The clergy replied that they recognized in their diocese no authority but that of their own bishop, Major General Leonidas Polk, who had ordered discontinuance of the prayer. Later in the fall occurred the famous incident at St. Paul's, recounted above, when the adjutant general, Colonel Strong, stopped the service and arrested the pastor.[16]

About the same time the minister of Christ Church Cathedral and Dr. John Fulton of Calvary committed the same offense. Since all three clergymen had formally registered themselves as enemies, Butler arrested them and sent them away to prison in New York. Then Chaplain T. E. R. Chubbock, an Episcopal lay reader of the Thirty-first Massachusetts, appeared with official orders at Christ Church and demanded the keys from the warden. The keys were surrendered, but the congregation thereafter refused to attend services and the church was closed.[17]

In line with Banks' conciliatory policy, Episcopal churches in the city were permitted to reopen on Christmas Day, 1862. But when the three exiled pastors returned in February in hope of regaining their pulpits, Banks denied them entrance to the city because they still refused to take the loyalty oath.

[15] General Orders 27, New Orleans, May 13, 1862; *Delta,* May 29, 1862.
[16] Special Orders 33; *Journal of Julia Le Grand,* 121-23; see Ch. Four.
[17] John S. Kendall, "Christ Church and General Butler," *L.H.Q.,* XXIII (1940), 1241-57.

Meanwhile, Chaplain Chubbock took over Christ Church, which became the place of worship for Federal officers who were Episcopalians.[18]

Later in the spring Banks formally requested the entire local clergy to read a proclamation by President Lincoln designating April 30 as a day of national fasting and prayer. Apparently the request was honored only in those churches having army chaplains. But with his reversal of policy prior to his departure for Vicksburg the general became stricter with the churches. In midsummer he had two of his chaplains seize the large Coliseum Place Baptist Church, near his official residence. In the absence of its pastor services there had been conducted by the trustees and the deacons.[19]

In the fall of 1863 northern Methodists induced the War Department to instruct commanding generals of occupied areas to cooperate with them in placing northern Methodist ministers in all churches of that denomination lacking "a loyal minister appointed by a loyal bishop." During the winter Methodist Bishop Edward A. Ames arrived to direct the program; he was immediately defied by the pastor of the McGehee Church on Carondelet Street. Banks had the pastor removed and also approved Ames' request that Chaplain E. Jones of the Thirty-fourth Indiana be appointed to the Monroe Street Methodist Church. Under the bishop's leadership a Union Ministerial Conference was set up, apparently so successful in its efforts that the *Era* reported the next spring that "all of the Methodist churches are now on the side of the Union."[20]

Meanwhile, northern Presbyterians had launched a similar program, and again Banks cooperated fully by appointing a commission to check on the loyalty of trustees of local Pres-

[18] *Ibid.; O.R.*, XV, 624; Palfrey to his family, April 5, 1863, *Palfrey Papers.*
[19] Provost Marshal James Bowen to Clergy of New Orleans, April 25, 1863; to Trustees of Coliseum Place Baptist Church, July 28, 1863; to W. D. Duncan, Aug. 29, 1863.
[20] *O.R.*, XXIV, pt. 2, 311; Robert A. Cross, *The History of Southern Methodism in New Orleans* (New Orleans, 1931), 34; *Era*, Jan. 19, 24, 1864.

byterian and Baptist churches. The commission found that most of the regular clergy of those churches were away in the Confederate army and that most of their trustees and deacons were disloyal. Consequently Banks turned all of the churches of those two bodies over to northern representatives. At the same time he ordered Episcopal lay readers to include a prayer for President Lincoln in their services. When those at St. Paul's and St. Peter's refused, the provost marshal appointed new boards of trustees for them. Ultimately northern rectors were found for all Episcopal churches. By the time Banks departed for Washington in the summer of 1864, therefore, he had achieved a loyal leadership of the local Protestant denominations. But no action was taken against lay church officers, who frequently absented themselves from services.[21]

The clash between the Federal authorities and the local Episcopal churches is easily explained. Theirs was traditionally the old southern church, and in New Orleans its vestry represented the mercantile aristocracy, which was more ardent in its support of the Confederacy. Most of all, its liturgy included a prayer for the President of the United States, which became the central point of dispute. Among the Presbyterians, Methodists, and Baptists there were many stanch supporters of slavery, though the last group was one of the smaller denominations in the city. Apparently local Lutherans, fairly numerous because of the recent German immigration, had no dissension with the authorities.[22]

The Roman Catholic Church, largest of the religious denominations, had little conflict with the Union military officials during the occupation. Luckily its service contained no prayer for any lay official, and its able Archibishop Jean

[21] Bowen to Rev. Charles Strong and D. H. Allen, June 4, 1864; to Thomas J. Dix, Jan. 28, 1864; to Wardens and Trustees of St. Peter's, St. Paul's, and Trinity Churches, Feb. 2, 1864; to Wardens and Vestry of St. Peter's and St. Paul's, Mar. 1, 1864; *True Delta*, Sept. 4, 1864.

[22] John Nau, "The Lutherans in Louisiana" (M.A. thesis, Tulane University, 1948).

Marie Odin, whose diocese was the second oldest in the nation, conveniently left on clerical duty in Rome in June, 1862, where he remained until after Butler's recall. Perhaps the Federals for various reasons simply wished to avoid trouble with the numerous Irish, particularly since the conquerors became so involved with the Episcopalians and later with other Protestant denominations. On one occasion Archbishop Odin was defied by Father Claude P. Maestri of the St. Rose de Lima Church, a Unionist and an abolitionist who incited Negroes against the whites. After Odin interdicted Maestri's church, he successfully appealed to Provost Marshal Bowen for assistance in forcibly ousting the rebel.[23]

During Odin's absence Father Ignatius Mullen, seventy-year-old pastor of St. Patrick's, openly defied Butler without punishment. But usually the Catholic clergy pursued more subtle tactics. When Banks requested the reading of Lincoln's proclamation in April, 1863, the priest at St. Mary's Italian Church read it in English, a language which most of his congregation did not understand. His colleague at Jesuits did not read it until the end of the service as his communicants were leaving. But in the summer of 1864 Banks did go so far as to place under house arrest Abbé Napoleon J. Perche, rabidly prosouthern editor of *La Propagateur Catholique,* whose publication he suspended.[24]

ON THE EVE of the war New Orleans had the best public school system in the South, one probably as good as that of the most progressive northern cities. With the unification of the three municipalties in 1852, however, the schools had not been similarly centralized, and French remained the language of instruction below Canal Street. The state supplied one-

---

[23] Roger Baudier, *The Catholic Church in Louisiana* (New Orleans, 1939), 413.
[24] *Ibid.,* 427; *Era,* April 28, 1863, May 28, 1864; *Journal of Julia Le Grand,* 269-70.

fourth of the funds for public education. A part-time normal school offering a two-year course had been established in 1858. Half of the city's white children attended nonsectarian private schools or parochial schools set up by the Catholics and the Lutherans. Then as later, women teachers predominated on the faculties of public schools.[25]

The outbreak of war inevitably brought some changes in curriculum and personnel. The Yankees were horrified to discover that the salaries of male teachers who had joined the Confederate army were still being paid. Confederate history had been substituted for American history, and much of the students' time was spent in singing the "Bonnie Blue Flag" and in other exercises to enhance their devotion to the southern cause.[26]

Butler and Military Governor Shepley quickly put a stop to such practices in the "nurseries of treason" and sought to reconvert local youth to Unionism. They purified the faculties by requiring them to take the loyalty oath in June, 1862, and reorganized the whole system before schools reopened the next fall. They unified it, made English the sole language, provided a single course of instruction throughout the city, and imported textbooks from the North. Obviously their main objective was identical with that which the Confederates had been pursuing before the capture: patriotic indoctrination of the rising generation. Because of the usual sensitivity of the public about schools attended by their offspring, the Federal program met considerable resistance from parents and students alike.

The system was administered by a bureau of education, consisting of the mayor and several other municipal officials. They in turn appointed as superintendent an ardent Union-

[25] *Delta*, Aug. 17, 1862; Henry Rightor, ed., *Standard History of New Orleans, Louisiana* (Chicago, 1900), 236-38; Elizabeth J. Doyle, "Nurseries of Treason," *J.S.H.*, XXVI (1960), 161-79. For a good description of the system before the war see Reinders, *End of an Era*.

[26] *Delta*, Aug. 17, 1862.

ist, John Butler Carter, and boards of visitors for each district whose chief function was to check on teacher loyalty. The boards were composed, in fact, almost exclusively of the leading members of the Unionist clubs—Michael Hahn, for instance, was active in this endeavor. Teachers were given only one-year appointments and were required to pass annual examinations, thus providing Butler's local machine with lucrative patronage. Salaries, including those of principals, ranged from $600 to $2,000 in boys' schools, from $600 to $1,250 in girls'; a motion in the constitutional convention of 1864 to increase them 25 percent was defeated.[27]

The school term ran five days a week from 9:00 a.m. to 2:30 p.m. and lasted from the third Monday in September through the last Friday in June. The curriculum was broad, including such subjects as Latin, Greek, French, botany, and trigonometry. In order to pass, students had to take oral examinations in June, perhaps the most novel of Yankee innovations. The bureau drew up a detailed manual of instructions for both parents and students, stipulating among other things that tobacco and profanity were strictly prohibited and that misbehavior would not be tolerated. This proved no idle threat, for three boys who stoned Jackson School because they had been suspended were sentenced to terms in the House of Refuge. In the spring of 1863 a violent dispute between the bureau and the various boards of visitors ended in the abolition of the boards.[28]

While most of the changes were good in theory, the Federal objective was more indoctrination than education. "The good of the scholar," commented the *Picayune* caustically in 1864, "is quite subordinate to that of the teacher, and especially to that of the politician, to whom she is an instrument or associate. . . . Parrots themselves, they produce par-

[27] Louisiana State Superintendent of Education, *Report, 1864;* Doyle, "Nurseries," *J.S.H.,* XXVI, 164-68.
[28] Doyle, "Nurseries," *J.S.H.,* XXVI, 165-66; *Delta,* Nov. 16, Dec. 4, 1862.

rots." So much time was spent in inculcating loyalty that half of the students went on strike in May, 1863, in protest against "musical patriotism."[29]

Confederate sympathizers in New Orleans boycotted the Federal system. If they could afford to, they sent their children to one of the city's 140 private schools, where most of the public school teachers dismissed for disloyalty found jobs; otherwise they simply kept them home. According to the superintendent's report for 1864, only 12,511 out of a total of 37,665 educables attended the forty-four public schools in operation. Thus only a third of the local youth attended during the occupation, in contrast to a half before the war. Certainly there was some social pressure on the citizenry to send their children to public school, but the Federals apparently exerted no overt force to compel them to do so.[30]

When Banks adopted his policy of severity early in 1863, he appointed special police to search for sedition in the private schools, where it was well known that expressions of antipathy for the Yankees and of sympathy for the Confederacy were common. During a raid on several fashionable girls' schools they discovered in one freehand sketches of the rebel flag in copybooks. The teacher, a British subject, denied all knowledge of the "treason," but Provost Judge A. D. Hughes fined her $100. When Madame Locquet's school on Camp Street was charged with the same offense, the proprietor tartly told the judge she did not think it any of her business if her students wanted to draw flags. Hughes promptly fined her $250, but the students took up a collection to pay part of it. Two weeks later Confederate flags were found in Jesuits' Boys School. The principal, Father Anthony Jourdan, pleaded that it was impossible for his staff to check on all the actions of the 250 boys, but Hughes decreed a $250

[29] *Picayune,* Nov. 11, 1864; Harrington, *Banks,* 95.
[30] State Superintendent of Education, *Report, 1864,* App. A and B.

fine for him. After Banks' departure for Vicksburg the drive slowed down and was not resumed until a year later.[31]

In the summer of 1864, after his defeat in the Red River venture, Banks bore down heavily on disloyalty in New Orleans. The successful establishment of a civil government under his friend Governor Hahn evidently made him feel freer to do so than formerly. Not only did he seek to abolish local businesses owned by Confederate sympathizers, but he also finally brought the local Protestant churches to heel. Then he proceeded to attempt a similar purge of private schools.

As he had done with local businesses, he appointed an investigating commission, among whose members were Dr. Dostie and Judge E. S. Hiestand, to screen all private school teachers and to report a "full description of such schools, . . . the objects for which they were organized, and their general influence upon their pupils and the community." The commission was stacked, for Judge Hiestand told the press he believed that many schools had been "gotten up within the last two years . . . with a design of keeping the children from what is vulgarly termed Yankee influence."[32]

The commission found what it was looking for, and fewer than half the schools met the test. In 50 of the 140 visited, loyalty was *not* being taught. Eleven principals, when asked if they would object to flying the United States flag over their desks, replied positively that they would. Six admitted that they were for the Confederacy, and five stated that they were neutral. All the Catholic schools and more than half of the nonsectarian ignored both the commission and its questionnaire. While the commissioners pronounced the Lutheran schools loyal, they were much disturbed that German was the language of instruction. Apparently few schools were

[31] *Delta,* May 9, 1863; *Picayune,* May 9, 13, 23, 1863.
[32] *Delta,* July 17, 1864; State Superintendent of Education, *Report, 1864,* App. B.

closed, however, and the drive stopped with Banks' departure for Washington in September. Actually it accomplished no more than the simultaneous attack on local businesses.[33]

The war closed institutions of higher learning in the city. Many students from the law and medical schools of the University of Louisiana (predecessor of Tulane), which had never had much of an undergraduate body, joined the Confederate army. Some professional students informally consulted their professors during the occupation. The new Medical School of Louisiana founded in 1856, which had 250 students when war broke out, closed its doors, and its building was used by the Federals as a general hospital.[34]

Federal interference with the basic social institutions of New Orleans, in view of the fact that it was in a war zone, can hardly be considered unduly onerous. Even censorship of the press was on the whole spasmodic; the *Picayune* and the *Bee* were frequently critical of official policies. The Catholic Church to a large degree was left alone. The Protestant ministry was in time Unionized, but communicants were not required to attend churches with whose pastors they disagreed. Nor were citizens compelled to send their children to public schools polluted by the Yankees, and private schools—which the report of the commission of 1864 showed to be largely disloyal—were not forced to change their ways. Had Butler remained in the city, the story might have been different, but there is little question that Orleanians outpointed General Banks.

[33] State Superintendent of Education, *Report, 1864*, App. B.
[34] Rightor, *Standard History*, 217.

NINE CIVILIANS AND SOLDIERS

*L*IKE POLAND, because of a sea-level terrain, Louisiana in the first century and a half of its existence was exposed to a succession of invasions. First, the French early in the eighteenth century removed the local Indians who dwelt in the narrow strip of land along the portage between Lake Pontchartrain and the river. After 1763, when Spain took over from France, a few Spaniards came in and settled there alongside their Latin brothers. As time passed and after the United States bought the area in 1803, an Anglo-American invasion began which increased steadily in intensity, particularly from the northeastern section of the nation. Toward the middle of the nineteenth century thousands of Irish and Germans arrived in New Orleans, making the city's population even more heterogeneous than ever. Included in this potpourri of humanity were the Negroes, both slave and free, who had been resident there since the French and Spanish regimes. Finally, in 1862, came the Yankee soldiers.

Thus throughout its existence the city had been forced to adjust itself to a constant influx of outsiders, diverse in origin and in tradition from residents whose families were themselves originally migrants. It cannot be said that the newer groups were ever fully assimilated, for surely there was a vast gulf between the *ancien population* on one hand and the Negroes and the shanty Irish of the 1850s on the other. Social exclusion in bilingual New Orleans, based on national origin, color, prior arrival, as well as class, was always a conspicuous fact in the ante bellum period. But if assimilation did not occur, the various groups somehow worked out a *modus vivendi*—at least a tenuous and unstable toleration.

The Yankee soldier presented a different problem. He did not immigrate to make money, nor had he left home because of dissatisfaction with local conditions, and in many instances he did not come of his own volition. He came or was sent to conquer, with no intention of making his sojourn any longer than was absolutely necessary. When it became evident during 1863 that the Federals were there to stay—that the war and the occupation would be of considerable duration—many citizens made an accommodation of sorts. In doing so, they were aided by their previous, and even recent, experience in adapting to outsiders in their midst as their forebears had done before them. Extended military occupation was unique in the city's history, and any specific comparison with past or subsequent decades is not entirely relevant. Understandably, it left a bitterness in local memories far greater than that of epidemics and depressions.

New Orleans had always been subject to calamities, both natural and man-made. It was constantly threatened and frequently smitten by yellow fever and cholera, hurricanes and floods. Life was hazardous at all times and, certainly for its lower classes, cheap. This conditioning made the process of adaptation to the new calamity—the Federal conquest— easier for those who chose to collaborate with the enemy within their gates.

The Louisiana metropolis was southern chiefly by virtue of geography, climate, its dependence upon staple-crop agriculture, and the presence of the Negro. It was European because of the persistence of a French tradition and a proletariat born in Germany and Ireland. It was western as a result of its commercial ties with the upper Mississippi Valley, American because it was a place where the lucky could make quick profits. Like all seaports and river towns, it had a tough, transient element in the population. These were the main factors which made for resistance or collaboration.

In general those who were native-born, both Latin Creoles and Anglo-Americans, resisted. Many of their menfolk, it should be remembered, were away fighting in the Confederate army; some of them had already given or in the future would give their lives for the southern cause. Julia Le Grand's brother Claude, for instance, who had shown promise as a sculptor, was wounded in Virginia in 1861 and his right arm had to be amputated.[1] Registered enemies were almost exclusively relatives of soldiers. On the contrary, those who were or became Unionists after the capture were mainly northern-born, Germans, or Irish.

This is not to say, reluctant though some of them had been to secede in January, 1861, that many local German, Irish, and northerners had not loyally supported the Confederacy before the capture. When hostilities broke out, some northerners left the city, like the newspaperman T. B. Thorpe who later returned with the Union army and became municipal surveyor. So did a few southern Unionists like John De Forest's fictional character, South Carolina-born Dr. Ravenel, who had been teaching medicine for twenty years at the University of Louisiana. Other northerners like Dr. Dostie and Benjamin Flanders were exiled by the Confederates.

But these three groups had already changed their citizenship or their residence once in their lifetime, and their attachment to their adopted community was simply not so deep in most cases as that of natives. By a process of natural selection they were more practical and perhaps more expedient. Despite their earlier southern loyalty, it was easier for them to accept the Federal conquest as a fortune of war with

[1] *Journal of Julia Le Grand*, 28-29.

which they must live. Though some were "Yanks for the money,"[2] many of them were intelligently trying to make the best of a bad situation for themselves and their community—not unlike the conservatives who cooperated with Banks in hope of saving slavery and other cherished institutions.[3]

Examples are numerous. German-born Christian Roselius and Michael Hahn were the most distinguished Unionists. Even more striking was the background of state officials elected in 1864. Secretary of State Stanislaus Wrotnowski had arrived from Poland in 1849, Attorney General Bartholomew L. Lynch from Ireland in 1851. State Treasurer Dr. James G. Belden (a nephew of Noah Webster), Superintendent of Education John McNair, and Auditor Dr. A. P. Dostie had all come from New York in the 1840s.[4]

History is sometimes a distortion of the facts not merely because of the prejudice of the historian but because of the bias of the written sources. Southern memoirs of the occupation period were written by the more sensitive people who resented it most strongly, women in particular. The great mass of folk, particularly the lower classes, seldom left a record of their feelings, which probably were not so extreme. Life had been almost unbearable to the poor for many years before the war; it merely brought them a change of masters.[5] Poverty had driven many an Irish girl into prostitution, and the wartime depression drove many more. The local underworld welcomed the Federals as new lambs to be fleeced at a time when the home market was running short, as did the Negroes, especially free men of color. With these groups, as

[2] Carrie Hyatt to Arthur Hyatt, July 6, 1864, *Hyatt Papers*, Louisiana State University Library.
[3] See Ch. Six. There were some exceptions. The uncle of New England Captain John G. Palfrey, who lived in New Orleans, opposed secession but refused to take the oath after the capture or even to speak to his nephew (Palfrey to his family, May 17, 1863, *Palfrey Papers*).
[4] Caskey, *Secession*, 108.
[5] Earl S. Niehaus, "The Irish in Antebellum New Orleans" (Ph.D. dissertation, Tulane University, 1961), Ch. XII.

well as with the northern businessmen and local Unionists, the Yankee soldier could find all the fraternization he needed.

Orleanians were traditionally disrespectful of law and even of a municipal administration of their own choosing; instinctively they defied the Federal invader when he took over their government. Various frustrations, already built up during the Confederate regime, were naturally directed against the conqueror. Men had lost work, martial law had been declared, and relief of the unemployed had been instituted before the Yankees arrived. Patriotism in some instances had begun to wane. Editor McGinnis charged that the Irish were being used as cannon fodder in Virginia, while planters' sons and those who had influence with the governor were given safer assignments. He advised his countrymen to join the Home Guards, and in late 1861 they formed the Louisiana Irish Regiment for that purpose.[6]

The depression of 1861-1863, in fact, would have made any local government unpopular with the citizenry, and the shortages of necessities and the concurrent inflation aggravated the bitterness. Stung with surprise and dismay at the city's capture, the populace at first turned on President Davis, whom they accused of betraying them, and on General Lovell. As Julia Le Grand put it, "Lovell, a most worthless creature was sent here by Davis. . . . He did little or nothing and the little he did was all wrong. . . . [He] knew not what to do; some say he was intoxicated, some say frightened."[7] But shortly they transferred all their frustrations and resentment to Picayune Butler, who so dramatically poured brine on their bleeding wounds.

EVEN AS HARMLESS a wild creature as a rabbit will resist when it is captured. During the early months of the occupa-

[6] Ibid., 401-402; True Delta, Oct. 13, 1861, March 7, 8, 1862.
[7] Journal of Julia Le Grand, 39-40.

tion, Federal soldiers were constantly insulted by the populace. "These people," observed one diarist, "are treated with the greatest haughtiness by the upper classes and rudeness by the lower. They know how they are hated and hang their heads." Captain John De Forest from New England expressed the antipathy more vividly through his major character, Captain Edward Colburne. "Our regiment was the first to reach the city," Colburne wrote a southern Unionist friend in New Haven, "and to witness the bareness of the once-crowded wharves, the desertion of the streets, and the sullen spite of the few remaining inhabitants. I suspect your aristocratic acquaintances must have all fled at the approach of the Vandal Yankees, for I see only Negroes, poor foreigners, and rowdies more savage-looking than the tribes of the Bowery. The spirit of impotent but impertinent hate in this population is astonishing. The ragged newsboys will not sell us a paper; the beggarly restaurants will not furnish us a dinner. Wherever I walk I am saluted by mutterings of 'Damned Yankee!'—'Cut his heart out!' &c. &c. I once more profess allegiance to your theory that this is where Satan's seat is. But the evil spirits who inhabit this city of desolation only grimace and grumble, without attempting any manner of injury."[8]

The initial hostility was almost universal in the city, but in one respect De Forest was wrong; all aristocrats had not left the city. The population consisted largely of women and men too old to fight, and hatred for the invader continued to be more intense in the upper classes, since they were hurt most in pride and pocketbook. After Butler executed Mumford, issued his Woman Order, required the loyalty oath, and seized the property of those who refused to take it, their hatred for the Yankees grew to infinite proportions. At the same

---

[8] *Ibid.*, 44; Captain Palfrey to his family, March 12, 15, 1862, *Palfrey Papers;* John W. De Forest, *Miss Ravenel's Conversion from Secession to Loyalty* (New York, 1867), 104. References in this chapter are to the Harpers' edition, New York, 1939.

time, since neither the yellow jack nor their beloved Beauregard came to rescue them, the general's stern measures forced circumspection upon most and considerably reduced open manifestations of hostility.

Without question there was much suffering on the part of previously opulent and middle class families during the depression and the inflation. Those who owned securities, businesses, or in many instances rental property saw their assets steadily diminish. Elderly gentlemen, according to Union Captain John G. Palfrey, often sought positions as clerks with the army. Some suffered from actual shortage of food, and insufficient nourishment increased the frequency and duration of perennial illnesses common to the locality. Added to these misfortunes were the spiritual hurt of Confederate defeat, frustrated hopes, injury or death to their soldier husbands, sons, and brothers on the field of battle, and lack of the usual social distractions. Southern women gave the Federal administrators endless trouble, but unless they went to extremes, they could usually do so with impunity because of their sex. They loathed the Federal soldiers and despised the new horde of northern businessmen who followed the army.[9]

Life was "always very monotonous and ennervating," wrote one young Creole wife to her army husband. Therefore it was increasingly difficult to find news to put in letters; "I rarely go out, I devote myself entirely to our two little angels." And in 1864 she informed him that "our enemies are just as amiable as ever towards us [but] they'll find me a damned rebel forever." Her mother-in-law Polyxene Reynes wrote one of her sons in 1862 that "we live like cabbages and turnips. . . . Misery begins to weigh heavily on each one." Some yielded to despair without the tone of hatred. "I often take a good cry over the wash tub," another woman told her

[9] Palfrey to his family, Nov. 12, 1863, *Palfrey Papers; Journal of Julia Le Grand*, 158-59, 181, 195-99, 227, 257-61, 301.

soldier husband, "and think how different things would have been if it had not been for this cursid [sic] war, sometimes I feel broken down and old."[10]

Often the young were quick to pick up the hatred of adults for the enemy. When the police raided the private school she attended, sixteen-year old Josephine Moore recorded in her diary that she hated northerners "with a deeper and more lasting hatred than ever before. Nothing evil could ever befall them at which I could not rejoice." Feminine indignation against the Federals reached its high point in the dramatic Battle of the Handkerchiefs in February, 1863.[11]

Because of the depression and the military situation, General Banks forbade the observance of Mardi Gras in 1863. The previous fall the *Picayune* had predicted the dullness of the months ahead. "How are we going to spend these long winter evenings?" it asked. "Of amusement we are likely to have a dearth. Itinerant lecturers will be few. The clubs are broken up. We shall not have many balls or parties."[12]

The most intimate and graphic account of the life of rebels during the first year of the occupation is the diary of Julia Le Grand, a philosophical, sensitive, and humanitarian woman for all her Confederate ardor. Born in Maryland, she was reared on her father's large plantation at Millican's Bend on the Mississippi in southern Louisiana. She and her sister Virginia were so impractical that they lost the fortune they inherited upon his death; eventually they opened a fashionable school for girls in New Orleans. After the capture they closed their small house on Prytania Street and moved to the home of an older woman friend for protection. Miss Le Grand was vehement in her excoriation of Butler and the Federals. "I do hate those bloody wretches who have made

[10] Uranie to Emile Reynes, Feb. 18, 25, 1864; Polyxene to Edouard Reynes, Feb. 19, 1862, *Reynes Family Papers*, Louisiana State University Library; Carrie Hyatt to Emile Hyatt, June 26, 1864, *Hyatt Papers*.
[11] *Moore Journal*, May 7, 1863, University of North Carolina Library; see Ch. Five.
[12] *Picayune*, Nov. 16, 1862.

war upon us," she confessed, "and I glory in our Southern chivalry. . . . This is a most cowardly struggle—these people can do nothing without gunboats." She was one of a group of ladies who pleaded with officials not to surrender the city. A registered enemy, she steadfastly refused to take the oath and evidently was with the group that departed in May, 1863.[13]

She frowned upon fraternization and sternly lectured two of her young friends who permitted a Federal naval officer to call upon them. If he "had been a gentleman," she told them, "he would not have entered your house as he did, knowing that true Southerners are compromised by receiving Federals." But her innate kindness led her occasionally to express sympathy for enemy soldiers, especially enlisted men. She was touched when one Union officer stopped at her gate and asked for some rosebuds to send to his wife. "These privates," she recorded on another occasion, "when they are Americans, have a sad and hopeless look, as if their hearts were aching for home." For expressing such sentiments some of her friends looked upon her as "half Yankee. . . . I accept a bloody triumph only as the least of two evils. . . . Men's suffering always excites me, let the men be who they may."[14]

The pages of her journal poignantly reveal how local rebels clung to hope, how they constantly cherished wild rumors that their deliverance would soon be at hand. The French fleet was about to relieve the city; Union soldiers were deserting and mutinying by the thousands; Farragut and the *Hartford* had been captured; Vicksburg and Port Hudson were absolutely impregnable. Hardly a week went by that someone had not talked to a Confederate spy who bore tidings of great joy, tidings that soon became common knowledge among the faithful, each of whom had been sworn to secrecy. The most sensational story had Stonewall Jackson,

[13] *Journal of Julia Le Grand*, 14-33, 43, 74.
[14] *Ibid.*, 63, 104, 161, 181, 243.

disguised as a wagoner, at Ponchatoula across Pass Manchac about fifty miles away; another account said he was a mere five miles from the city. Even as late as 1864 Polyxene Reynes could exult upon McClellan's nomination by the Democrats that "news from the North is marvelous."[15]

In the same year Gus Mandeville, working as a clerk in the city, wrote more objectively to his sister that he tried "to keep posted as far as the papers post us," but he was "tired of reading so many war lies." He felt that "a Peace candidate is of no avail, that the War is bound to go on for years or until like the Kilk[enny] Cats are both used up."[16] In both North and South, reports of battles in the press were confusing throughout the war, each side claiming victory for several days or even a week before the truth was known and conceded. Cut off from Confederate information, New Orleans became one huge rumor factory.

Grant's capture of Vicksburg was definitely the turning point of the Federal occupation, partly because it stimulated economic recovery but also because, as Miss Le Grand had predicted, "should Port Hudson fall, or Vicksburg, thousands of hearts would lose hope to struggle." Before Christmas 1862, 1,100 registered enemies had left with Butler's permission. Banks encouraged the 2,000 remaining to take the oath, but he refused Unionists' demands to publish the names of the recalcitrant. In fear of insurrection when the troops left for the attack on Vicksburg, the provost marshal ordered them all out by May 15. Later he restricted the order to men of military age only, and upon Banks' advice he finally canceled it entirely to prevent information from being carried to the enemy. One thousand had already left, however, and 76 took the oath. Only 778 remained in 1864, according to an estimate by the provost marshal, and Banks

---

[15] *Ibid.*, 212-14, 235, 240; Polyxene to Edouard Reynes, Jan. 2, 1864, *Reynes Family Papers*.
[16] Gus Mandeville to his sister, Sept. 3, 1864, *Henry D. Mandeville Papers*, Louisiana State University Library.

ordered these deported on June 23; but some were still departing the following October.[17]

Yet so many took the oath after the surrender of Vicksburg, and so many who had taken it previously became active Unionists, that Polyxene Reynes confided to her son that "we are learning every day the sad truth, love of money is stronger than love of country for the mass of men." Mrs. Reynes, until then a registered enemy, herself took the oath, which all along many had regarded as a mere "formality of circumstance." The latecomers soon learned that oathtaking and Unionism were leagues apart. In the normal course of living, citizens had to appear in court or deal with the military municipal officials on some matter or other. The Federals now had their revenge for previous insults by discriminating against the recalcitrant in various ways, and there was no appeal from their decisions. The assistant quartermaster general, who exercised great power, even ruled that ardor for the southern cause in 1861 was evidence of disloyalty two years later. Regular officers, according to one northern observer, were more humane in their dealings with civilians than volunteer officers. After the summer of 1863, in most matters the Yankees clearly held the upper hand.[18]

In general, the Latin Creoles as a group never accepted Federal officers socially. The *ancien population* had never liked Americans anyway, though at higher levels they had formed business and marital alliances with them. They had, in fact, always been practical about using Americans for their own ends. A few Creole belles, lacking southern beaus, attended the fancy balls given by General and Mrs. Banks; undoubtedly some of them, like De Forest's "doublefaced" Mrs. Larue, managed to run with both the hares and the

[17] *Journal of Julia Le Grand*, 246; *O.R.*, XV, 57; *True Delta*, May 12, 1863; *Picayune*, Oct. 17, 1864; Doyle, "Civilian Life," 224-26.
[18] Polyxene to Edouard Reynes, Jan. 1, 1864, *Reynes Family Papers*; *Journal of Julia Le Grand*, 282; *Era*, April 2, 1863; Doyle, "Civilian Life," 226-30, 307; Hoffman, *Camp*, 65.

hounds. Mrs. Larue was frank to admit that Don Juan was her favorite hero. Her niece Lillie Ravenel, at first an ardent rebel, became loyal when she found herself snubbed by her old friends because of her father's Unionism, and she married a Federal colonel. Older women were more bitter, but after Butler tamed the local ladies, they usually took out their spite in private letters or in singing the "Bonnie Blue Flag." At least, since the Federals left the Catholic Church alone, they were not subjected to interference in their religious worship.[19]

Latin Creole men, recalling Mumford's fate, were evidently more circumspect. Though many of them had lost their fortunes in aiding the Confederacy or were proscribed for refusing to take the oath, a few were practical enough after Vicksburg to face reality. As Banks' investigation of 1864 proved, they still controlled local businesses like the utilities and the banks, and they shared to some degree in the returning prosperity. Some even cooperated with the Federals; Aristide Miltenberger and F. J. Ducourge, for instance, served on Banks' investigating commission. Captain Palfrey, needing bricks for fortifications and knowing the slowness of his own quartermaster department, negotiated with a certain Mr. Blanc for their local purchase.[20] Local Anglo-American aristocrats also collaborated. When Colonel Carter succumbed to temptation and decided to sell government ships for his own profit, he made a deal with Mr. Hollister, former secessionist and an old resident of high social position who had taken the oath.

ON THE EVE of the declaration of war against Germany in 1917, Woodrow Wilson remarked that "when a war got

---

[19] Harrington, *Banks*, 94; Southwood, *Beauty and Booty*, 275; De Forest, *Miss Ravenel*, Ch. XI.
[20] See Ch. Seven; Palfrey to his family, April 9, May 17, Oct. 11, 1863, *Palfrey Papers*, De Forest, *Miss Ravenel*, Ch. XXX.

going it was just war and there weren't two kinds of it."[21] Half a century before, General Sherman had said the same thing succinctly in his famous statement that war is hell. The whole Civil War generation found this out for themselves, but the Yankees who were so unlucky as to be sent to the swamps of southern Louisiana caught more than their share of hell—as the diaries of the enlisted men who bore the greatest impact of it graphically attest. Camping on the banks of the Wabash or the Potomac is one thing; on the lower Mississippi or Bayou Teche it is quite another. Worst of all, they arrived in May at the beginning of the long hot summer. Had the capture occurred in October, the situation would have been drastically different. Probably not until the jungle fighting in the Pacific islands in World War II did American troops again fight in such acute discomfort and in such a difficult terrain.

The foot soldiers and the line officers, it should be remembered, bivouacked in tents at camps outside the city proper. Enlisted men might occasionally get a pass to visit town, and some officers of higher rank or on special duty found more comfortable quarters in the city itself. Nevertheless, to both groups the experience was not unlike that of living in a foreign land. What struck them most about New Orleans, judging by their letters and diaries, was the unbearable summer heat, the vicious fauna that inhabited the semi-inundated terrain, the open sin of the city, and the Negro.[22]

But they were only incidentally troops of occupation in a combat zone, for they were on their way to kill or be killed. Consequently, their basic reaction was that of soldiers to the imminence of death. Encouraged by patriotic sweethearts and sisters, they had come on a holy mission to save the Union by committing mayhem on their southern brothers.

[21] John L. Heaton, *Cobb of "The World"* (New York, 1924), 268-70.
[22] Frank M. Flinn, *Campaigning with Banks* (Lynn, Mass., 1887), and Lawrence Van Alstyne, *Diary of an Enlisted Man* (New Haven, 1910), are good accounts of the soldier's reaction.

Some, it is true, had hired themselves as substitutes for the money or had been drafted, but whatever the cause, they found themselves together in the same predicament. While the response of different individuals to danger varies, the basic response in war is much the same. "Smothering despair within their souls by songs, licentiousness, and wine," wrote Tolstoi, "men will trail along, torn from peaceful labor, from their wives, mothers, and children—hundreds of thousands of simple-minded, good-natured men with murderous weapons in their hands—anywhere they may be driven."[23] So it was in New Orleans.

An army moves on its belly, goes an old adage, but since its objective is mass killing, it also requires attention to other of its physical and spiritual wants. Many troops in Louisiana were sick most of the time or dying from diarrheal infections and fevers, forcing the medical corps to work overtime.[24] Besides the doctors, the Federals brought with them a fair number of chaplains to minister to the soul. In addition to voicing assurance of bliss in the hereafter, a chaplain has the more difficult job of the rationalization of murder; he must convince his charges that murder is moral and then administer the last rites to them if they become the victims.

Such ministrations have seldom been sufficient for men going into combat. As Tolstoi suggests, invariably they seek stronger and more carnal means of forgetting the fate awaiting them. Even when stationed in their own homeland, soldiers acquire an unerring knack for ferreting out women, food, and drink. At times food might have been short in New Orleans, but women never were. The medical director of the Military Division of the Western Mississippi estimated that within two years the Gulf Department lost from 50,000 to 100,000 days of service from its men as a result of veneral

---

[23] Leo N. Tolstoi, "Christianity and Patriotism," *Works* (Centenary ed., London, 1928-1937), XX, 489.
[24] Van Alstyne, *Diary*, 81-96; Palfrey to his family, June 14, 1863, *Palfrey Papers*.

disease.²⁵ So many of them married while in the city that relief for their families—who could not live on the enlisted man's thirteen dollars a month—was a major problem.

Alcoholic beverages of various types had always flowed freely in New Orleans; thanks to their higher income, Federal officers probably obtained more than their share. In September, 1862, Butler forbade the purchase of liquor by enlisted men and threatened his officers with court martial if they were seen drinking in public. But such severe regulations did not long remain in force. White men in the tropics frequently take to drink, and these were caught in a Louisiana summer. Imbibing was induced largely by the initial fear of the fever and of combat, as well as by the strain of acclimatization. De Forest's Colonel Carter advised his sick New England friend Captain Colburne, a teetotaler, to indulge moderately in order to ward off illness. The official policy was usually vacillating, though in 1864, the provost marshal recommended to Banks a crackdown because of the heavy drinking among army laborers and soldiers. Thereupon the general formally prohibited the import of spiritous liquors except by special permit from him, but he promptly issued so many permits that the results were meager.²⁶

New Orleans had always been full of dives, not just on Gallatin, Girod, and St. Thomas streets, but all over the city. Forty-five places sold liquor in the six blocks on St. Charles between Canal Street and LaFayette Square. During the war new names were invented for old establishments, falsely attributed to "Yankee riff-raff" who followed in the wake of Farragut's fleet. The "barrel-house" was a joint where patrons drank cheap adulterated liquors; they could order brandy, Irish whisky, and wine—but their choice made little difference as to contents. Failure to refill resulted in ejection by

²⁵ Dr. Edward P. Vollum to C. T. Christensen, Aug. 27, 1864, Doyle, "Civilian Life," 73.
²⁶ *Ibid.*, 133-36; General Orders 11 and 93, 1862; De Forest, *Miss Ravenel*, 111-12; Palfrey to his family, Jan. 18, 1863; *Palfrey Papers*.

the proprietor; continuance frequently ended in the patrons being doped and "rolled." For the more discriminating and opulent there were the "concert-salons," where customers could also find music, dancing, food, floorshows, and girls (forerunners of the modern "B-drinkers"). The first of these, the St. Nicholas, did not open on St. Charles until 1865; so apparently the war years were the gestation period of this type of establishment.[27]

Gambling has always been a major opiate of soldiers; it requires few props, while women and liquor are sometimes unavailable. Men can pitch pennies and shoot craps or play poker for matches, nickels, or dollars. New Orleans had long had organized gambling and racing which the police left alone as much as they did prostitution unless there were specific complaints. Many apocryphal stories have come down about the experiences of Federal officers and paymasters with three-card monte and the like; undoubtedly they have some factual basis, though it is rarely recorded in Union memoirs. Supposedly Butler closed the gambling houses, but he allowed those who would pay a fee to continue and cut his brother Andrew in on the "take." Like many another Butler story, no evidence exists to support it. No general has ever been able completely to suppress gambling among his officers and men, and few have attempted it. But organized gambling was such a problem for the Federals that General Hurlburt closed all houses in 1864 and theaters on Sundays as well. His order was strictly enforced until the end of the occupation.[28]

In short, soldiers will be soldiers and New Orleans offered the whole gamut of diversions. On the other hand, Federal troops were unusually well disciplined during the occupation. They were typical American boys of their day, usually reared in God-fearing Christian homes in the Northeast and North-

[27] Asbury, *French Quarter*, 228, 318-22.
[28] *Ibid.*, 225-29; *Delta*, July 16, 1862; Special Orders 292, New Orleans, Oct. 28, 1964; *Picayune*, Oct. 29, 1864.

west and disinclined toward debauchery and disobedience before they joined the army. At the outset Butler put fear into their souls by executing several men for plundering. Stationed outside the city and in training for combat, most of the time their officers kept them busy on marches and in drills. The rest of the time many of them were too tired or too sick to seek diversion outside the bunk. When they came back from a major battle, like that of Port Hudson, they might be briefly allowed the freedom of the city. One-third of the persons arrested in New Orleans during the war years were women, but only 12 percent were soldiers. Even if the provost marshal or their uniform saved the troops, this proportion is amazingly low, and complaints against them occur rarely in memoirs of the period.[29]

Two northern enlisted men published a record of their experiences in the Gulf Department, Frank M. Flinn of the 38th Massachusetts Volunteers in his *Campaigning with Banks* and Lawrence Van Alstyne of the 128th New York in his *Diary of an Enlisted Man*. Van Alstyne's account is more vivid and intimate, since it was written on the spot and almost daily. In his first months in Louisiana he was sick much of the time, and his journal is filled with accounts of the ills and deaths of his buddies, his tribulations with sadistic or inefficient officers, and the ordinary traumatic experiences of the rookie soldier. Then health, maturity, and humor came to his rescue, and he began to look around him. He had difficulty in accustoming himself to body lice, snakes, alligators, and especially mosquitoes, which he called the "pest of our lives." On a march from Camp Parapet above the city to Pass Manchac on the way to Ponchatoula, he noted that he "thought we had them [mosquitoes] in camp, but we did not. It was only the skirmish line; the main body is here."[30]

[29] Shugg, *Origins*, 59; *Bee*, Jan. 5, 1865; Doyle, "Civilian Life," 130-32, 142.
[30] Van Alstyne, *Diary*, 81-105.

But he did enjoy the beauty of the cypress trees with their many knees protruding above the water, the Spanish moss, the shellfish of the Gulf, and the bright color of the subtropical flora which abounded in the area. In New Orleans for reassignment after his return from Port Hudson, Van Alstyne rented a cheap room on Gravier Street, from which he had to move because of the heat, the bedbugs, and the cockroaches. While there he enjoyed the best meal he had eaten in a year, the thrill of seeing General Grant, and the luxury of undressing to go to bed. But he lacked the money to ride the mulecars out to Lake Pontchartrain.[81]

As MIGHT be expected, Union officers have left the fullest description of their impressions of the city and its life. Possessing in general a better education and background, more leisure and money, they often lived in fashionable quarters downtown and came more frequently into contact with residents. Some were chaplains like George H. Hepworth of Boston (author of *The Whip, Hoe, and Sword*), concerned mainly with the Negro, social problems, and things of the spirit. Since they were usually puritans, they missed much of the color of the region. Their memoirs are generally dull, although occasionally they show real insight into southern life.

At the other extreme was Hepworth's aristocratic fellow Bostonian John G. Palfrey, son of the famous New England historian and clergyman and a graduate of Harvard and West Point, who rose from the rank of captain to general while on duty in the Gulf Department. An engineer, Palfrey was in charge of the defenses of Ship Island, but he spent much time in the city and participated in all the major campaigns in the area. His weekly letters to his mother and sisters (still unpublished) constitute one of the most human, critical, yet

[81] *Ibid.*, 174, 176-78.

not unsympathetic accounts ever written about life in the Crescent City.

His room on Baronne Street he thought good, as were his meals, though the price was excessive. He easily accustomed himself to brandy cocktails for breakfast and champagne during the day, both of which he regarded as good for one's health in the subtropics. While insults from women and children caused him at first to call the city "this off-scouring of creation," once he became acclimated, he liked it more than he disliked it. He commented on the bad sidewalks, the dirt, the cockroaches, snakes, and mosquitoes, but he loved the flowers and the trees which flourished in the winter when his native New England was bleak and snowbound. The local duckhunting was the "most exciting" he had ever experienced. He attended Christ Church and the French Opera House, the "loveliest theater" he had ever seen. Few Creole ladies attended, he noted, but despite their rudeness he thought New Orleans women beautiful.

He himself did not associate with them, though some of his brothers officers did, and he commented humorously in one instance on how wild the local navymen had gone over a southern belle down from Natchez on a visit. He partied frequently with fellow officers and their wives, or with their wives alone when their husbands were absent on duty. Evidently his mother, knowing the ways of men, feared the worst, for he once wrote in answer to her concern that he would not marry a woman "brought up among slaves for all the riches of the South." An excellent officer, able to make the best of his lot and even to enjoy his temporary abode, he never overcame his New England prejudices. He refused to become commanding officer at Ship Island because Negro troops were stationed there, and he confessed that he was never really happy "more than eight hours from Boston."[32]

[32] Palfrey wrote almost weekly letters to his mother and his sisters Anna and Sarah during 1863 and 1864. They are uncataloged and scattered throughout the *Palfrey Papers* in the Houghton Library at Harvard.

The most gifted of northern officers stationed in New Orleans was John W. De Forest of New Haven, Connecticut, who had been living in Charleston with his father-in-law at the time of the Sumter crisis. Some critics consider the vivid account of New Orleans during the occupation in his *Miss Ravenel's Conversion from Secession to Loyalty* (1867) the greatest Civil War novel. De Forest had lived in Europe and had written several works before the war; in 1874 William Dean Howells, editor of the *Atlantic Monthly*, in his review of *Miss Ravenel's Conversion* said of him that "so far he is really the only American novelist."[33] Like his major character Captain Colburne, De Forest recruited a company in Connecticut and served as their captain in Louisiana for almost three years. His work is noted for its realism, its insight into feminine character, and its freedom from anti-southern bias. Having lived several months a year in Charleston, he knew the South, and his novel is as authentic a memoir on New Orleans as the letters Captain Palfrey wrote to his family.

The scene opens in 1861 in the town of New Boston (New Haven) in the Yankee state of Barataria, where, because of his Unionism, Dr. Ravenel of the faculty of the University of Louisiana had fled with his rebel daughter. There they meet Yale graduate Edward Colburne and a Virginia-born West Pointer, Lieutenant Colonel Carter, who had stayed with the Union. Colburne falls in love with Lillie, but Carter, a suave, hard-living man of the world, seems unaffected by her charms. The colonel helps Colburne get a commission, and they sail with Butler to New Orleans, where the Ravenels follow them after the capture. To the sorrow of his friend Colburne, Carter soon falls in love with Lillie Ravenel and she with him; despite Dr. Ravenel's reluctance the two are married. Soon Carter, on a mission

[33] *Atlantic Monthly*, XX (1869), 170-72, XXIX (1878), 365, XXXIV (1883), 229.

to New York, is seduced by his wife's mother's sister-in-law, the fabulous Creole widow Mrs. Larue, who happens to be traveling on the same ship. Later the truth inadvertently reaches Lillie, and her father takes her north to forget her grief. General Carter is killed on the retreat from the Red River in 1864, fighting valiantly as usual.

De Forest sketches on a large canvas, but with careful, colorful detail, all the major aspects of wartime life in Louisiana from contraband trade to Banks' reorganization of Negro labor on the plantations. His battle scenes at Port Hudson and his description of a field hospital equal, if they do not surpass, Stephen Crane's *Red Badge of Courage*.[34] Equally superior are his vignettes of Negroes and the Yankees' experiences with them.

One group of Federal officers were diehard abolitionists, like Chaplain Hepworth, General Phelps, and B. Rush Plumly, who set up Banks' Negro school system. They saw in the Negro nobility of soul and an opportunity for moral uplift. A larger group of officers disliked slavery but, like Captain Palfrey, wanted no contact whatever with the freedmen. For the same reason Brigadier General Weitzel, Butler's ablest subordinate, at first declined the leadership of the LaFourche expedition in 1862. Northern enlisted men generally shared this antipathy. But most Federals, whether they wished to or not, were forced into some contact with Negroes, and many of them developed a degree of realism about them.

De Forest's Captain Colburne was one of these. Despite the captain's resistance, his boy Henry had thrust himself upon him, giving up a job on the levee which paid three times as much because it worked him "nuff to kill a horse." Colburne despairingly informed Dr. Ravenel: "I am as much of an abolitionist as ever, but not so much of a 'nigger-worshipper.' I don't know but that I shall yet become an

[34] Gordon Haight, Introduction to De Forest, *Miss Ravenel*, ix-xvi.

advocate of slavery. I frequently think that my boy Henry will fetch me to it. He is an awful boy. He dances and gambles all night, and then wants to sleep all day. . . . In order that he may not be disturbed in his rest by my voice, he goes away from camp and curls up in some refuge which I have not yet discovered. I pass hours every day in shouting for Henry. Of course his labors are small and far between. He brushes my boots in the morning because he doesn't go to bed until after I get up; but if I want them polished during the day—at dress parade, for example—it is not Henry who polishes them. When I scold him for his worthlessness, he laughs most obstropolously [sic]. . . . For his services, or rather for what he ought to do and doesn't, I pay him ten dollars a month, with rations and clothing. He might earn two or three times as much on the levee at New Orleans; but the lazy creature would rather not earn anything; he likes to get his living gratis, as he does with me."[35]

IN MANY RESPECTS the city which the Federals occupied in the spring of 1862 bore little resemblance to the old New Orleans. The physical setting, of course, was the same; but even before they came, normal urban life had been severely disrupted by the war. Comparative vital statistics, therefore, have little meaning. The reduction of the crime rate, for instance, resulted from stricter enforcement under martial law; and though a fever epidemic was avoided, the incidence of several other infectious diseases increased, as it did in all centers of troop concentration before World War II. To care for the wounded as well, new hospitals were established; the Charity, which normally treated about four hundred patients, had twice that number by 1864, two-thirds of whom were soldiers.[36]

[35] De Forest, *Miss Ravenel*, 240-41.
[36] New Orleans *Times*, June 3, 1864.

During that year the city came alive again with economic and social bustle, even though members of the cast had changed somewhat. Restaurants and theaters were crowded. The gigantic celebration of Hahn's and Banks' victory in the spring election provided the citizenry with the customary excitement of Mardi Gras. As 1865 started, the political future remained uncertain but the end of the war was clearly in sight. Life had begun to move in old familiar channels and, whatever might follow, the ordeal of occupation would soon be over.

TEN THE NEGRO DURING THE OCCUPATION

O*N THE EVE* of the war the Negro population in New Orleans, roughly 13,000 slaves and 11,000 free persons of color, presented certain contrasts to that of the South at large. There were many mulattoes—80 percent of the free persons of color had white blood, as did some of those who were legally slaves. Though interracial marriage was forbidden, white men of both upper and lower classes, even married ones, had taken colored women as concubines without interference from civil authorities. The offspring of such unions could inherit property if the mother were free. Miscegenation had begun in the colonial period, and a tolerant French and Spanish background permitted its continuance after 1803. The number of mulattoes was also increased by a constant immigration from the West Indies, where the custom of mixed cohabitation had long been common. As a natural result, among southern cities only Baltimore had more free persons of color than New Orleans.[1]

The size of the slave and the free groups had declined both relatively and absolutely in the prewar decade. Increasing restrictions, climaxed by legislative prohibition of manumission in 1857, had induced some migration of free persons back to the islands and to Europe. And as early as the 1840s the Irish had begun to replace slaves as common laborers. Many of the latter had developed skills and were hired out locally by their masters; others were sold or sent to nearby plantations as the price of cotton and sugar rose. Thus those who remained in the city moved up economically to a higher level of the urban proletariat.

The aristocracy among the free Negroes was a propertied and well-educated group related to some of the oldest local families. Those who had descended from the *ancien population,* in fact, were called "colored creoles," proud of the fact that they had formed a battalion which fought against the British in 1815 under General Jackson. Colored Orleanians had attained free status through manumission or through purchase of their freedom by their fathers, their relatives, and sometimes by themselves. Though they had traditionally enjoyed a certain social and economic status, they remained in 1860 an anomalous class, accepted fully neither by the whites above or the blacks below. Outside observers like Connecticut-born Frederick Law Olmstead and the native historian Gayarré agreed that caste lines were more rigid among colored residents—griffes, sacratas, quadroons, marabons, and metifs—than among whites. Some free persons of color owned slaves, whom they looked down on even more than white masters did.[2]

Among them were businessmen and planters, doctors and teachers, but not lawyers. Some were wealthy, like Thomas Lafon, a real estate broker worth $10,000 in 1860 who became the richest of his race after the war, or Nelson Fouchon, a migrant from Cuba who became a successful beer merchant. Beneath this top level was a larger group of petty bourgeoisie and skilled laborers, composed of grocers, tailors, barbers, masons, and carpenters, and female seamstresses, nurses, and boarding-house operators. City Surveyor Thorpe told the constitutional convention of 1864 that free persons of color

---

[1] *Eighth Census of the United States* (1860), 615; Donald E. Everett, "Free Persons of Color in New Orleans, 1803-1865" (Ph.D. dissertation, Tulane University, 1952), 1-11.
[2] Frederick L. Olmstead, *Journey in the Seaboard States* (New York, 1856), 583.

paid taxes on $13,000,000 worth of property; Reconstruction Governor Warmoth made an even higher estimate.[3]

The large slave population in the South could prove a military asset if the blacks remained peaceably at their labor on the plantations, thus making more white men available to the army. Yet they were also potentially a great source of danger, should they rebel or be incited into insurrection. The concentration of free Negroes in New Orleans heightened the danger because they might lead such a revolt. The threat, of course, had long been recognized, and to meet it some legal restrictions had been placed on the activities of free colored persons. The local French consul told Alexis de Tocqueville on his visit in 1832 that he thought the whites had erred in not "taking in" at least the upper levels of the group; "by repelling the mulattoes . . . the white aristocracy gives the slaves . . . the only weapon they need to become free: intelligence and leadership."[4] In the ante bellum period, in fact, almost as many alleged insurrection plots were discovered in Louisiana as in Virginia.

Nevertheless, colored veterans of the Battle of New Orleans had been publicly honored and even given pensions, but not the franchise for which some of them hoped. When invasion threatened again in the spring of 1861, fifteen hundred free men of color assembled in a downtown meeting, organized themselves into military companies, and offered their services to Governor Moore. Moore formally incorporated them into the Louisiana militia as the Native Guards, but General Lovell politely refused their offer to serve as escorts for Union prisoners of war, though he urged them to be ready for "a more important occasion." Evidently Confederate authorities hesitated to run the risk of using the Native Guards in combat or for any critical duty. The colored

---

[3] *Debates in the Convention,* 216; Everett, "Free Persons of Color," 194-229; Henry C. Warmoth, *War, Politics, and Reconstruction* (New York, 1930), 43.

[4] George W. Pierson, *Tocqueville and Beaumont in America* (New York, 1938), 631.

companies, most of which provided their own arms and uniforms, spent the rest of the year in drills and parades.[5]

Many of the Native Guards, no doubt, were motivated by loyalty to the Confederacy. Some told Butler later that they enlisted because of fear of retaliation if they refused; certainly as a group they hoped that the South might reward them for their action by social or even political concessions. But Governor Moore's fine words could not hide the fact that the Native Guards had been rebuffed by the authorities, and consequently they disobeyed orders to leave the city when Farragut's fleet approached. Soon after the capture, a group of colored officers called on Butler to inquire about the status of their companies, tacitly making him the same offer they had originally made the Confederates. The general did not give them a definite answer, but he began correspondence with Secretary of War Stanton on the subject. With slaves pouring into the city from adjacent parishes, the Federals recognized the danger of an insurrection. Finally the threat of a Confederate counterattack and the lack of reinforcement from the North induced Butler to reactivate the colored brigade in August, 1862. "They are free," he wrote Stanton; "they have been used by our enemies, whose mouths are shut, and they will be loyal."[6]

Within two weeks one thousand men had enlisted, forming the first Negro regiment which was officially mustered into the United States army, on September 27, 1862. Though two other regiments were soon activated, so many volunteers enlisted that all of them could not be accepted. White officers were assigned to the field grade posts, allegedly because of the lack of military training of the colored volunteers, who were appointed as line and noncommissioned officers. Prominent among the latter were Captains "Old Jordan" Noble, who had served as drummerboy at Chalmette in 1815, and

[5] *Picayune,* April 21, 1861, Jan. 10, 1862; *Crescent,* April 27, 1861; *O.R.,* XV, 556.
[6] Parton, *Butler,* 516-17; *O.R.,* XV, 442, 549, 557.

P. B. S. Pinchback, later lieutenant governor of the state during Reconstruction.

Many of the mulattoes were so lightskinned—"about the complexion of the late Mr. Webster," according to Butler—that a few passed for white and actually enlisted in white companies of both the Union and Confederate armies. The general insisted that he had never armed slaves, but many of the recruits had recently been emancipated under his orders or those of military courts on one ground or another. According to one member of the Native Guards, Joseph T. Wilson, who subsequently wrote the history of the corps, probably half the volunteers had not been legally emancipated, since all the recruiting officers required of applicants was an oath that they had been manumitted.[7]

Butler continued to request official confirmation of his action from the War Department and President Lincoln, but none came and he finally informed Stanton that he assumed silence meant consent. Though the general was highly regarded by his new troops, he encountered open opposition from the majority of his officers, particularly the West Pointers who doubted that Negroes would fight, and from the local press and residents whose fear of insurrection greatly increased after Lincoln issued the Emancipation Proclamation in September, 1862. The matter came to a head when Butler assigned the first two regiments of the Native Guards to protect the Opelousas Railroad and supply lines on Weitzel's expedition into the Lafourche-Teche parishes in November. General Weitzel protested that the presence of colored troops would incite slaves in the area into insurrection and asked to be relieved of their command. Butler argued at some length with his subordinate in defense of the colored troops, but in the end he compromised by placing the regiments under an independent command.[8]

[7] Joseph T. Wilson, *The Black Phalanx* (Hartford, 1888), 179, 196, 473; Parton, *Butler*, 517-18; *O.R.*, XV, 559, Ser. 3, III, 101.
[8] *O.R.*, XV, 162, 164, 166, 171, 628.

BANKS SHARED the West Pointers' skepticism about colored troops. Upon assuming command of the Gulf Department he found their morale extremely low because of clashes between the white field and the colored line officers, most of whom in both groups, according to his assistant adjutant general, were decidedly inferior men. He proceeded to eliminate colored officers by court martial or reexamining boards, and most of those who survived, like Pinchback, found themselves in such an uncomfortable position that they resigned. New commissions were given only to whites, with the result that the morale of Negro troops was still further lowered, especially since most of the white officers were incompetent and some were even sadistic.[9]

After he received formal approval from Stanton of Negro enlistment in March, 1863, however, Banks determined to expand the group to eighteen regiments of five hundred men each and changed its name to the Corps d'Afrique. Apparently at the time he intended to use them only on noncombatant duty to relieve white troops for actual fighting. "The Government makes use of mules, horses, uneducated and educated white men," he declared; why should it not use the Negro "for the cause in which he is as deeply interested as other men." But the Negrophobia of his white officers and men, as well as the fear of reducing the supply of equally needed plantation laborers, caused him shortly to halt the recruiting program until Lincoln, having at last made up his mind, sent General Daniel Ullman to the department with authority to enlist a Negro brigade. To block Ullman, Banks stepped up recruiting and raised 10,000 troops by August, more than in any other military department.[10]

Prior to that date Banks had finally yielded to repeated petitions from the Native Guards that they be given a

---

[9] *O.R.*, XXVI, pt. 1, 689; R. B. Irwin, *History of the Nineteenth Army Corps* (New York, 1893), 49; Wilson, *Black Phalanx*, 175; Palfrey to his family, April 19, 1863, *Palfrey Papers*.
[10] Harrington, *Banks*, 112; O.R., Ser. 3, III, 101.

chance at combat. He took the First Regiment (which contained the largest number of mulattoes) and the Third with him for the attack on Port Hudson. In the bloody but unsuccessful assault on May 27, 1863, they lost twenty-nine men and three officers, thereby removing any doubt in his mind about their fighting mettle. "No troops could have been more determined or more daring," Banks reported, and he later wrote Lincoln that the ultimate victory "could not have been accomplished at the time it was but for their assistance." Before the surrender of Port Hudson in July he used 3,000 troops from the various colored regiments, of whom 100 were killed. New Orleans Negroes gave a tremendous funeral to Captain André Cailloux, who was slain in the first assault in May, but whose body was not recovered until July 8 because the Confederates refused to permit reclamation of Negro dead under a flag of truce. During the siege Confederate General Kirby Smith wrote to his subordinate General Richard Taylor urging him to give no quarter to colored troops or their white officers. For the next six months reports of atrocities committed on colored prisoners of war in Louisiana were investigated, and early in 1864 the Federals issued a formal threat of retaliation. Lincoln had issued a similar decree the previous summer.[11]

Though they proved their valor at Port Hudson, the Corps d'Afrique was not employed thereafter in any military action. Constant conflicts arose between white and colored troops, and the antipathy of the New Englanders for Negroes could not be ignored. In one instance at Ship Island, the Thirteenth Maine Regiment defiantly refused to join in battalion parade or drill because some of their white officers would be subordinate to the colored. Because of previous friction, a Federal gunboat at the island actually fired on colored troops when they retreated in an engagement. Open fighting was

[11] *O.R.*, XXVI, pt. 1, 45, 68-70, 689, Ser. 2, VI, 21-22, 961; Wilson, *Black Phalanx*, 217; Irwin, *Nineteenth Army Corps*, 174; Harrington, *Banks*, 112-13.

narrowly averted at Algiers between the famous Mims battery and the Second Regiment when one of the latter's guards stopped a white soldier with a lighted pipe from entering an ammunition shed. Men of the Thirteenth Maine declared that they could not "acknowledge a negro their superior, by virtue of any shoulder straps he might wear." Upon its transfer to Baton Rouge in May, 1863, the Fourth Regiment, which contained many recently emancipated slaves, was heckled by shouts that "niggers have no business to be soldiers."[12]

But the chief deterrent to the use of the Corps d'Afrique in combat was the extreme incompetence of its white officers. As Banks himself admitted, this inferiority continued despite his determined efforts to improve their caliber. Competent white officers like Captain John Palfrey simply refused assignment to colored units, and in typical army fashion white commanders unloaded their undesirable and unfit subalterns on black companies. A dramatic example was the "mutiny" of the Fourth Regiment at Fort Jackson against Lieutenant Colonel A. C. Benedict in December, 1863. Benedict habitually cursed, kicked, struck, and imposed cruel punishments upon his men for trivial offenses. Banks insisted upon a court martial and drove him out of the service, then replaced him with Colonel Charles R. Drew, who proved equally sadistic. The best tribute to the Union's Negro soldiers in Louisiana, observed one scholar, is the fact that they served under such officers most of the time with obedience in the garrison and courage in the field.[13]

THE CIVIL WAR resulted in the abolition of the institution of Negro slavery in 1865 by a constitutional amendment.

[12] Wilson, *Black Phalanx*, 208-12; Everett, "Free Persons of Color," 298-99; Harrington, *Banks*, 110.
[13] Harrington, *Banks*, 111-12.

But progress toward that goal during the war was gradual and often halting, because at any given time specific action was taken largely on military grounds; i.e., with a view to the probable effect upon public opinion in the North, the South, and abroad, and the concomitant influence upon the outcome of the war. From the beginning of hostilities Congress, the President, and commanding generals in the different theaters all participated in the formulation of policy. Their common objective was the preservation of the Union or, in simple terms, victory for the United States. As Lincoln well put it in his reply to Horace Greeley in August, 1862, if by so doing he could save the Union he would free no slaves, all slaves, or only some of them.

Some mention has been made above of national and local actions affecting slavery in Louisiana. Until his death Lincoln favored compensated emancipation because he regarded the North and South as equally responsible for the institution, but his initial plan in 1861 was rejected by the border states which had not seceded. At the same time he countermanded orders of Generals Frémont and Hunter freeing slaves in conquered areas. Prior to his Emancipation Proclamation, announced in September, 1862, to become effective the following January 1, Congress had passed several measures. These prohibited the return of slaves who had escaped from disloyal owners, and freed (1) slaves in hostile military service; (2) Union slave-soldiers, but with compensation to their owners; (3) slaves of persons supporting the rebellion; and (4) slaves of rebel owners fleeing to Union lines. These laws could be put into effect in any southern region conquered by the Federals, and they gave Butler legal authority for the emancipation of certain categories. All that he added were those belonging to French and British subjects, on the valid grounds that their nations had abolished slavery.[14]

Lincoln's proclamation, hardly as strigent as the congres-

---

[14] Randall, *Civil War*, 477-98.

sional Confiscation Act of 1862, specifically exempted from its provisions the conquered area of Louisiana. In no way did it rescind that act, which Butler did not enforce in regard to slaves belonging to owners absent in the Confederate army. Nor did it have any local effect other than increasing the chances of and the fear of an insurrection.[15] The Federals had faced in New Orleans, ever since the capture, the more pressing problem of a heavy influx of Negroes, slave and ex-slave. Slaves on plantations in Federal Louisiana were still legally slaves, as they were in the border states. General Banks assured their masters that the war was not being fought against slavery.

But Banks' major project in 1863, as well as Lincoln's, was the restoration of civil government in the state. This put them both in somewhat of a dilemma. They were determined to keep the old planter class from regaining control and restoring in full the constitution of 1852, yet they hoped for planter support of their reconstruction program. They knew also that only a free-state government had any chance of acceptance by Congress and the northern public. Despite his earlier exception of Louisiana, the President now insisted upon emancipation as a *sine qua non* of civil restoration; "the adverse element," he warned Banks, "seeks insidiously to preoccupy the ground." Fortunately, both the moderate and radical wings of local Unionists agreed.[16]

Banks felt safe, therefore, in suspending the slavery provisions of the old constitution of 1852 when he called for a state election by proclamation on January 11, 1864. He did so under his military powers, the identical grounds upon which Lincoln had previously based his proclamation. Four months later the state constitutional convention voted to abolish slavery, though it recommended that Congress compensate loyal owners. In Louisiana, as in the nation, the

[15] *Journal of Julia Le Grand*, 58-9.
[16] See Ch. Six.

institution was formally suspended by military order and later abolished by constitutional amendment.

In addition to the political problem of slavery, the migration of Negroes to Union lines in increasing numbers confronted Butler and Banks with a serious threat to the security of their troops—as it did Grant in Tennessee and Federal commanders elsewhere in the South. In depression-ridden New Orleans, where thousands were already on relief and many were almost starving, the crisis was even more acute. Not only yellow fever, but other diseases which broke out in the crowded quarters occupied by the new arrivals, could decimate the army; cohabitation with colored women, by increasing the venereal rate, reduced its efficiency. And, for all their official calm, both Federal generals surely realized that local conditions and the Negroes' misunderstanding of Lincoln's proclamation could set off an insurrection.[17]

To meet the danger Butler took several practical steps, and a month after his arrival Banks issued a general order decreeing a "fight or work" policy. Unless they joined the army, unemployed Negroes would be sent out of the city to work on privately owned or government-confiscated plantations. Individuals could choose their masters under a government-guaranteed contract, but once they made their choice, they were bound to service for one year. In return they received quarters, rations, medical care, and wages as high as ten dollars a month, or by mutual agreement they could work on a sharecropping basis.

Unless they provided an honest day's labor from dawn to dusk, they would suffer stipulated penalties, but not flogging. To maintain general order and health, certain restrictions were placed on their activities; e.g., possession of firearms and liquor was usually denied them. Ultimately the Gulf Department employed 50,000 workers on 1,500 estates under this program, probably the most successful of its kind in the

[17] Butler to Stanton, May 25, 1862, *Butler Papers;* Delta, Nov. 5, 1862.

occupied South. It contributed immeasurably to the war effort by releasing white Union soldiers for combat and by producing food for the city and cotton for export to the North and to England.[18]

Neither planters nor Negroes were enthusiastic about the results, but during wartime no experiment in a free-labor system had much chance for conspicuous success. Nor did Banks receive the credit he hoped and deserved in the North. Radicals like Horace Greeley and Wendell Phillips attacked his action; better "the bullet from . . . Jeff Davis," said Phillips, "than . . . serfdom from General Banks." But abolitionist Chaplains Hepworth and E. M. Wheelock, who personally investigated the operation, were loud in their praise, and Lincoln and northern conservatives were more than satisfied.[19]

Nevertheless Banks accomplished his main objective, the reduction of the Negro population in New Orleans. However logical the fear of residents about arming the black men, the results confirmed the general's belief that induction of the colored men in the army would actually increase their control over them. Had the necessity arisen, enough white troops were available to suppress a revolt. The much-publicized Fort Jackson "mutiny," as pointed out above, was merely an isolated protest against a sadistic commander, but occasional violence by members of the Corps d'Afrique reported in the press kept citizens alarmed. They were disturbed also by the restiveness of their servants; Miss Le Grand's maid Julie Ann, for instance, ran away with several hundred dollars. The Federals too faced similar problems. Putting Negroes into uniform did not change their character at once, and at least some got out of the army as easily as they

[18] *O.R.*, XV, 666-67; Harrington, *Banks*, 105. In Ch. XVIII and XIX of *Miss Ravenel*, De Forest gives an excellent account of the operation of one such plantation.
[19] Hepworth and Wheelock to Banks, April 9, 10, June 28, 1863, Banks to his wife, Oct. 20, 1871, *Banks MSS;* New Orleans *Tribune*, Oct. 12, 1864; Harrington, *Banks*, 106.

got in it. One of them confessed to a friend that he had tried "sojerin" for a while but had finally decided to go back to "niggerin."[20]

Banks included the education of Negro children in his labor system, raising funds from a special property tax and army levies on cotton, sugar, and molasses. At first progress was slow because of opposition from natives as well as from some of his own officers. By the end of 1864 a special Board of Education for Freedmen, under Chaplains Plumly and Wheelock, had set up a hundred schools in the occupied parishes with an enrollment of 10,000 students. A majority of the teachers were white women from New Orleans Unionist families. Night and Sunday schools were also opened for colored adults, and one white teacher was assigned to each Negro regiment.

By October, 1863, seven schools were operating in the city with seventeen hundred students and twenty teachers. A year later Plumly reported that both the number of schools and the enrollment had doubled. Probably because of pressure from Banks, the constitutional convention voted for the continuance of these segregated schools, though it first toyed with a proposal that each race pay its proportional costs through separate taxes.[21]

THE OCCUPATION gave free men of color ample opportunity to exert pressure on the Federals for political and social concessions. This they did through their newspapers, the weekly *L'Union* and its successor the *Tribune,* and by direct action. Butler permitted them to ride on streetcars with the whites and to testify in court, but a return to former restrictions seemed imminent when Banks, worried about rumors

---

[20] *Delta,* Sept. 16, 17, 18, 1862, Mar. 20, 1863; *Picayune,* Aug. 5, 1862; *Journal of Julia Le Grand,* 58-59.
[21] *Report of the Board of Education for Freedmen, 1864;* Doyle, "Civilian Life," 288-90; Harrington, *Banks,* 108-10.

of insurrection, arrested numbers of them for violation of the curfew and for assembling in public meetings without permits.[22] Their enlistment in the army and their performance at Port Hudson, however, brought a favorable change in attitude on the part of the new commander and sympathy from the *Times,* the organ of the radical Unionists. Negro leaders, accordingly, started a determined movement for the franchise.

Toward that end they held a number of meetings during 1863. At the first of these, chaired by Nelson Fouché of *L'Union* in late June at Economy Hall, ten veterans of the Battle of New Orleans were elected vice presidents. Plans were laid for the celebration of the Fourth of July and a petition for suffrage for free colored persons.[23] At a second meeting in November, where according to the *Times* "more white American than African" blood was present, the plea of the radical Dr. Dostie against pressing demands for the franchise was ignored. François Boisdoré replied that free Negroes had waited long enough for the promises of 1815 to be honored; iliterate Germans and Irish who could sign their names only with ×'s had been allowed to vote, and he threatened to take the matter to President Lincoln if local authorities did not act. Captain Pinchback put the issue even more succinctly. If his group were denied the vote, it should not be subject to military draft: "they did not ask for social equality, and did not expect it, but they demanded political rights—they wanted to be men."[24]

The assembly then drafted a petition to Military Governor Shepley, citing the Declaration of Independence and the recent opinion of United States Attorney General Edward Bates that freeborn persons of color were citizens, and asking to be included in the governor's current registration of loyal

---

[22] W. M. Brown, *The Negro in the American Rebellion* (Boston, 1867), 177-82. See Ch. Five.
[23] *L'Union,* June 30, 1863.
[24] New Orleans *Times,* Nov. 6, 1863.

voters. They did so on three grounds: their military service in 1815 and 1863, their payment of taxes on a sizable amount of property, and their education. Shepley did not reply immediately, but later he passed on their request to General Banks, who also temporized. Meanwhile, delegates from two of the free colored clubs were seated by the Louisiana Convention of the Friends of Freedom, an organization formed by local white Unionist groups which eventually became the Republican party in the state.[25]

Dissatisfied with the failure of the military authorities to respond, in January 1864, the Union Radical Association selected an emmissary to go to Washington and present its demands to Lincoln and his cabinet. Before the emmisary's departure a special commissioner appointed by the President arrived in the city and told an overflow crowd in Lyceum Hall that he had been sent to "ascertain their wishes." At his suggestion a committee was appointed to draw up resolutions in general terms, without any specific mention of the franchise, and plans were made to invite the famous Negro leader Frederick Douglass to New Orleans at once.[26] At this point came the gubernatorial election.

Hahn and the moderates opposed extension of the franchise even to free men of color and made the issue a key one in the campaign. T. J. Durant, a leading radical, openly favored extension and, according to the *Era,* so did the radical's candidate Flanders until he realized the unpopularity of that position and "attempted to hedge out of it." After Hahn's victory the colored men proceeded with their original plan, and in March a delegation arrived in Washington with a petition, signed by more than a thousand property owners, asking for suffrage on the three grounds cited in the meeting of the previous November.

Lincoln turned them down. He admitted that his action

[25] *American Annual Cyclopedia, 1863,* 591-92; New Orleans *Times,* Nov. 9, 1863.
[26] New Orleans *Times,* Jan. 20, Feb. 9, 1864.

was determined purely by political expediency, not concern for justice, and directed singly toward restoration of the Union. In his opinion extension of the franchise would not contribute to that end. Yet shortly he wrote Hahn a private letter suggesting that limited extension might be considered by the constitutional convention.[27]

The convention soon exhibited its Negrophobia in a provision, passed on May 10 by a vote of 68 to 15, stating that the "legislature shall never pass any act authorizing Negroes to vote, or to immigrate into this state under any pretense whatever." Though a minority led by T. B. Thorpe continued to press for some compromise, a limited franchise measure was rejected later in the month 53 to 23. At this point General Banks, possibly prodded by Lincoln but equally afraid of a hostile congressional reaction, appeared before the body and persuaded it to grant the legislature power to extend the franchise to "other persons" on any of the three basic grounds already advanced. The prohibition on the entrance of free Negroes into the state was also rescinded.[28]

After the war Banks stated that a military order granting suffrage to all Negroes would have been unacceptable to officials in Washington and to the country at large. But he did try to arrange a case in the Federal Circuit Court in New Orleans whereby all men with more white than colored blood would be declared white and would thus acquire the ballot. Such a decree, it was estimated, would have included about thirty thousand colored residents of the state. According to the general, "a few men, who wanted to break the bundle of sticks without loosening the band, defeated it. The President gave me too much to do . . . or it would have been accomplished."[29]

[27] *Era,* Feb. 21, Mar. 16, 17, 1864. See Ch. Six.
[28] *Journal of the Constitutional Convention of 1864,* 71; *Debates in the Convention,* 216, 250, 301. Caskey, *Secession,* and Shugg, *Origins,* discuss the movement fully.
[29] *American Annual Cyclopedia, 1864,* 479-80.

A measure to that effect, the so-called "Quadroon Bill," was introduced in the convention, but it was defeated 47 to 23. Later in the fall the state senate defeated an identical bill by a vote of 20 to 4. Some of the senators, like editor Alfred C. Hill of the *Era* who favored limited extension on the basis of taxation or education, objected to this method because it would place "a premium on prostitution," since colored women would seek white fathers for their children. The local press was also generally opposed, even the *Tribune*, which argued that such a law would increase the rigidity of caste lines among the colored population, dividing it into "white, white-washed, and blacks." The war ended, therefore, without the legislature's taking any action under the power granted it by the new constitution.[30]

During the extended debate free colored persons held frequent rallies and founded the *Tribune*, which at once struck a militant note. Its opposition to all efforts to divide mulattoes from Negroes led future Governor Warmoth to accuse it of seeking to make Louisiana a "Negro state"; the *Picayune* charged that it was being used as a front by disgruntled white leaders. The *Tribune* fought ratification of the constitution and advocated instead that Congress act in the matter, as it did subsequently in passing the fourteenth and fifteenth amendments.[31]

To the *Tribune's* chagrin, local white radicals joined Dr. Dostie in opposing the demand for the extension of the franchise. George Denison wrote Chase that any attempt to force it upon the convention "would be futile." Abolitionist Major R. B. Plumly wrote William Lloyd Garrison that the free Negroes were not ready for the ballot. He also accused some of them of sympathy for the Confederacy and added that they were "bitterly hostile to the blacks, except as a

---

[30] New Orleans *Tribune*, Nov. 16, 1864; *Debates in the Convention*, 547; *Louisiana Senate Debates, 1864*, 45-50.
[31] New Orleans *Tribune*, Sept. 6, Dec. 6, 1864; Warmoth, *Reconstruction*, 32; *Picayune*, Sept. 5, 1864.

slave." Garrison himself refused to support their cause. Another local chaplain, Thomas W. Conway of the Louisiana Freedman's Bureau, aroused the *Tribune's* ire by reviving the old project of African colonization.[32]

Having failed to obtain from the whites the franchise for themselves alone, free men of color finally came out boldly for universal suffrage for all Negroes. To close ranks with the freedmen, in January, 1865, they held a weeklong convention in New Orleans and formed a local branch of the national Equal Rights League. As much as possible they avoided publicity about their direction of the new movement, but the contemporary press did not mention a single ex-slave as one of the leaders. Foreshadowing the subsequent course of events, they joined with a few white radicals like Thomas Durant at the Republican State Convention—which met in the city in September, 1865—and nominated Henry Clay Warmoth for governor. In the election the conservative candidate Wells defeated Warmoth, but the Freedman's Bureau permitted Negroes to vote for the first time in "voluntary polls." Among them, according to the *Tribune,* were 1,000 freeborn soldiers, 2,000 emancipated soldiers, 5,000 other freeborn colored men, and 8,600 other freedmen.[33]

In most of the South, political reconstruction did not begin until the end of the war. In Louisiana, on the contrary, the various issues had been debated and voted on in the convention and the legislature long before Lee's surrender. Early in 1865 local Negroes, scalawags, and carpetbaggers were in the process of forming a party which, despite defeat in its initial bid for power, would soon gain control of the state.

[32] Denison to Chase, July 10, 1863, "Chase Correspondence"; *Delta,* Dec. 4, 1864; New Orleans *Tribune,* Dec. 2, 7, 1864.
[33] New Orleans *Tribune,* Dec. 21, 1864, Jan. 8, Sept. 14, Dec. 13, 1865; Everett, *Free Persons of Color,* 366.

EPILOGUE

THE PERSISTENCE of the Civil War in the collective memory of the South is still obvious a century later. Such persistence is understandable. As C. Vann Woodward observes in *The Burden of Southern History,* one of the ways in which the South differs distinctly from the rest of the nation is that it has suffered defeat in a long war. For more than a generation after the Revolution, Tory ladies in New York City closed their shutters on the Fourth of July. For an even longer period after the expulsion of James II, English Royalists prayed for the return of the Stuarts.

Unsouthern though it was in many respects and reluctant to secede in 1861, New Orleans had never faltered in its defense of slavery. It took its defeat in 1865 as bitterly as the rest of the South, and it has contributed its share to the southern legend and the southern postmortem. However mild its war experience, nowhere else in the conquered region was the ordeal of Reconstruction more traumatic. With the reelection of Governor Wells in November, 1865, ex-Confederates were again in control of the state, and the legislature proceeded to pass the famous "black codes" reducing freedmen to peonage. Violence broke out in New Orleans in the summer of 1866 when a few members of the constitutional convention of 1864 reconvened in Mechanics Hall in an attempted coup to enfranchise the Negro. A riot ensued in which thirty-four Negroes were killed and more than two hundred wounded.

Under the congressional act of March, 1867, Louisiana was occupied by Federal troops commanded by General Philip Sheridan. He interpreted the terms of the act so strictly that half of the white citizens of the state were disfranchised in the election for delegates to a new constitutional convention, but all adult male Negroes could vote. The Republicans, therefore, elected all but two of their delegates, half of whom were white and half black by previous agreement. The constitution of 1868 enfranchised Negroes and provided for full equality between the races in public schools and on common carriers. In the state election of that year the Republicans easily elected Henry C. Warmoth, who was more a scalawag than a carpetbagger, as governor, and P. B. S. Pinchback, a mulatto, as lieutentant governor.

Under the new constitution the governor had almost dictatorial powers; for instance, he appointed local police, registrars, and returning boards which could throw out votes at will in any election. Taxes soared and hundreds of thousands of dollars went into graft, more to the benefit of "a small band" of white leaders than to the black masses who gave the Republicans their power at the polls. Legislative sessions, which had cost on an average a hundred thousand dollars in the prewar period, now cost almost a million. During the decade of military occupation the state debt rose from eleven to fifty million dollars, and state taxes from 37 cents per $100 in 1866 to $2.15 in 1871. In New Orleans alone the sheriff made 37,000 seizures for taxes between 1871 and 1873, and its population was estimated to have dropped 30,000 within two years. Whites of all classes blamed conditions on the Negroes and formed White Leagues which took revenge upon freedmen all over the state; the *Bulletin* estimated that 14,000 Orleanians were members. A clash in the city between the governor's metropolitan police and the league in September, 1874, killed twenty-seven men and wounded one hundred.

Dazzled by easy access to booty, the Republicans split into two factions. Hardly had the Warmoth-Pinchback regime taken office when it was opposed by customhouse officials led by William P. Kellogg and United States Marshal Stephen

B. Packard. Since the latter were backed by congressional Republicans, the customhouse crowd replaced Warmoth and Pinchback in 1872 with Kellogg and a mulatto, C. C. Antoine. Probably the Democratic-Conservatives, who nominated John McEnery, won the state election in that year, but the returning board counted them out. President Grant used Federal troops to install Kellogg and to put his Republican supporters in control of the legislature. Much of the time during the next four years Louisiana actually had two governors and two legislatures, but Grant constantly used troops to support Republican claimants. Racial violence increased as the economic situation grew worse with the onset of depression in 1873. The election of 1876 was a replica of that in 1872, but when Republican Hayes was given the vote of Louisiana, along with that of Florida and South Carolina, and thereby the presidency, he kept his promise and removed troops in April, 1877. As part of the bargain he recognized Democratic ex-Confederate Francis T. Nichols as legal governor. Ten years of Reconstruction had done as much injury as four years of war.

It is pertinent to ask if the undeniable decline of the Crescent City in postwar decades was simply a consequence of the damage it suffered in the Tragic Era. Cultural historians stress the fact that war accelerates developments already underway, either in ascending or descending ratio. In a sensational book banned in the South, *The Impending Crisis* (1857), North Carolinian Hinton R. Helper used the federal census of 1850 to prove that his section was falling behind the free states, particularly those in the upper Mississippi Valley, in the value of its agricultural production. This he blamed on the institution of Negro slavery, for which he contended the nonslaveholding white yeoman paid the price.

Other factors which persisted in the post bellum period, it is now conceded, were probably more responsible for this economic lag: a one-crop agriculture which placed the southern region at the mercy of a foreign market it could not control; a system of social values which attached undue prestige to the investment of available capital in land and slaves, thereby accelerating overproduction of the staples; and the resulting regional self-insufficiency which increased its cost of production and its cost of living.

The war compounded this lag. Since it was fought on southern soil, the extensive physical destruction plummeted land values. The emancipation of slaves wiped out two billion dollars of available capital, in addition to all the losses of individuals in Confederate bonds and money. Because the war led to the adoption of a national policy of paternalism for the businessman, all farmers—even those in the Middle West—were hurt increasingly by a vicious governmental discrimination. The New South of the Henry Gradys had no alternative other than to seek absentee capital from the victorious North, for which southern Bourbons received their huckster's cut. The masses, pursuing their old god, sank deeper and deeper into tenancy and sharecropping. Not until 1900—when the rest of the nation had moved far ahead—did the South regain its economic position of 1860. And not until the middle of the twentieth century did it finally begin to diversify its economy.

The decline of New Orleans in national rank in population was roughly parallel with the economic decline of its section. In 1840 it was third in the nation and the leading port in value of exports. By 1860 it was sixth in population, and New York had again moved ahead of it in exports. In 1880 it was tenth, in 1900 twelfth, in 1930 sixteenth. In the 1950s its rival, Houston, moved ahead of it as the largest southern city.

The significant fact, however, is that its rate of decline during the twenty years *after* the war was roughly the same as that during the twenty years *before,* and that this rate has remained constant for the past century. The basic cause was quite evident before the guns fired on Sumter in 1861. In the preceding six years the city's receipts of western products dropped from an average of 60 percent of its total trade to less than 20 percent. With the advent of the railroad other American cities, from New York to Mobile, succeeded in diverting many of the exports of the Mississippi Valley to their harbors. No matter what New Orleans did, it had lost the bulk of this trade permanently, and therefore its main chance for national predominance.

On the basis of hindsight it can be argued that local businessmen, had they possessed the acumen and the energy of those in New York and Chicago, could partially have offset their inevitable loss of the upper valley trade by developing contacts with other areas more quickly. Undoubtedly they were slow in expanding their markets in Texas and in Latin America. They might have regained some of the valley trade had they improved port facilities and deepened the mouths of the river. (In 1962 New Orleans handled more grain than any American port.) They should have built more railroads to extend the boundaries of their southern market and invested more of their capital in ocean shipping and local industry. But this argument resembles the older one in philosophy as to whether the chicken or the egg comes first. There was only so much capital in New Orleans, and it continued by long habit to go where the largest profits had always been—into cotton and sugar.

In the 1850s the city became much more of a southern than a national metropolis. As such, its decline was definitely accelerated by the economic consequences of the Civil War. Being a river port and an ocean port, it retained certain competitive advantages like cheaper transportation rates; but its main profit came more and more from the value of the southern products it marketed and from the purchasing power of the hinterland to which it sold a variety of goods.

For this market, whose purchasing power and production decreased as a direct result of the war, it had to face increasing competition from Memphis up the river and later from the new Texas towns.

The economic decline of the city, it should be emphasized, has been relative—not absolute. Men continued to make big money there and still do. And this decline is by no means an unmixed evil. Many Americans and Europeans regard the contemporary city as the most attractive in the nation, with the possible exception of San Francisco. It pursues the dollar, but it also pursues without much inhibition the pleasures of the flesh and to some extent those of the spirit. Among American cities it is a typical and unusually tolerant. Without apology its residents abandon work for Carnival Balls or the racetrack, for golf or hunting and fishing; and no city exceeds it in disregard for the law. Probably nowhere else could 100,000 unanswered traffic summons be torn up to at the end of every year with such equanimity. Had New Orleans become a metropolitan giant, it is doubtful that it could have preserved its charm and provinciality.

Surely its location in the middle of a swamp would under any circumstances have retarded greater growth because of the physical impediments to expansion. The city grew without much consideration of geographical rationality. In fact, no city should have been located where New Orleans is. Since it is already more than one hundred miles from the gulf by river, a more logical site would have been the higher ground at Baton Rouge another hundred miles upstream, above normal floods and far more healthy. As the *Illustrated London News* said in 1853, truly it was built "upon a site that only the madness of commercial lust could have ever tempted men to occupy."

The Civil War aggravated the factors responsible for the economic retardation of the South, and the largest southern city inevitably felt the effect. Despite the risks, big profits had attracted northern capital and northern entrepreneurs to the ante bellum metropolis. When the local rate of profit declined in the 1850s, the flow of men and money from the North began to slow down; it would have continued to do so, even had war not come, as long as that decline continued. The big profits of the war years revived the flow temporarily, but those profits arose from an abnormal set of circumstances. With the advent of peace in 1865 the steady continuation of the prewar lag caused northern capital to seek more lucrative locations. It was not to come again to New Orleans in any quantity until almost a century later, when the discovery of rich deposits of oil and sulphur in southern Louisiana once more made high return on investments possible.

BIBLIOGRAPHY

OFFICIAL DOCUMENTS

A main source for any Civil War study is *War of the Rebellion: A Compilation of the Official Records of the Union and Confederate Armies* (Washington, 1880-1901), and the companion title, *Official Records of the Union and Confederate Navies in the War of the Rebellion* (Washington, 1894-1922). Of special pertinence for New Orleans in the latter is *Inquiry Relating to the Fall of New Orleans*, Ser. 2, I, 639-716, which includes correspondence between General Lovell, Governor Moore, and President Davis. Eyewitness accounts of the capture of the city and negotiations leading to the surrender may be found in the semiofficial *Battles and Leaders of the Civil War*, R. U. Johnson and C. C. Buel, eds. (New York, 1884). An official military investigation of corruption in the Gulf Department, supressed by Secretary of War Stanton, is *Report of the Special Commission*, New York, Sept. 23, 1865 (also called *Smith-Brady Report*), in the National Archives, Record Group 94, v. 737.

Since the city remained under martial law throughout the occupation, municipal records are filed in the National Archives, Old Army Records, Record Group 94. Included are separate volumes of the Correspondence of the Commanding General and the Provost Marshal, Register of Foreigners, Register of Registered Enemies, Permits Granted for Importation, Police Reports of Seizures and Arrests, Cashbook of the Provost Marshal's Office, and the Correspondence and Receipt Book of the Sequestration Commission. General Orders of the Gulf Department, bound by years from 1862 to 1865, are in the Howard Tilton Library, Tulane University, but of course they may also be found in the *Official Records*.

State documents include *Journal and Debates* of the Constitutional Convention of 1864; *Senate Debates* and *House Debates* in the Louisiana legislature for 1864-65; State Superintendent of Education, *Report,* 1864; and *Report of the Louisiana Board of Education for Freedmen,* 1864.

NEWSPAPERS

The New Orleans Public Library has in typescript separate histories of New Orleans newspapers, edited by Charles Youngman, 1938. The following were published during the Civil War:

Bee	*Picayune*
Commercial Bulletin (stopped 1862)	*Times* (started 1863)
Crescent (stopped 1862)	*Tribune* (started 1864)
Delta (changed to *Era* 1863)	*True Delta*
Era (1863-1864)	*L'Union* (weekly 1862-1864)

War correspondents' accounts appeared regularly in the New York *Herald* and the New York *Tribune.*

An influential monthly journal published in New Orleans was *De Bow's Review,* prewar series, 1846-1862, mainly written by the editor, J. D. B. De Bow.

LETTERS AND MEMOIRS

The papers of the commanding generals include *Butler's Book, Autobiography and Personal Reminiscences* (Boston, 1882), his *Private and Official Correspondence,* Jessie A. Marshall, ed. (Norwood, Mass., 1917), and James Parton, *General Butler in New Orleans* (New York, 1864), a contemporary panegyric. The letters of General Banks are in the Essex Institute, Salem, Mass. I have consulted them but not the smaller collection (mostly letters from Lincoln) at the Illinois State Historical Society. The latter is covered thoroughly in Fred H. Harrington's excellent biography.

The fullest accounts by residents of New Orleans are *The Journal of Julia Le Grand,* Kate M. Rowland and Mrs. Morris E. Croxall, eds. (Richmond, 1911), and Marion Southwood, *"Beauty and Booty," the Watchword of New Orleans* (New York, 1867). These are supplemented by several manuscript collections in the Louisiana State University Library: the *Reynes Family Papers,* the *Hyatt Papers,* and the *Henry D. Mandeville Papers.*

Letters of local Unionists are also an important source, particularly those of Treasury Agent George S. Denison to his chief, Secretary Salmon P. Chase, in American Historical Association *Annual Report, 1902,* 312ff, and to his family in Vermont, in *Louisiana Historical Quarterly,* XXIII (1940), 1132-1240. Emily H. Reed, *Life of A. P. Dostie* (New York, 1868), includes letters and speeches of the fiery New York-born resident who had been exiled by the Confederates.

Among the memoirs of Federal soldiers are Lawrence Van Alstyne, *Diary of an Enlisted Man* (New Haven, 1910), Frank M. Flinn, *Campaigning with Banks* (Lynn, Mass., 1887), and Chaplain George H. Hepworth, *The Whip, Hoe, and Sword* (Boston, 1864). The best of these are the letters of Captain John G. Palfrey to his family in Boston, in the *Palfrey Papers,* Houghton Library, Harvard University. With them, in spirit at least, must be classed John W. De Forest's novel, *Miss Ravenel's Conversion from Secession to Loyalty* (New York, 1867), for the scene is laid in the New Orleans area where the author himself served during the war as captain of a New England company. James T. Wilson, *The Black Phalanx* (Hartford, 1888), might also be regarded as a memoir, since Wilson served in New Orleans as a member of the Corps d'Afrique. Henry Clay Warmoth, governor during Reconstruction who served as a provost judge during the occupation, recounted his experiences in *War, Politics, and Reconstruction* (New York, 1930).

Other contemporary sources are:

Robert G. Barnwell, *The New-Orleans Book* (New Orleans, 1851)
O. S. Clark, *The 116th Regiment of New York Volunteers* (Buffalo, 1868)
W. C. Corsan, *Two Months in the Confederate States* (London, 1863)
George N. Gordon, *A War Diary of Events in the War of the Great Rebellion* (Boston, 1882)
John C. Gray, *War Letters* (New York, 1927)
W. Hoffman, *Camp, Court, and Siege* (New York, 1877)
R. B. Irwin, *History of the Nineteenth Army Corps* (New York, 1893)
Frederick L. Olmstead, *Journey in the Seaboard States* (New York, 1856)
DeWitt Roberts, *Southern Sketches* (Jacksonville, Ill., 1865)
Clara E. Solomon, *Diary, 1861-1862,* typed copy, Louisiana State University Library

BOOKS, ARTICLES, AND MONOGRAPHS

J. E. Alexander *Transatlantic Sketches* (London, 1833)
Herbert Asbury, *The French Quarter* (New York, 1936)
Roger Baudier, *The Catholic Church in Louisiana* (New Orleans, 1939)
M. L. Bonham, Jr., *British Consuls in the Confederacy* (Columbia University Studies in History, Economics, and Public Law, XLIII; New York, 1911)
J. D. Bragg, *Louisiana in the Confederacy* (Baton Rouge, 1941)
W. M. Brown, *The Negro in the American Rebellion* (Boston, 1867)
Harriet Cale, "Cultural Life in New Orleans in the 1850's" (M.A. thesis, Louisiana State University, 1945)
G. M. Capers, *Biography of a Rivertown* (Chapel Hill, 1939)
W. M. Caskey, *Secession and Restoration of Louisiana* (Baton Rouge, 1938)
R. T. Clark, "The German Colony in New Orleans during the Civil War," *Louisiana Historical Quarterly*, XX (1937), 997ff
E. M. Coulter, "Commercial Intercourse with the Confederacy in the Mississippi Valley, 1861-1865," *Mississippi Valley Historical Review*, V (1918-19), 378ff
R. A. Cross, *The History of Southern Methodism in New Orleans* (New Orleans, 1931)
T. E. Dabney, "The Butler Regime in Louisiana," *Louisiana Historical Quarterly*, XXVII (1944), 487-536
Jefferson Davis, *The Rise and Fall of the Confederate Government* (New York, 1881)
E. J. Doyle, "Civilian Life in Occupied New Orleans (Ph.D. dissertation, Louisiana State University, 1955)
E. J. Doyle, "Greenbacks, Car Tickets, and a Pot of Gold," *Civil War History*, V (1959), 347-62
E. J. Doyle, "Nurseries of Treason," *Journal of Southern History*, XXVI (1960), 161-79
C. L. Dufour, *The Night the War Was Lost* (New York, 1961)
D. L. Dumond, ed., *Southern Editorials on Secession* (New York, 1931)
D. E. Everett, "Free Persons of Color in New Orleans, 1803-1865" (Ph.D. dissertation, Tulane University, 1952)
Shelby Foote, *The Civil War, a Narrative* (New York, 1958)
F. H. Harrington, *Fighting Politician* (Philadelphia, 1948)

R. S. Holzman, *Stormy Ben Butler* (New York, 1954)
H. P. Johnson, "New Orleans under General Butler," *Louisiana Historical Quarterly*, XXIV (1941), 434-536
J. H. Johnson, *Red River Campaign: Politics and Cotton in the Civil War* (Baltimore, 1958)
J. S. Kendall, "Christ Church and General Butler," *Louisiana Historical Quarterly*, XXIII (1940), 1241-57
J. S. Kendall, *History of New Orleans* (Chicago, 1922)
Achille Murat, *America and the Americans* (New York, 1849)
John Nau, "The Lutherans in Louisiana" (M.A. thesis, Tulane University, 1948)
J. H. Neill, "Shipbuilding in Confederate New Orleans" (M.A. thesis, Tulane University, 1940)
E. S. Niehaus, "The Irish in Antebellum New Orleans" (Ph.D. dissertation, Tulane University, 1961)
M. E. Owen, "Presidential Elections in New Orleans, 1852-1860" (M.A. thesis, Tulane University, 1956)
J. H. Parks, "A Confederate Trade Center under Federal Occupation: Memphis, 1862 to 1865," *Journal of Southern History*, VII (1941), 289-314
G. W. Pierson, *Tocqueville and Beaumont in America* (New York, 1938)
E. P. Puckett, "The Attempt of New Orleans to Meet the Crisis in Southern Trade with the West," *Mississippi Valley Historical Association Proceedings*, X (1919-20), 491-98
J. G. Randall, *The Civil War and Reconstruction* (Boston, 1937)
R. C. Reinders, *End of an Era* (New Orleans, 1964)
Henry Rightor, ed., *Standard History of New Orleans, Louisiana* (Chicago, 1900)
A. J. Roberts, "The Federal Government and Confederate Cotton," *American Historical Review*, XXXII (1926-27), 262-75
C. B. Rousseve, *The Negro in Louisiana* (New Orleans, 1937)
R. D. Shugg, *Origins of the Class Struggle in Louisiana* (Baton Rouge, 1939)
Harold Sinclair, *The Port of New Orleans* (New York, 1942)
G. M. Smith, *Confederate War Papers* (New York, 1884)
L. C. Soule, *The Know Nothing Party in New Orleans* (Baton Rouge, 1961)
J. G. Tregle, "Early New Orleans Society: A Reappraisal," *Journal of Southern History*, XVIII (1952), 20-36
H. A. Trexler, "The Confederate Navy Department and the Fall

of New Orleans," *Southwest Review*, XIX (1933), 88-102

M. C. Vernon, "General Butler and the Dutch Consul," *Civil War History*, V (1959), 263-75

J. B. Walters, "General William T. Sherman and Total War," *Journal of Southern History*, XIV (1948), 456-66

R. B. Way, "Commerce of the Lower Mississippi Valley in the Period, 1830-1860," *Mississippi Valley Historical Association Proceedings*, X (1919-20), 57-69

R. S. West, Jr., *Lincoln's Scapegoat General: A Life of Benjamin F. Butler, 1818-1893* (New York, 1965)

B. I. Wiley, *Southern Negroes* (New Haven, 1938)

J. E. Winston, "Notes on the Economic History of New Orleans," *Mississippi Valley Historical Review*, XI (1924-25), 200-27

J. D. Winters, *The Civil War in Louisiana* (Baton Rouge, 1963)

INDEX

Advocate, 111, 177-78
Alcoholic beverages, 12, 205-26, 209
Algiers, La., 37, 44, 60, 221

Banks, General Nathional P., assumes command in New Orleans, 104-11; and Negroes, 106-108, 219-26, 229; and local Unionists, 108-12, 126-44; evaluation of, 112, 174-76; and Port Hudson campaign, 115-16; trade policy of, 158, 162-69; attacks local businesses, 159-61; and newspapers, 178-80; and churches, 182-85; and schools, 188-90
Banks, 152, 154, 156, 159-61; in 1860, 45; Butler's action on, 64, 85, 91, 101; under Confederates, 79-80
Baptists, 183-84
Barker, Jacob, 118, 124, 158, 177-78
Baton Rouge, La., 35, 48, 221, 237; battle of, 70, 75, 93, 113
"Battle of the Handkerchiefs," 109, 198
Beauregard, General P. G. T., 35, 61, 69-70, 86, 88, 93, 98, 197
Bee, 15, 92, 176-77, 179-80
Benjamin, Judah P., 6, 19, 34, 37, 110, 141
Blockade, Confederate, 82, 146-49
Blockade, Federal, 27, 31, 52, 80, 82, 146-48
Bulletin, 21, 92, 176-78, 233
Bullitt, Cuthbert, 126, 160
Butler, Andrew, 83-84, 161, 165, 168
Butler, General Benjamin F., and fall of New Orleans, 39, 47, 48, 59; militry career of before New Orleans, 55-59; initial action of in New Orleans, 60-76; and "Woman Order," 66-69; and Mumford, 69-71; evaluation of, 72-76, 87-88, 174-76; and efforts at recovery, 81-85; speculation of, 82-84; and confiscation of property and taxes, 85-86,

Butler, B. F. (continued):
107, 155-56; and yellow fever, 88-89; and oath of allegiance, 90-94, 121-23, 128-29; and clergy, 92; and Negroes, 94-96, 217-18, 222, 226; and foreign consuls, 98-103; removal of, 103-104; farewell address of, 105; and newspapers, 177-78; and churches, 181-82; and schools, 186-87

Cairo, Ill., 25, 80, 148
Camp Moore, 45, 66
Camp Parapet, 95, 207
Canby, General E. R. S., 117, 140, 142, 181
Carrollton, La., 60, 63
Chalmette, La., 34, 43, 63
Charity Hospital, 14, 82, 212
Chase, Secretary Salmon P., 84-85, 111-12, 126, 130, 164-68, 178, 180
Churches, see specific denomination
City Railroad, 160-61
Confication Act of Congress, 1862, 55, 86-87, 93, 96
Conscription, 78, 150, 162, 224
Constitutional convention of 1864, 120, 128, 132-33, 137-41, 229-30
Contraband trade, 82-85, 98, 101, 107, 161-71
Corps d'Afrique, 111, 219, 221, 225
Cotton, 2, 3, 11, 27, 79-85, 146-54, 161-71
Courts, 121, 130
Creoles, 6-9, 12, 20, 159, 193, 201-202
Crescent, 30-31, 92, 176, 178
Crime, 12, 207, 212
Currency, 64, 81, 85, 91, 151, 159-61, 170

Davis, Jefferson, 26ff, 61, 182, 195
De Bow's Review, 3, 4, 21, 147
De Forest, John W., 193, 196, 201, 205, 210-12, 241

Delta, 68, 92, 100, 130, 176, 178-79
Democratic party, 12, 19-23, 176
Denison, George S., 84, 87, 108, 110, 127, 130, 136, 152, 180, 230; and wartime trade, 162-69
Department of the Gulf, 60, 74, 102, 105, 117-119, 136
Dostie, Dr. A. P., 78, 91, 109-10, 124, 126, 143-44, 159, 189, 193-94, 227, 230
Duncan, General J. K., 41-42, 50
Durant, Thomas J., 91, 126, 132, 137, 141, 228, 231
Durrell, Edward H., 129, 136, 138

Elections, congressional, 1862, 91-92, 123; congressional, 1864, 123, 133-36, 141; congressional, 1863, 131; constitutional convention, 1864, 133, 137-41
Emancipation Proclamation, 55, 87, 94, 121, 131, 218, 222, 224
Episcopalians, 14, 107, 182-84
Era, 130, 150, 178-81, 183, 228, 230
European attitude, 26-27, 52, 69, 75, 103, 174

Farragut, David G., 31-50, 59, 72, 81, 114, 146, 168, 199
Federal soldiers, 67, 71, 192, 196-97, 199, 202-12; prejudice against Negro, 96, 209, 211, 218-19
Fellows, J. Q. A., 135-36
Flanders, Benjamin, 78, 91-92, 110, 118, 122, 124, 126, 129-30, 134-36, 142, 193, 228
Food shortages, 79-82, 150-51, 170
Foreign (European) Brigade, 45, 48, 63, 65, 99
Foreign consuls, 75, 86, 98-103, 108, 165
Fort Jackson, 29, 40-41, 50, 59, 66, 69, 221
Fort St. Philip, 29, 40-41, 43, 50
"Free Market," 44, 80, 151
French fleet, 21, 69, 70
French language, 15, 176, 185
French residents, *see* Creoles

Gallatin Street, 12, 205
Gambling, 12, 205-206
Gayarré, Charles E. A., 9, 12, 18, 214
Germans, 5, 7, 12, 24, 127, 184, 193, 227
Grant, General U. S., 75, 85, 114-17, 164, 206, 208, 224, 234

Hahn, Michael, 78, 91-2, 110, 112, 118, 124, 126-44, 180, 187, 194, 228-29
Halleck, General Henry W., 103-104, 116-17
Hartford, flagship, 40, 43, 47, 134
Hepworth, Chaplain George H., 106, 211, 225
Hill, A. C., editor, 178-79, 230
Hopkins, Commander George N., 36, 42
Hurlburt, General Stephen A., 117-18, 142, 160, 180, 205

Industry, 4, 36, 149
Irish, 5, 7, 9, 12, 14, 24, 77, 127, 185, 193-95, 214, 227

Johnson, General Joseph E., 34, 45, 115
Johnson, Reverdy, 84, 102, 104, 121, 165

Kennedy, Hugh, 143, 179-80
Know Nothing party, 14, 19-20, 73, 127, 176

Laborers, economic condition of, 9-10, 20, 34, 77-79, 150-54, 171; and politics, 127, 140
Lafayette Square, 49, 205
Lake Ponchartrain, 5, 30, 168, 191, 208
Leeds foundry, 36, 52
Le Grand, Julia, 88, 108, 174, 193, 195, 198-200, 225
Lincoln, Abraham, 21-23, 52, 55, 77; and Butler, 57, 59, 82, 91, 94, 96, 102-103, 218; and Banks, 105, 111, 117, 219-20, 223-25; and free-state government in Louisiana, 121-22, 125-44, 173-74; and franchise, 139, 228-29; and slavery in Louisiana, 222-24
Louisiana, ironclad, 36, 42, 44, 50
Lovell, General Mansfield, 28-47, 61, 63, 195, 216
Lutherans, 184, 186, 189

Manassas, ram, 37, 38, 43
Mardi Gras, 13, 136, 198, 213
Mays, Thomas P., 140, 158
McClelland, General George B., 25, 60, 74-75, 200
McGinnis, John, 177, 179, 195
Memphis, 5, 12, 20, 24, 58; capture

INDEX

Memphis (continued):
of, 25, 31, 52, 54, 75; conditions of after capture, 76, 118, 161, 167, 237
Merchants (resident), 15, 154-58, 170
Metarie race-track, 13, 97
Methodists, 14, 193-84
Mexico, 103, 116, 167
Mississippi, ironclad, 36, 46
Mississippi River, 2, 4, 5, 25, 28, 29, 35, 83, 147-48, 168, 193, 203
Mitchell, Captain John K., 42, 50
Mobile, Ala., 31, 74, 81, 99, 113, 116
Monroe, Mayor John T., 20, 46-51, 61-69, 80, 127, 144
Moore, Governor Thomas O., 30, 31, 35, 38, 69, 79, 80, 82, 216
Mumford, William B., 49, 60

Negroes, slave and free, in 1860, 5, 10, 14, 24, 214; in army, 77, 95, 111, 217-21; Butler and, 94-97; Federal prejudice against, 96, 209, 211, 218-19; Banks and, 106-107, 111, 211-12, 219-26, 229; in politics, 125-44, 226-31; *see also* Slavery
Newspapers, 92, 176-81; *see also* specific paper
New York, 1, 3, 4, 6, 8, 12, 54, 168, 236
New York *Tribune*, 127, 178, 181

Oath of allegiance, 64, 86, 92-94, 99, 123, 134, 157
Opelousas railroad, 16, 52, 65, 80, 218

Palfrey, Captain John G., 197, 202, 208-209, 241
Palmer, Benjamin, 21, 181
Parton, James, 49, 61, 65, 90, 94, 96, 102
Peabody, Judge Charles A., 103, 121, 160
Phelps, General John W., 95-96
Picayune, 21-23, 71-77, 82, 92, 108, 111, 136, 150, 176-81, 187, 190, 198, 230
Pinchback, P. B. S., 144, 218-19, 227, 233-34
Pleasant Hill, 113, 117
Plumly, Chaplain R. B., 226, 230
Polk, General (Bishop) Leonidas K., 37, 182
Population, of New Orleans, 1, 6, 121, 235-36
Porter, Commander David D., 29-50, 59, 114, 116, 166

Port Hudson, Miss., 75, 111, 115, 148, 169, 199, 207, 220
Presbyterians, 181, 183-84
Prostitution, 12, 194, 204

Red River, 52, 80-81, 83, 115-16, 119, 137, 148, 153, 166, 169, 173
Registered enemies, 93, 107, 110-11, 199, 200
Republican party, 103, 141
Reynes, Polyxene, 197, 200, 201
Robb, James, 8, 15, 161
Roberts, De Witt, 21
Roman Catholics, 14, 184-86, 189, 190, 202
Roselius, Christian, 8, 12, 24, 91, 123, 126, 128, 138, 194
Rozier, John A., 22, 91, 124, 126, 137

St. Charles Hotel, 13, 61, 62
Schools, 15, 110, 139, 185-90, 226
Scott, General Winfield, 57, 87
Seward, William H., and Butler, 69, 71, 100, 102, 104; and Banks, 105, 111, 130, 175
Shepley, General George F., 69, 85, 91, 112, 121, 129, 131, 132, 133, 136, 165, 182, 186, 227-28
Sherman, General William T., 18, 54, 76, 85, 114, 118, 145, 166
Shiloh, 25-26, 40
Shinplasters, 81, 161
Ship Island, 30, 31, 40, 66, 70, 208-209, 220
Sinclair, Harold, 3
Slavery, 10, 94-97, 106-107, 125, 134, 139; abolition of in Louisiana, 221-24, 139
Slidell, John, 8, 13, 19, 20, 110, 141, 176
Smith, General Kirby, 113, 220
Smith-Brady report, 118-19, 136, 164, 166
Soulé, Pierre, 9, 19, 47, 62-65
Southwest Pass, 34, 40
Southwood, Marion, 88, 89
Stanton, Edwin M., 60, 74, 100, 103, 119, 217, 219
Stevenson, John A., 37, 41
Stith, Mayor Gerard, 20, 127
Sugar, 2, 3, 11, 80, 83, 101, 146-54, 169, 170
Sumner, Charles, 141-42

Taylor, General Richard, 75, 113, 114-17, 164, 220

Texas, 104, 116, 122, 148, 151, 167, 236, 237
Thorpe, Colonel T. B., 89, 112, 129, 193, 215, 229
Times, 130, 135, 136, 140, 178-81, 227
Trade, before 1860, 1-5; in 1861, 80-82; wartime statistics for, 146-48; and depression, 1862-63, 148-52; and recovery, 152-54; overall decline of 235-36
Tribune, 180, 181, 226, 230-32
True Delta, 21, 61, 73, 92, 135, 138, 176-79
Twigg, General David, 31, 35, 86

L'Union, 180, 226-27
Unionists, in 1860-61, 22-24, 46, 48, 78, 127; under Butler, 70, 88, 90-92, 96; under Banks, 108-12, 122-23, 126-44, 201

University of Louisiana, 18, 24, 190, 210

Van Alstyne, Lawrence, 207-208
Vicksburg, 25, 31, 48, 74-75, 83, 111, 113-19, 132, 148, 152, 167-68, 173, 199, 200

War correspondents, 127, 178, 180
Warmoth, Henry C., 144, 216, 230-31, 233-34
Weitzel, General Godfrey, 39, 75, 113, 129, 211, 218
Wells, Governor J. Madison, 118, 124, 143, 232
Whig party, 15, 19-20, 176

Yellow fever, 5, 11, 14, 73, 88-89, 224

Zacherie, Dr. Issachar, 118, 149, 166

www.ingramcontent.com/pod-product-compliance
Lightning Source LLC
Chambersburg PA
CBHW022055160426
43198CB00008B/238